Online
Journalism
Ethics

Online Journalism Ethics

Traditions and Transitions

Cecilia Friend and Jane B. Singer

M.E.Sharpe
Armonk, New York
London, England

Library of Congress Cataloging-in-Publication Data

Friend, Cecilia
  Online journalism ethics : traditions and transitions / Cecilia Friend, Jane B. Singer.
    p. cm.
  Includes bibliographical references and index.
  ISBN 978-0-7656-1573-2 (cloth: alk. paper); ISBN 978-0-7656-1574-9 (pbk.: alk. paper)
  1. Online journalism. 2. Journalistic ethics. I. Singer, Jane B., II. Title.

PN4784.O62F75 2007
174'.907—dc22   2006036291

To the journalists

who maintain their own integrity and that of their work,

whatever the medium

Contents

List of Exhibits

Acknowledgements

This book drew inspiration from many sources, including the outstanding journalism published online and the work of many keen thinkers in journalism ethics, particularly Bill Kovach and Tom Rosenstiel, and the writers and editors of the *Journal of Mass Media Ethics* and *Media Ethics*.

Special thanks go to the scholars and professional journalists who contributed directly to this volume, many of whose insights are included here and whose collective wisdom informed this work. Those whose dialogues on the book's topics are especially appreciated include Bob Berkman, Pablo Boczkowski, Ann Brill, Connie Davis, Mark Deuze, Jonathan Dube, Thomas Hanitzsch, Chris Harper, Bruce Henderson, Mike Kittross, Mindy McAdams, Nora Paul, John Pavlik, Thorsten Quandt, Jan Schaffer, Carole Tarrant, Eric Ulken, Stephen Ward and Lee Wilkins.

Closer to home, we are grateful to our students, who over the years consistently raise exactly the right questions, and to our colleagues in the School of Journalism and Mass Communication at the University of Iowa and at Utica College, whose pursuit of knowledge across a broad spectrum of topics has consistently enriched us.

For their support and advice, we also thank those who have directly shaped and enhanced the contents of this book: our editors at M.E. Sharpe, Niels Aaboe, Lynn Taylor, Henrietta Toth, and copyeditor Laurie Lieb; and our manuscript reviewers, Dean Ann Brill of the William Allen White School of Journalism and Mass Communications at the University of Kansas and Dean Paul Voakes of the School of Journalism and Mass Communication at the University of Colorado-Boulder.

In addition, Cecilia Friend would like to thank Dean Steve Neun and Utica College for personal and professional support. Deepest appreciation goes to Donald Challenger, true partner and friend, for his encouragement, advice and understanding.

Introduction
The Practice and Promise of Journalistic Ethics in a Digital World

Cecilia Friend and Jane B. Singer

This is a book about the future of journalism.

In a world of digital media in which anyone can be a publisher, in which there are few if any technological or financial barriers to producing and disseminating information, in which concrete and finite media products such as a newspaper or a television news broadcast have been replaced by an amorphous and constantly changing agglomeration of billions of seamlessly interconnected bits—where does the journalist fit in? Why do we need such a person, and what purpose does he or she serve? Is there any future at all for what we know as journalism?

We think the answer rests less on what journalists do—basically, gathering and sharing information, which lots of other folks online are doing, too—but on how and why they do it. It rests, that is, on ethics.

Ethics, broadly defined, is a discipline dealing with what is good and bad, as well as with moral duty and obligation.[1] It is a uniquely human concept and an explicitly social one, tied to systems of value and custom shared within and among groups of people.[2] Professions are examples of such a group, and in fact all professions incorporate a normative or ethical dimension in their self-definitions of who they are and what they do that distinguishes them from other groups or individuals.[3]

There is an ongoing debate about whether journalists are professionals—and another about whether online journalists are journalists.[4] We suggest laying both controversies to rest. Journalists consider themselves professionals; they feel loyalty to a particular set of shared ideals and norms,[5] as discussed below. And while the medium in which they work affects the nature of specific tasks, it does not inherently make those tasks any more or less journalistic. A third debate has been whether the ethical guidelines created by and for journalists who work in traditional media apply equally to journalists who work in this significantly different online world.[6] Much of this book deals in one way or another with that issue.

The more profound question, and one that is central to this book, is this: Who is a journalist in the first place? We think ethics provides the crux of the answer. A journalist in our society is someone whose primary purpose is to provide the information that citizens of a democracy need to be free and self-governing;[7] someone who acts in accordance with a firm commitment to balance, fairness, restraint, and service;[8] someone whom members of the public can trust to help them make sense of the world and to make sound decisions about the things that matter. In the open, participatory, and gloriously raucous online world, it is these broad principles—and the concrete ways they are enacted day to day, by individual journalists around the world—that are defining the journalist and determining the future.

Organization of the Book

Online Journalism Ethics is divided into eight chapters, the last one including a conclusion that summarizes the book's main themes and points to the future for digital journalism. We are concerned here specifically with journalism, primarily the production of news content, rather than such fields as advertising or public relations, where the loyalties of practitioners are necessarily different; we touch on those areas from time to time throughout the book but do not make them our focus. Each chapter concludes with a case study that we hope will help you think about the issues in a concrete way. First, in this introduction, we offer an overview of the premises that have guided our thinking and writing. In addition to the framework you have just read, these premises include the guidance offered in both professional codes of ethics and by other authors, as well as fundamental ideas about ethics offered by key philosophers and thinkers throughout history.

Chapter 1, "Traditions, Conventions, and Ethics," explores the history of journalism news conventions and such principles as independence and objectivity in the context of technological change, primarily as it has been enacted within the United States. Journalists tend to see their ethical codes and policies as absolute, but newsroom ethics are closely tied to the mechanisms by which news is produced and the culture that has grown up around those mechanisms. For example, the notion of objectivity in reporting the news is closely connected to the conventions of the inverted pyramid as a storytelling device—conventions that stemmed in part from the commercial development of the telegraph in the nineteenth century. This chapter looks at traditional newsroom ethics as products of their time and place, raising the question of the degree to which those ethics may be transferred to and transformed by a new media environment.

In Chapter 2, "Newsrooms Go Online," we offer a brief historical overview of online journalism, summarize the nature of online news and its audience at mid-decade, then deal further with the question, "Who is a journalist?" As noted above, in an environment in which anyone can be a publisher, the answer is not as straightforward as it may appear. After considering some of the possibilities, we use the traditional journalistic role of gatekeeper as a means of digging deeper into the nature of journalism as it goes digital.

"Gathering and Sharing Information" is the subject of Chapter 3. The Internet explosion has been a gold mine for reporters, whose main job is gathering information. This chapter explores the parameters for assessing and using information from Internet sources, including verifying that information and judging its accuracy. It also addresses the growing practice of transparency so readers and viewers can better understand, comment on and participate in the journalistic enterprise.

Chapter 4 focuses on "Ethics and the Law." Although the two realms are distinct, many of the ethical issues facing journalists also have legal implications. For instance, this chapter examines the blurred lines between what is a public arena and what is a private conversation on the Internet. It also considers other legal areas that are being contested in the online environment, including copyright, libel laws, shield laws, and jurisdictional issues.

Blogs and bloggers are generating heat for journalists in a variety of ways, and in Chapter 5, we consider "Bloggers and Other 'Participatory Journalists.'" As the number and kind of blogs have exploded, news producers and consumers are wearing multiple hats—sometimes at the same time. This chapter explores a variety of related issues, including how bloggers' ethics overlap with those of journalists, the blogger's self-described role as watchdog on the watchdogs, and the role of journalists in editing and overseeing blogs.

Chapter 6, "Beyond Blogs: Other Interactive News Forms," continues the discussion of the interchangeable roles of producers and consumers of information with a closer look at interactivity, a hallmark of digital journalism. In this chapter, we consider news organizations' responsibility in the era of citizen journalism, as well as issues raised by instantaneous online polling and increasing reader participation in the news conversation.

Chapter 7 is devoted to "Commercial Issues and Content Linking." Commercial issues are a particular area of pressure for all journalists, including those working online. In a digital environment, journalists must grapple with ways of adapting traditional notions about how to deal ethically with proprietary information, sponsored content, and advertisers. The design and nature of the medium itself make it difficult to separate editorial content and commercial content in the same way they are separated in print and broadcast. This chapter looks at the traditional church-state issues and how news organizations are handling them in an interactive, hyperlinked, multimedia medium.

The last chapter, "Cross-Platform Journalism, Partnering, and Cross-Ownership," considers the accelerating move toward multiplatform publishing by news organizations. The ability to create digital text, audio, and video content has transformed the way stories can be told, simultaneously transforming individual newsrooms and reigniting culture clashes among journalists who work in different media. At the same time, one result has been a recognition that public service ethics translate across platforms. This chapter also considers the ethical obligations of managers and media companies to their employees, as well as implications for the consolidation and the suppression of competition and diverse voices.

Practical Foundations

Throughout this book, you will encounter references to various frameworks related to the practice of ethical journalism. Two in particular deserve a bit of explanation before we begin. One is the code of ethics developed and revised over the years by the Society of Professional Journalists (SPJ). The other is a book that explicitly considers journalism within the social context of democracy, *The Elements of Journalism: What Newspeople Should Know and the Public Should Expect,* written by Bill Kovach and Tom Rosenstiel in 2001.

SPJ drafted its first ethics code, based on an earlier one from the American Society of Newspaper Editors, in 1973 and has modified it several times since. The current version, which is reprinted in full in Appendix A, was adopted in 1996. It emphasizes the role of the press as a vehicle for public enlightenment, the "forerunner of justice and the foundation of democracy." The code identifies the duty of the journalist as furthering those ends "by seeking truth and providing a fair and comprehensive account of events and issues." It offers four guiding principles—seek truth and report it, minimize harm, act independently, and be accountable—and a range of concrete actions journalists should take to attain those principles. For instance, one aspect of truth-telling is to "tell the story of the diversity and magnitude of the human experience boldly, even when it is unpopular to do so."[9] Minimizing harm includes being sensitive when interviewing or photographing people affected by tragedy or grief. Independence includes avoiding both real and perceived conflicts of interest; accountability encompasses inviting dialogue with the public about journalistic conduct.

At times, these guidelines seem to offer conflicting advice for journalists. For instance, most professionals see truth as journalism's most fundamental ethical principle, but the truth can sometimes be painful. The code's authors suggest that choices be evaluated along a continuum: How much harm is necessary in order to tell how much important truth? What is the optimal way to maintain independence from both external and internal pressures while remaining accountable to the public?[10] Accountability, a controversial new guiding principle added to the latest version of the SPJ code only after much debate over its relationship to the press's constitutionally protected freedoms,[11] has proved especially interesting in an online environment. Bloggers, for instance (discussed further in Chapter 5), delight in serving as watchdogs on the watchdogs, holding journalists accountable by enthusiastically pointing out real or perceived errors in fact, judgment, or ethical behavior. In general, Americans' expectations of transparency and accountability online seem to be growing, manifested in a desire for clear separation between online news and advertising content, prominent display of corrections and clarifications, and the ability to contact both editors and reporters through e-mail.[12]

Online journalists, by the way, have their own organization, which offers a set of principles that corresponds broadly to the SPJ code. The Online News Association has more than 600 professional members who gather or produce news for digital presentation.[13] The organization's founding principles—its statement of core ethics for online journalists—can be found in Appendix B.

Virtually all professions have their own code of ethics, intended to act as the group's conscience and to offer guidance that is simultaneously less subjective than personal beliefs and less rigid than a legal mandate.[14] But a code of ethics does not create ethical behavior; the strength of a code rests largely on its legitimacy and power in the eyes of those for whom it is written. The SPJ code, for instance, does not include penalties for those who violate it; its value lies almost solely in the extent to which individual journalists voluntarily adhere to it.[15] This perceived legitimacy is perhaps particularly important in the online medium, where standards are continually evolving as new forms of communication and new types of communicators jostle for position. It is just those pressure points that this book explores.

Codes tend to be somewhat narrowly focused. Throughout this book, we also draw on the ideas offered earlier this decade by Bill Kovach, founding director of the Committee of Concerned Journalists, and Tom Rosenstiel, who heads the Project for Excellence in Journalism, in their 2001 book, *The Elements of Journalism.* Kovach and Rosenstiel start with the premise that "the primary purpose of journalism is to provide citizens with the information they need to be free and self-governing";[16] they then explore how journalists can best fulfill this task. The book is a splendid blend of pragmatism and principle. Beginning with an obligation to truth and a central loyalty to citizens, it urges careful thought about journalists' roles, rights, and responsibilities in our society, as well as concerted action to support, preserve, and strengthen them. A list of the authors' key points is provided in Appendix C.

Kovach and Rosenstiel consider a host of associated changes, not least of them technological changes that are creating new ethical pressures on our twenty-first-century media. Among the many ideas directly relevant to us here and explored in the chapters that follow are the speed of information delivery, the challenges related to verification, the commercial pressures facing online media, the increasingly contested notion of privacy, the vastly expanded nature of civic discourse, and the increased need—and opportunity—for transparency. Online journalism has enormous potential to enhance the democratic purpose that has been the press's social and ethical foundation for centuries. It also has the potential to sidetrack both journalists and their audience, particularly if we forget what we have learned over the centuries:

> The elements of journalism have been forged and tempered in three hundred years of experience and testing in the marketplace of competing forms of information. They stem from the function that news plays in people's lives. . . . Civilization has produced one idea more powerful

than any other—the notion that people can govern themselves. And it has created a largely unarticulated theory of information to sustain that idea, called journalism. The two rise and fall together.[17]

Philosophical Foundations

The ethical codes guiding journalists are practical in nature; they focus on such day-to-day concerns as source relations, conflicts of interest, and the need for accuracy in reporting. The wise counsel provided in *The Elements of Journalism,* while broader in its scope, similarly sets its frames of reference within a professional context. But the underlying ideas are hardly new, and they are not limited to journalistic conduct. Although innumerable thinkers over the ages have developed many philosophical concepts about ethics that are useful to today's journalists, a fairly small set of approaches are particularly applicable. This book is primarily concerned with issues for readers to think and talk about rather than with specific ethical decisions, but a few key ideas will be helpful before beginning.

The concept of perhaps the broadest application to journalism is utilitarianism, which connected ideas about ethical behavior to notions of freedom and democracy as they emerged in the eighteenth and nineteenth centuries. Utilitarianism emphasizes a rational use of freedom to choose the act that will produce the greatest good for the greatest number of people. Perhaps its best-known proponent is the nineteenth-century British philosopher John Stuart Mill, who holds that actions are right in proportion to the degree of happiness they bring.[18] The journalistic notion of public service, the foundation of professionalism, rests largely on utilitarianism: Journalists may perhaps cause individual discomfort or even harm, but doing so may be justifiable if it leads to a benefit for the society at large. The exposure of corporate or political wrongdoing, for instance, may make those doing the wrong uncomfortable, but it is ethically justifiable and even desirable if it produces a benefit for people in general that outweighs the potential harm to the individual.

Utilitarianism demands a consideration of the consequences of a particular act: Will it have a positive or negative effect on the public? An alternative approach to ethics focuses on the rightness of the act itself, with relatively little concern for the results. Philosophers refer to this idea as duty-based ethics, meaning that people have an ethical obligation to rationally identify their duty and then act in accordance with it.

An ethical duty can thus be thought of as a sort of moral rule to follow. The eighteenth-century German philosopher Immanuel Kant offers a clear articulation of this approach. His "categorical imperative" states that an ethical person must identify and follow a primary duty, one that he or she would want everyone else to follow, all the time and in every circumstance.[19] For journalists, for instance, a primary duty is to tell the truth, meaning that all journalists should always be truthful in reporting and presenting information. The fact that truth may sometimes be painful should not deter journalists from pursuing it to the best of their ability, Kant would advise.

Of course, in the real world, people have multiple duties, and these often conflict. The four guiding principles of the SPJ code, for instance, offer obligations that may pull in different directions, such as both telling the truth and minimizing harm, or being both accountable and independent. One philosopher who offers a helpful way out of this dilemma while still emphasizing the need to identify and adhere to clear moral obligations is William David Ross, a twentieth-century Briton. Ross offers a typology of duties, grouping them into sets that include duties of gratitude, justice, and beneficence.[20] He also ranks the various duties, placing greatest importance on the duty to do no harm. Such an approach encourages people to follow their duty and consider the consequences of doing so when deciding which duty takes precedence in a particular situation. For example, while a journalist might value the full disclosure of information (in an account of a rape on a local college campus, say), he might ethically decide to withhold a piece of that information (such as the name of the victim) if its harm seems to significantly outweigh its benefit.

These approaches, while different in important ways, all emphasize the ethical action. Another valuable way to consider journalism ethics focuses instead on the actor—the person making a choice about whether or not to do something. Ultimately, being ethical involves a personal decision, and the ancient Greek philosopher Aristotle was one of the first to propose that ethics is not something people possess; rather, it is something they do. Through time and practice, Aristotle says, one can develop the habit of making wise decisions in a range of situations, ultimately becoming a happy and virtuous person (and helping build a happy and virtuous society) in the process. In particular, Aristotle emphasizes the value of moderation in making such choices—that is, avoiding the extremes and seeking a "golden mean" somewhere between excess and deficiency.

For example, an editor working on a story about a local murder might reject both an extremely gruesome photo (excess) and the option to run no photo at all (deficiency), instead choosing a photo that complements the story without sensationalizing it. Aristotle would approve of such a choice. (If the editor followed the guidance of a different philosopher, she might well come to a different decision. What would Kant suggest? How about Mill?)

One final philosophical approach that is especially relevant in the online world also emphasizes the importance of the individual but directly connects that individual to the broader society. Existentialism has been explored and advanced by a number of thinkers, mostly Europeans, over the past 200 years, notably nineteenth-century Danish philosopher Soren Kierkegaard and Jean-Paul Sartre, a twentieth-century Frenchman. It combines the sometimes conflicting goals of individual autonomy and personal responsibility, emphasizing the need not only to make personal choices freely but also to stand behind those choices once made and to consider their effects on other members of society. We suggest that the unprecedented freedom to publish in a digital environment should, for the journalist, be connected with acceptance of responsibility for content and its likely effects. In other words, the online journalist must freely choose to be responsible in order to fulfill a long-standing social role based on trust.[21]

Journalists may or may not recognize the philosophical names or terms outlined here, but it is likely they draw on these ideas every day, regardless of the medium in which they work. As you read this book, think about which approach you might find most helpful in dealing with the issues raised in gathering and presenting information online.

Conclusion

The application of such principles to issues raised in the practice of online journalism is the subject of this book. As we said at the start, we believe that the distinction between journalism and other forms of publication rests primarily on ethics—as does, ultimately, the journalist's professional survival. How the journalist does his or her job will be fundamental to whether that job continues to hold any value, or even to exist at all, in a world in which anyone can be a publisher—but not necessarily a journalist.

One likes to think of ethical standards as distinct and separate from the temptations and pressures of the moment. That is, after all, what defines ethics: principles of conduct that stand outside the contingencies of place and time, a kind of protected, communal mental space to which we retreat when things get complicated or move too fast. When one measures the ethical implications of an act, a statement, or a choice, it is measured against what noble and enlightened predecessors have done in similar straits, against models and systems of behavior that have worked in situations roughly analogous to one's own.

Behaving ethically, then—in journalism as in life—is in some ways a process of abstraction and metaphor. Forced to choose a course of action that sacrifices one important value in order to serve another, one extracts the essence of the conflict and looks for antecedents that resemble it in ways that matter. Aristotle teaches the importance of virtue, warning that the means cannot justify the end; therefore, it is unethical to take down the corrupt mayor, however much he deserves it, by publishing unfounded rumors of cocaine use and strip-club visits. My religion says I should treat others the way I want to be treated; therefore, I will not publish the name of the woman who was raped on her way home from work last night unless she gives me permission. *Washington Post* Executive Editor Ben Bradlee made Bob Woodward and Carl Bernstein find multiple sources to verify the claims of Deep Throat as they chased the Watergate story; therefore, the story about booster payments to local college athletes needs to be held to the same standard.

Because decisions about ethics always take place in a realm of traditions and antecedents, they are inherently conservative. Ethical principles change slowly and only on the basis of extensive, convincing evidence. This is as it should be. A function of journalistic ethics is to lend continuity and stability to some shared idea of what is "good." What kinds of coverage appropriately balance the rights of individuals against the needs of the public? Which approaches to reporting and presenting the news best serve a participatory democracy in which useful information is chronically diluted and warped by political spin, celebrity voyeurism, and hidden agendas?

But while the intransigence of journalistic ethics can be useful in the day-to-day business of putting out a newspaper or doing an evening news broadcast, such an approach can devolve into a form of absolutism. Ethical guidelines come to be seen as eternal verities that supersede circumstance. The truth is that professional codes and principles are closely tied to the dynamics of the newsroom culture and the larger culture in which they evolve. And, as shown throughout this book, they are tied as well to the technologies by which the news is gathered, produced, and understood.

As you read this book, we hope you will keep an open mind about the ethics of journalism that is grounded in time, place, and technology. What happens to journalistic ethics when they are transferred to, and transformed by, a digital environment? What, if any, traditions and models can we bring with us to this new world of blogs and citizen journalism sites and multimedia presentation and 24/7 deadlines? And what does the transformation to a new order reveal about the very nature of journalistic ethics?

This book will help those who are or will be working online to think about issues and situations before they arise, in order to be prepared when decisions have to be made quickly, even instantaneously. To embrace the creativity of the Web and its possibilities—all it might imply about democracy, community, participation, and the value of individual voices—does not require that we abandon hard-won principles and standards, but it does require that we interrogate them deeply. It requires, too, that the digital realm be envisioned not as a tool for doing old things in new ways, but as a means of passage to an entirely different place. As with all such passages and transformations, that place will bear some resemblance to this one, but perhaps—probably—not in anticipated ways. Our work, on this threshold, is to imagine an ethics of the unexpected.

Notes

1. Merriam-Webster Online Dictionary, "Ethics," Merriam-Webster OnLine, 2006, www.m-w.com/dictionary/ethics.

2. Roger Crisp, "Ethics," in *Routledge Encyclopedia of Philosophy,* ed. E. Craig (London: Routledge, 1998), www.rep.routledge.com/article/L132.

3. Margali Sarfetti Larson, *The Rise of Professionalism: A Sociological Analysis* (Berkeley: University of California Press, 1977).

4. Jane B. Singer, "Who Are These Guys? The Online Challenge to the Notion of Journalistic Professionalism," *Journalism: Theory, Practice and Criticism* 4 (May 2003): 139–163.

5. Philip Patterson and Lee Wilkins, *Media Ethics: Issues and Cases,* 5th ed. (New York: McGraw Hill, 2005).

6. Deuze and Daphna Yeshua, "Online Journalists Face New Ethical Dilemmas: Lessons from The Netherlands," *Journal of Mass Media Ethics* 16, no. 4 (2001): 273–292; Robert I. Berkman and Christopher A. Shumway, *Digital Dilemmas: Ethical Issues for Online Media Professionals* (Ames: Iowa State Press, 2003).

7. Bill Kovach and Tom Rosenstiel, *The Elements of Journalism: What Newspeople Should Know and the Public Should Expect* (New York: Crown, 2001), p. 17.

8. Ted Gup, "Who's a Journalist—I," *Media Studies Journal* 13 (Spring/Summer 1999): 34–37.

9. Society of Professional Journalists, "Code of Ethics," 1996, http://spj.org/ethicscode.asp?.

10. Jay Black, Bob Steele, and Ralph Barney, *Doing Ethics in Journalism: A Handbook with Case Studies,* 3rd ed. (Boston: Allyn and Bacon, 1999).

11. Ibid.

12. Project for Excellence in Journalism, "Online: Public Attitudes," *The State of the News Media 2006,* 2006, http://stateofthenewsmedia.com/2006/narrative_online_publicattitudes.asp?cat=7&media=4.

13. Online News Association, "Reporting Excellence Online," 2005, www.journalist.org.

14. Black, Steele, and Barney, *Doing Ethics in Journalism.*

15. Ibid.

16. Kovach and Rosenstiel, *Elements of Journalism,* p. 17.

17. Ibid., p. 193.

18. John Stuart Mill, utilitarianism, www.utilitarianism.com/mill1.htm, and John C. Merrill, *Journalism Ethics: Philosophical Foundations for News Media* (New York: St. Martin's Press, 1997).

19. Immanuel Kant, *Fundamental Principles of the Metaphysic of Morals,* trans. Thomas Kingsmill Abbott, www.gutenberg.org/etext/5682.

20. Patterson and Wilkins, *Media Ethics.*

21. John C. Merrill, *Existential Journalism* (Ames: Iowa State University Press, 1996); Jane B. Singer, "The Socially Responsible Existentialist: A Normative Emphasis for Journalists in a New Media Environment," *Journalism Studies* 7 (February 2006): 2–18.

Online
Journalism
Ethics

1

Traditions, Conventions, and Ethics

Cecilia Friend

Journalists and scholars largely see journalistic ethical codes and principles as transcending time and place, but newsroom ethics are closely tied to the culture in which they develop and the technology by which news is produced. For example, the emergence of objectivity as an ideal in reporting the news is derived in part from the conventions of the inverted pyramid as a storytelling device and the commercial development of the telegraph in the nineteenth century that gave rise to those conventions.

Practices that once might have been tolerated, if not officially sanctioned, such as eavesdropping at government officials' office doors, have morphed into a pervasive wariness toward all types of surveillance as electronic looking, listening, and lurking become easier. And the range of taboo images and information—from shattered bodies to the names of rape victims—has steadily shrunk, first under the influence of televised war images from Vietnam, the Middle East, and Somalia, then in response to the ubiquity of personal data on the Web.

Journalistic ethics, then, is always in a position of delicate and uneasy equipoise with culture, technology, and history. Ethical standards must wield their influence outside the daily riptides of deadline pressure, shaky sources, and dubious methods. The standards are, by definition, abstractions—models and maps. Yet changing times do alter they way we think about or apply some traditional standards. And such changes may themselves pull in quite different directions, as with the many newspapers that have pledged to exorcise racial and ethnic bias from their pages even as they shift news-gathering resources from urban to suburban desks.

This chapter explores traditional newsroom ethics as a product of their time and place; the degree to which those ethics may be transferred to a new media environment; and, in particular, how ethical principles are transformed as they are both appropriated and contested in the digital realm.

History of Journalism Conventions and Principles

Claims of fairness, balance, and truthfulness in news are hardly a modern phenomenon. American publishers have voiced them since well before the American Revolution, according to David Mindich.[1] But throughout the era of the Revolutionary War press and the partisan press that followed it, most domestic newspapers were marked by a narrow political slant or driven by primarily mercantile interests. Before the 1830s, newspapers were "expensive, partisan and sedate."[2] Journalism in the modern sense had not yet been born.

The advent of the penny press in the 1830s saw the rise of a more popular daily journalism that targeted the masses with a mix of crime and human interest stories.[3] Political news was not altogether ignored, but the financial success of these cheap newspapers made them economically independent of the political parties that had previously underwritten them. The working-class audiences attracted to the egalitarian rhetoric of these mass-circulation newspapers turned them into big business and brought wealth to their owners. By the early 1900s, newspapers around the country were following the model of the successful penny city papers in Boston and New York: putting audience tastes and interests ahead of political interests and instant financial gain in a strategy of long-term financial growth.[4]

In some markets and newsrooms, of course, this financial independence was accompanied not by a larger journalistic vision, but only by a larger appetite for pandering—that timeless tradition that Jill Geisler has described as "bodybags and beauty tips, house fires and health hints."[5] An influential few, however, understood that financial independence was the necessary condition for ideological and intellectual independence. Adolph Ochs, who bought the *New York Times* in 1896, codified this new philosophy of disinterest in his first edition, in a pledge that would become his legacy: "To give the news impartially, without fear or favor, regardless of party, sect or interests involved."[6]

As policies of editorial independence took hold, editors and writers increasingly began to regard journalism as a profession and think of themselves as its trained practitioners. With the emergence of a professional ethos, journalistic principles such as those espoused by Ochs began to be articulated, debated, and institutionalized as ethical standards grounded in broad ideals of independence and nonpartisanship.

In 1912, a group of editors formed a professional association around a code of ethics that placed independence above all other principles. The American Society of Newspaper Editors' code said in part, "Freedom from all obligations except that of fidelity to the public interest is vital. Promotion of any private interest contrary to the general welfare, for whatever reasons, is not compatible with honest journalism. . . . Partisanship, in editorial comment which knowingly departs from the truth, does violence to the best spirit of American journalism; in the news columns it is subversive of a fundamental principle of the profession."[7]

Nearly a century later, those ideals are echoed with remarkable fidelity in a recent well-received book about journalism principles, *The Elements of Journalism: What Newspeople Should Know and the Public Should Expect,* by Bill Kovach and Tom Rosenstiel. Their first principle is that journalism's first obligation is to the truth. The second is a reiteration of Ochs's declaration: Journalism's overriding loyalty is to the public. "Allegiance to citizens is the meaning of what we have come to call journalistic independence."[8]

This is not to say, however, that the intervening decades have left Ochs's notions of the truth and the public interest unchallenged. While they are the foundations on which the twentieth century's most lasting journalistic legacies were built, both independence and its corollary, objectivity, have been the source of confusion, inquiry, and criticism. The terms have often been used as synonyms for other ideas, Kovach and Rosenstiel point out, including disengagement, disinterestedness, and detachment: "These terms are a confusion and reflect a fuzzy understanding."[9]

Independence, the Inverted Pyramid, and Objectivity

Michael Schudson in *The Power of News* observes, "In historical perspective there is nothing more striking than the transformation of journalism from the nineteenth-century partisan press to the twentieth-century commercial-professional press."[10] Central to that transformation in the latter part of the nineteenth century was the emergence of a new way to tell stories. The inverted pyramid, which begins with the most important information and ends with the least important, supplanted earlier chronological and expository forms over a span of several decades. With its emphasis on the "facts" of who, what, when, where, why, and how, the inverted pyramid signaled a shift not only in the way news stories were shaped but also a shift in the worldview of the society it chronicled. The inverted pyramid also brought with it a fresh ethical framework for how writers should approach their work.

While no one can say precisely where and why the idea of the inverted pyramid story format took hold, journalists were certainly influenced by the telegraphic transmission of news during and following the Civil War.[11] The telegraph's compressed messages highlighting the most dramatic pieces of information may have provided a model for modern news reporting, Schudson says.[12] The telegraph was only one of many scientific innovations of the era. Journalists of the new century, already influenced by their new prestige, affluence, and independence, were undoubtedly also affected—if only by diffusion—by an emerging empirical and scientific worldview[13] as well as the movement toward realism in literature and art.[14]

Schudson characterizes this newsroom paradigm of the era as a "naïve empiricism"—a faith in the power of observation, evidence and "neutral" language to convey things as they really are.[15] Reporter Ray Stannard Baker noted, "Facts, facts piled up to the point of dry certitude, was what the American people really wanted."[16] By the turn of the century, most writers had abandoned the older news story formats of narrative convention or emphases on points of view and embraced the inverted pyramid, with its hierarchical ordering of facts and events. "The world has grown tired of preachers and sermons," Clarence Darrow wrote in 1893; "to-day it asks for facts."[17]

Mindich summarizes the impact of this historical transition as a revolution. "The importance of the inverted pyramid, which supplanted the chronological style of antebellum news writing, is difficult to overstate," he says. The inverted pyramid produced an ethic of "straight" news and ushered in an era of "objective" news writing.[18]

And Kovach and Rosenstiel point out that the transition ultimately involved not only storytelling techniques, but the semiotics of the news— the design and placement of information to construct new meanings. "In essence, the press swapped partisan loyalty for a new compact—that journalists would not harbor a hidden agenda. Editorials and political opinion, which before had mixed with and sometimes even constituted the news on the front page, were now set apart by space or label. From these simple decisions—things that seem obvious today—much of today's standard journalistic ethics were formed."[19]

But while the inverted pyramid's focus on facticity and the growth of the ideals of objectivity and independence may have been a vast improvement over the verbal brawls of the partisan press, the new story form was not simply an objective, factual account of events—a mirror of the world as it is. Journalists writing in the inverted pyramid format were now forced to decide, however unconsciously, which parts of an event to include in the shortened story form and which story elements were more important than others. This interpretive dimension is, of course, present in any act of communication, but in the inverted pyramid it is typically hidden by a detached tone and nonnarrative sequence. "News, as we imagine it in its ideal state, is all information, no form," Schudson says. "The [inverted pyramid] news story informs its readers . . . but in a specific way. Its meaning lies in the instructions it tacitly gives about what to attend to, and how to attend to it."[20]

While the inverted pyramid story form and journalistic objectivity are certainly not synonymous, they are closely related philosophically and historically. The emergence of the form—the "methodology" of the inverted pyramid—was a necessary condition for the institutionalization of the principle; the principle validated the form. And despite the somewhat illusory nature of an "objective" new story, objectivity became quite literally enshrined as a journalistic ideal. It was "elevated to the status of a commandment: That shalt tell the news 'straight!'" Mitchell Stephens says.[21] Mindich also evokes the sacred in talking about objectivity: "If American journalism were a religion, as it has been called from time to time, its supreme deity would be 'objectivity.'"[22]

Criticisms of Objectivity

Despite objectivity's dominance as an ethical precept and the inverted pyramid's preeminence as the news story's form over the last century, the inherent flaws in both have been the subject of strenuous debate and criticism for more than half that time.[23] Most modern journalists would concede that pure objectivity is impossible. They recognize that the conventions of the inverted pyramid pose a number of inherent difficulties and that no one operates in a cultural vacuum or without personal biases.

Journalists cannot simply reflect reality. Breaking events into discrete facts, narrowing a story's focus, and imposing organization in the inverted

---

Exhibit 1.1
Objectivity and Hypertext

Mindy McAdams, with her former student Stephanie Berger, wrote "Hypertext," which discusses the nature of hypertext versus traditional journalistic storytelling and includes a discussion of objectivity. McAdams is the Knight Chair for journalism technology and the democratic process at the University of Florida and author of Flash Journalism: How to Create Multimedia News Packages *(2005). The article was published in the peer-reviewed* Journal of Electronic Publishing, *published by the University of Michigan Press.*

A hypertext story is a web of links that allows readers to either read the parts of the story in sequence from beginning to end or jump to topics by selecting a highlighted word or phrase embedded within the document.

Hypertext
Mindy McAdams and Stephanie Berger

Excerpts from "Journalism: 'Objectivity'" Thread

Will hypertext compromise journalism? That question rests on the possibility that stories told in the (multilinear) manner described here will be less fair, less credible—even less factual—than traditional print journalism.

Journalists often use the term "objectivity" as a shorthand to represent all matters concerning fairness, credibility, and accuracy. Many argue that "objectivity" went out of fashion in the mid-20th century as intellectuals conceded that all people (including journalists) have biases. . . .

Journalistic objectivity, nevertheless, retains currency as an ideal. . . . To approach the question of objectivity in hypertext, it will be useful first to determine the journalistic practices in which objectivity might apply. . . .

The practices of the journalist in selecting (and omitting) and presenting (or ordering) information—the practices of authoring—constitute the situation in which objectivity might be applied.

According to press critic Jay Rosen, "What is insidious and crippling about objectivity is when journalists say: 'We just present you with facts. We don't make judgments. We don't have any values ourselves.'

(continued)

Exhibit 1.1 *(continued)*

That is dangerous and wrongheaded" (Glaberson, 1994). The structure of a news story is largely determined by the values of the journalist and journalism institutions; these values affect the decisions made in the act of authoring.

Because a hypertext structure is multilinear—a collection of linked components—the standards of fairness and balance, and implications of bias and influence, will be manifest in the links themselves (Fredin, 1997).

Excerpts from "When Hypertext Is Better" Thread

Hypertext enables writers to skirt issues raised by the use of predefined writing formulas such as the inverted pyramid of traditional news stories which present facts in decreasing order of importance, the narrative path fixed and loaded with value judgments.

Some newspaper readers stop after a few paragraphs, satisfied that they've read the "most important" information. But what they got is the part of the story the writer believes is most important. Other readers skip through an article, trying to find a perspective relevant to them.

In contrast to linear stories with distinct beginnings, middles, and endings, hypertexts generally have multiple possible entry points, many internal threads, and no clear ending (Murray, 1997). This makes hypertext especially suitable for stories with numerous components. Unlimited storytelling space makes it so no component need be omitted in the process, which can lead to more objective journalism.

With a good hypertext, readers can foreground their own perspectives by first clicking links to the parts of the story they see as more important, then reading the remaining parts in any order (Fredin, 1997). In a unilinear story (i.e. print tradition), readers, reading conventionally, see first what the writer thinks matters most. In a well-crafted hypertext, readers immediately select what matters most to them. They spend less time sifting through facts as filtered through the writer's mind. Readers' choices allow them to avoid a form of information overload brought on by the choices of the writer.

Source: Mindy McAdams and Stephanie Berger, "Hypertext." *Journal of Electronic Publishing* 6, no. 3 (2001), www.press.umich.edu/jep/06–03/McAdams/pages/.

pyramid add subjective distinctions.[24] Journalists rely on witnesses and sources with restricted points of view, not to mention personal agendas. Language itself is not value-free and can shift meanings from person to person. The views journalists present to their audiences "vary depending on where in this large world journalists direct their small allotment of attention," Stephens says.[25]

Journalists also bring to their work their own upbringing, class and cultural attitudes, and personal beliefs. They are influenced by the routines and conventions of the work place. "Media consensus, in some instances, arises from a broad class and racial bias in society as a whole and the taken-for-granted angle of vision of mainstream journalists," Schudson says.[26] That kind of cultural bias is evident in every era, recently in both the U.S. and Arab media's reporting on the Iraqi war. U.S. media rely mostly on U.S. government officials and other American sources, and the media's views are generally pro-American; Al Jazeerah relies mostly on Arab government officials and sources, and its views are generally pro-Arab. Both claim to be fair and balanced; each frequently charges the other with slanting the news.

Reporters, whose jobs often focus on the workings of government, business, and society, must routinely rely on officials in those fields as sources for their news stories. What they get is the officials' point of view—spin—on the issues of the day. In the telescoped inverted pyramid form, those official pronouncements often lead the story and can constitute the greatest part of the news. That can lead to a negative kind of detachment, one that gives journalists a distanced, even ironic stance toward political life. In trying to give both sides to every story, inverted pyramid writers often create both the appearance of conflict, even when conflict may be minimal, and a false balance. Using the "he said/she said" model to achieve story balance can leave reporters vulnerable to manipulation.

During the 1950s, for example, many reporters relied on congressional testimony and the theatrical pronouncements of Senator Joseph McCarthy about the proliferation of communists in the government, in Hollywood, and in other realms of society. Coverage of this grinding daily cycle of aggressive, official accusations and often defensive, private denials was typically accurate and mechanically balanced. It also exposed some of the deepest flaws in the inverted pyramid form and the objective stance by legitimizing hysteria and polarizing debate.

Mindich cites an older example of how supposedly balanced coverage combined with widespread cultural biases failed readers in the coverage of lynching in the 1890s. The *New York Times* "balanced" its coverage by saying that, on the one hand, lynching is evil; on the other hand, "Negroes are prone" to rape. Ida B. Wells, the muckraker and anti-lynching crusader, was one of the few contemporaries to recognize that such "balance" merely served the status quo and offered "a skewed and dangerous construction" of reality. "In the case of lynching, 'objectivity' failed the truth. . . . The truth lay outside the rhetoric of 'objectivity.' . . . Wells was not 'objective,' but perhaps some journalists ought not be," Mindich says. He points out that Wells was practicing what now would be called public or civic journalism in an attempt to overcome the flaws of objectivity.[27]

The public journalism movement that began getting national attention in about 1994 was a reaction against an entrenched doctrine of journalistic detachment. It attempted to engage citizens in a variety of ways, including sponsoring public forums and galvanizing communities to find solutions to substantive issues. It emphasized cooperation rather than conflict, action rather than passivity, and large contexts rather than specific news events, especially the kind of staged political events that have become standard in recent decades. It tried to involve audiences in gathering and evaluating the news—a precursor to the interactive methods central to the blogging movement and subject to many of the same criticisms (which will be addressed later in this chapter and in subsequent chapters).[28]

Objectivity's Defenders

Although the abuses and methodological dangers of objectivity have become apparent, it is difficult to write it off entirely as an ideal, and a number of scholars and journalists now argue that the debate needs to be refined and reframed, not ended. Mindich and others, notably Kovach and Rosenstiel, say that despite objectivity's exalted position as journalism's most celebrated practice, it is also its least understood.[29] Objectivity has always been difficult to define as a philosophical concept, and in the century since its newsroom ascension, its definition has been made even more problematic by advances in cognitive and language studies. Kovach and Rosenstiel, in fact, argue that a misunderstanding of the *original* meaning of objectivity has led to most of its problems and criticisms. They say the term grew out of a recognition that journalists were full of unconscious bias and needed a method for testing information; the word was not meant to imply that journalists could be purged of bias. What journalists sought was "a transparent approach to evidence—precisely so that personal and cultural biases would not undermine the accuracy of their work." The original idea was that the *method* be objective, not the journalist.[30]

Others also have attempted to clarify the idea of objectivity, some by breaking it down into simpler components, such as fairness, impartiality, and balance. Kovach and Rosenstiel argue that even these terms are too ambiguous; they call for a reinvigorated "discipline of verification" to replace the murky nomenclatures that can be distorted and subverted. The foundation of this discipline of verification would include the following:

1. Never add anything that was not there.
2. Never deceive the audience.
3. Be as transparent as possible about your methods and motives.
4. Rely on your own original reporting.
5. Exercise humility.[31]

Schudson, and some others, though, suggest that we have outgrown the ideal of objectivity altogether. They believe the inverted pyramid and the quest for objectivity have themselves become a source of media bias, and they recommend that we begin the groundwork for what Mindich calls a "post-objective profession."[32]

Technology, Interactivity, and the New Media

The idea of abandoning objectivity as journalism's highest ideal resonates with many practitioners of new media. They invoke its inherent limitations and distorted evolution, along with the unprecedented ability of the Internet to engage readers, as good reasons for rethinking journalistic conventions for a new century.

A complementary movement away from objectivity can be seen in the resurgence of literary and narrative journalism efforts in the mid-1990s.[33] Writers for daily publications, such as Roy Peter Clark, Thomas French, and Mark Bowden, as well as an earlier generation of magazine writers such as John McPhee, Norman Mailer, Joan Didion, and Tracy Kidder, brought the first-person narrative back into news writing. Public journalism projects by 300 daily papers, some in conjunction with local broadcasters, from 1994 to 2001 were also in part a reaction against the traditional posture of detachment.[34] Even the shrill, vociferous jousting of tabloid TV and talk radio may be viewed as precursors to the move toward more outspokenness and partisanship that is one of the hallmarks of the new media.

It is, of course, not surprising that technology and its influence on society have fueled the charge to transform the current media model. New technology also set the stage for the emergence of the inverted pyramid and objectivity. Though it would be overly simplistic to make too much of the parallels, both the telegraph and the Internet threatened the hegemony of established media not only by creating new storytelling possibilities accompanied by new economic models, but also by bringing a degree of practical reality to the time-honored ideal of journalism as a public conversation. Internet technology has empowered anyone with a computer to create a media outlet with a potential audience of millions. And millions have.

News as Conversation

One factor driving this new media phenomenon is a dissatisfaction with the traditional model of journalists gathering and presenting an information "product" to an audience—a one-way street. Even when the audience is given some opportunities to express itself in letters to the editor or comments on print or network organizations' Web sites, the communication model remains more monologue than conversation. The mainstream media in 2006 are still dabbling in experiments in two-way communication with their audience—setting up readers' forums, accepting photos, allowing (but often closely monitoring) some citizen blogs. In the meantime, some journalists and thousands of wired citizens, unconstrained by tradition or training, have launched an incredible variety of expansive, inclusive media networks—including influential political blogs and grassroots music-sharing exchanges, communal data-gathering efforts such as Wikipedia and independent war coverage—and found some novel approaches to financing their efforts, including directly appealing to the public and using interactive Yellow Pages.

The Web's interactive capability has been the most dominant feature of the new media landscape. It has spawned passionate, public conversations among a throng of diverse voices and perspectives and led to the return of a point-of-view style of news writing. New media practitioners see this alternative media model as broader than, superior to, yet a faithful extension of the traditional press ideal of creating community and of keeping the citizens of a democracy informed and engaged.

The *Economist* quotes both Dan Gillmor, formerly of the *San Jose Mercury News* and author of *We the Media: Grassroots Journalism by the People, for the People,* and no less a powerful press baron than Rupert Murdoch echoing Clarence Darrow's plea to rescue the world from "preachers and sermons." Yet the terms have radically shifted; the contemporary "preachers" are the established print and network media, their "sermons" the consensual "important" stories told in conventional detached fashion. Today's youth "don't want to rely on a god-like figure from above to tell them what's important," Murdoch told the American Society of Newspaper Editors in April 2005. "And they certainly don't want news presented as gospel." And yet "as an industry, many of us have been remarkably, unaccountably, complacent." Gillmor agrees. "The tone in these new media is radically different. For today's digital natives," he says, "it is anathema to be lectured at. Instead, they expect to be informed as part of an online dialogue."[35]

Who Is a Journalist?

That, of course, means expanding both the notion of what journalism should be and the definition of who is a journalist. This topic is examined in depth in Chapter 2 and subsequent chapters, but it is useful to review its origins here in the context of the emergence of blogs and the citizen journalism movement.

Gillmor, who now makes the cause of citizen journalism the central theme of his work, sees interactivity as the core of a new media ethic. "The online world has . . . brought forth an ethic that we in mass media would do well to adopt: the willingness to engage with our audiences," Gillmor writes in "What Professional and Citizen Journalists Can Learn from Each Other." He calls the new ethos "part of an emergent ecosystem."[36]

New media practitioners and many citizen journalists or bloggers base much of their work on the idea that their readers know more about most subjects than they do. "Readers can help us understand our subjects better. They can give us facts we did not know. They can add nuance. They can ask follow-up questions. And, of course, they can tell us when we are wrong," Gillmor says.[37] This attitude of openness is, of course, common to most good journalism; it reflects Kovach and Rosenstiel's injunction to "exercise humility."[38] What differs in the digital world is that the pool of knowledgeable sources is both huge and self-selecting, and that—in "pure" blogs, at least—they enter the conversation on roughly equal footing with the journalist host. Gillmor recognizes that this represents both a continuity and a disconnect between digital and mainstream media. His goal is to teach citizen journalists how to combine the "fervor, knowledge and talent that exists out at the edges of the digital network" with the best practices and principles of traditional journalism.[39]

Jonathan Dube, creator of the Web site Cyberjournalist, editorial director for the Canadian Broadcast Corporation's Web site, CBC.ca, and an award-winning print and online journalist, envisions the online conversation as a kind of civic model of populist democracy. "The Internet is creating unprecedented levels of interaction between citizens and journalists—from blogs to forums—even to the point of citizens becoming journalists," Dube says in his posting "Journalism = Community = Democracy." He sees that as "a fantastic development for the future of journalism and democracy."[40] And K. Daniel Glover, who writes the Beltway Blogroll for the *National Journal*, likens bloggers to government's inspectors general (IG) and calls them not citizen-journalists but independent watchdogs of both government and journalism. "Just as IGs are not part of the agencies they oversee, bloggers are neither part of government nor journalism, but they keep a wary and watchful eye on both," Glover says. "And in so doing they provide a valuable check against the arrogance, inadequacies and abuses of all four estates."[41]

What often goes unmentioned, though Gillmor clearly recognized it, is the often symbiotic relationship between mainstream media and citizen bloggers. Most bloggers depend heavily on the information supplied by mainstream media—criticizing it, commenting on it, and sometimes adding to it. Traditional journalists, in turn, often look to blogs to see what news is igniting Web chatter. Some TV networks and magazines even offer "blog watches," reporting on what prominent bloggers are writing about. Nevertheless, the dominant rhetoric in the meeting of old and new media has thus far been the language of collision rather than collusion.

Bloggers Versus Traditional Media

Technology has been central to this shift from the old ethic of the reporter's objectivity in gathering information and presenting it to an audience in the inverted pyramid style to the new collaborative, conversational

Exhibit 1.2
Bloggers' Code of Ethics

The Bloggers' Code of Ethics was written by Jonathan Dube, an award-winning print and online journalist and now editorial director for the Canadian Broadcast Co.'s Web site, CBS.ca. Dube posted the code, modeled on the Society of Professional Journalists Code of Ethics, on his own Web site, CyberJournalist, in April 2003. CyberJournalist.net is a news and resource site that focuses on how the Internet, convergence and new technologies are changing the media.

Be Honest and Fair

Bloggers should be honest and fair in gathering, reporting and interpreting information. Bloggers should:

- Never plagiarize.
- Identify and link to sources whenever feasible. The public is entitled to as much information as possible on sources' reliability.
- Make certain that Weblog entries, quotations, headlines, photos and all other content do not misrepresent. They should not oversimplify or highlight incidents out of context.
- Never distort the content of photos without disclosing what has been changed. Image enhancement is only acceptable for technical clarity. Label montages and photo illustrations.
- Never publish information they know is inaccurate—and if publishing questionable information, make it clear it's in doubt.
- Distinguish between advocacy, commentary and factual information. Even advocacy writing and commentary should not misrepresent fact or context.
- Distinguish factual information and commentary from advertising and shun hybrids that blur the lines between the two.

Minimize Harm

Ethical bloggers treat sources and subjects as human beings deserving of respect. Bloggers should:

- Show compassion for those who may be affected adversely by Weblog content. Use special sensitivity when dealing with children and inexperienced sources or subjects.

(continued)

Exhibit 1.2 *(continued)*

- Be sensitive when seeking or using interviews or photographs of those affected by tragedy or grief.
- Recognize that gathering and reporting information may cause harm or discomfort. Pursuit of information is not a license for arrogance.
- Recognize that private people have a greater right to control information about themselves than do public officials and others who seek power, influence or attention. Only an overriding public need can justify intrusion into anyone's privacy.
- Show good taste. Avoid pandering to lurid curiosity.
- Be cautious about identifying juvenile suspects, victims of sex crimes and criminal suspects before the formal filing of charges.

Be Accountable

Bloggers should:

- Admit mistakes and correct them promptly.
- Explain each Weblog's mission and invite dialogue with the public over its content and the bloggers' conduct.
- Disclose conflicts of interest, affiliations, activities and personal agendas.
- Deny favored treatment to advertisers and special interests and resist their pressure to influence content. When exceptions are made, disclose them fully to readers.
- Be wary of sources offering information for favors. When accepting such information, disclose the favors.
- Expose unethical practices of other bloggers.
- Abide by the same high standards to which they hold others.

Source: Jonathan Dube, "Bloggers' Code of Ethics," CyberJournalist, April 15, 2003, www.cyberjournalist.net/news/000215.php.

ethic. But the roots of what has sometimes turned mainstream media and citizen journalists into adversaries go deeper—to the question of what medium and which methods best serve society and democracy. For those in each camp the answer is different, and the animosity between them is sometimes palpable.

One high-profile skirmish between the two camps of what one journalist calls the twenty-first-century information war[42] involved a successful attack on one of the country's most prominent journalists, the dean of network news, Dan Rather.

It began when *60 Minutes II* aired a story on September 8, 2004, that president George W. Bush had gotten preferential treatment during his time with the Texas Air National Guard. Rather cited four memos as evidence. Bloggers attacked the evidence as forged, and accusations, evidence, and commentary flashed around the Web, as well as traditional media. Ultimately, CBS admitted it could not back up its assertions.

An independent commission hired by CBS to examine the affair called the newscast the result of "myopic zeal" and concluded that the documents used could not be verified.[43] Despite the backtracking, a now-former CBS executive referred to bloggers as "a guy sitting in his living room in his pajamas."[44] The bloggers, ecstatic, were at least as unkind to CBS and the mainstream media (or MSM, a shorthand some use as an insult): "NOTE to old media scum . . . We are just getting warmed up!" wrote one cryptically named blogger, Rrrod, on the politically conservative Web site FreeRepublic.com. "I don't want to overstate the extent of my glee over the Dan Rather imbroglio now known as 'Memogate,'" wrote Jonah Goldberg, editor of *National Review Online*. "But it may well be the Greatest Story Ever."

The aftermath of the bloggers' assaults on Rather and the story led to the firing of a star CBS producer and the forced resignation of three high-level executives. It has also been cited as a factor in Rather's early retirement.

The CBS debacle also became the focal point for vituperation on both sides, not only because it was a major election-year story but because it intersected a number of ethical flashpoints: claims of partisan, ideologically driven reporting; the anchor-as-reporter illusion nurtured by TV news; the timing of campaign-season bombshells; and the lingering significance, if any, of Vietnam-era comportment by public figures. Most important was the fact that the story ultimately hung on a single, dubious source—a fault that mainstream media were as eager to condemn as digital media. Nevertheless, the drama was cast by bloggers primarily as an old- vs. new-media morality tale that exposed not only the rusty machinery of newsroom checks and balances, but also the mainstream media's hypocrisy.

New Media—Traditional Ethics

It is necessary to note, though, that bloggers who criticize the mainstream media for ethical lapses sometimes do not set the ethical bar so high for themselves. Matt Drudge, the Internet muckraker who was treated as a pariah by mainstream journalists until he broke several major stories on his Drudge Report site in the late 1990s, acknowledged that only about 80 percent of the information he posted was verifiable facts. The rest? Rumor and gossip.[45] According to Alex S. Jones, a former Pulitzer-Prize winning *New York Times* journalist and now director of the Joan Shorenstein Center on the Press, Politics and Public Policy at Harvard University, most bloggers disdain objectivity and the ethics of the profession as outdated and hypocritical: "Bloggers, with few exceptions, don't add reporting to the personal views they post online, and they see journalism as bound by norms and standards that they reject. That encourages these common attributes of the blogosphere: vulgarity, scorching insults, bitter denunciations, one-sided arguments, erroneous assertions and the array of qualities that might be expected from a blustering know-it-all in a bar."[46]

As blogging gains influence and adherents, though, some citizen journalists are attempting to revise their image and their work by setting up their own ethical standards based, at least in part, on the traditions of journalistic ethics. Jonathan Dube has created a model Bloggers' Code of Ethics on his CyberJournalist.net site based on the code of ethics of the Society of Professional Journalists. He says responsible bloggers should recognize that publishing imposes certain ethical obligations, even on those who do not consider themselves journalists and who therefore think they should not be expected to adhere to the profession's standards. They still have a responsibility to their readers, the people they write about, and society in general, he says. "Integrity is the cornerstone of credibility," and following an ethical code will "convey to their readers that they can be trusted."[47]

In May 2005, *New York Times* columnist Adam Cohen called for bloggers to heed their colleagues and their readers by holding at least the most prominent bloggers to "the same high standards to which they hold other media." The largest bloggers, in fact, are no longer outside mainstream media, despite their attempts to demonize it, Cohen argues, citing their annual coverage of the national political conventions and the World Economic Forum at Davos, Switzerland, since 2004. Traditionally, reform movements have held themselves to higher standards than the institutions they attack, he points out. "As blogs grow in readers and influence, bloggers should realize that if they want to reform the American media, that is going to have to include reforming themselves."[48]

Exhibit 1.3
Dialogues: Online Journalism Ethics:
Objectivity as the Journalistic Ideal

The following comments are excerpts from an online discussion with journalists and scholars in October 2004 in preparation for this book. Short biographies of the participants follow the discussion.

Stephen Ward (Canada)

I am an advocate and defender of the ideal of objectivity in journalism. I agree that all ideals and concepts, such as objectivity, have to be understood from within the context in which they are espoused—their space and time. I disagree that all scholars see objectivity and ethical principles as absolute. . . .

News reporting is enhanced when guided by *correctly understood* standards of objectivity. I do not defend the traditional notion of journalism objectivity—the idea of a reporter neutrally describing some objective reality, without any interpretation or perspective. The usual manner in which this idea is understood is to adopt a primitive positivism of fact—to insist that the reporter somehow stick just to the facts, and by implication, resist any selection, perspective or any other editorial activity. I think this is a false model of reporting, and of what objectivity requires. . . .

What I propose is that we reform the ideal of objectivity by reforming the ideas behind it. . . . What we need is a more sophisticated, defensible notion that acknowledges the valid criticisms of objectivity, yet retains its important elements. . . .

First, we need to acknowledge the obvious fact—cheerfully—that all forms of journalism involve some degree of perspective, interpretation and editorial selection and choice. . . . Second, we should reject the view of the journalist as a "recorder" and replace it with the journalist as an active inquirer into public events and serious issues. Then, we can ask: What objective standards are available to test our interpretations and our inquiries for such things as accuracy, impartiality, balance and other component ideas of the objective stance? Objectivity in this sense is . . . epistemic and fallible; it is about applying, as best we can, the best available standards of objectivity to our newsgathering and news

(continued)

Exhibit 1.3 *(continued)*

writing. Objectivity is not about eliminating passion or perspective or interpretation—it is about testing those interpretations with a set of ethical standards that disciplines and methodologically tests our impassioned inquiry. . . .

Chris Harper (United States)

I worked for that great bastion of objectivity, the Associated Press, after I graduated from Northwestern. Thirty years later, I have many problems with the notion of objectivity.

Let us keep in mind that objectivity in journalism is more or less an American invention. We have modified it to fairness and balance in recent years. Also, objectivity seems to me to be more of a business decision than an ethical foundation. If one is objective, one tends to offend less often. Therefore, one sells more newspapers or television ads or Web ads. . . .

I have worked in a variety of countries, mainly in Europe and the Middle East, for Newsweek and ABC News. Objectivity is far from the foundation of journalism in many democratic countries. In fact, I think that outright partisanship is a pretty good approach for a journalist. As a reader or viewer, I know exactly what the journalist's sentiments are.

In a world of journalism without objectivity, fairness, or balance, I know where journalists stand on issues. I know what agendas are likely to be set. I have a good idea of how reporters will frame a story. I know what their biases are. It makes my life as a news consumer a lot easier.

Online journalism, particularly bloggers, have had a profound impact on the world of "objective" journalism by pointing out the lack of objectivity, the lack of fairness, and the lack of balance from whatever political perspective you might choose. I doubt that traditional journalists will turn objectivity on its head, but the online world is already doing it. The only traditional medium that gets it is radio, where news and sports talk dominate the AM dial. . . .

Furthermore, since I don't think that objectivity provides an ethical foundation for journalism, it should be easier to cast aside what's really a writing style primarily practiced in the United States and Canada and move toward the more analytical approach of Europe and the Web.

(continued)

Exhibit 1.3 *(continued)*

Thomas Hanitzsch (Germany)

I agree that we need a more sophisticated understanding of objectivity in journalism. . . . We need a set of qualitative criteria that prevent journalists from presenting the news in a distorted or, even worse, partisan way. . . . If we abandon any kind of objectivity in journalism, we consciously expose journalism to being instrumentalized by politicians and other external sources. We would take away from journalism its legitimization as an essential force of democratic societies. . . . If people calling themselves journalists advocate a particular (political) stance, they don't subscribe to journalism but to (political) public relations. . . .

Let me pose a radical thesis: Journalism does not need any kind of "professional" ethics. If anything, journalism needs a common set of shared conventions. Ethical principles are connected with particular cultural understandings of morality. These normative values usually apply to a society as a whole, not only to journalists. A journalist subscribes to the same ethical principles as any other individual in a given society or culture. Sometimes people think that journalists, because of their power to influence public opinion, should be better humans than are their readers, viewers and listeners. . . . If we talk about ethics, we mean cultural values that manifest in norms and codes of conduct. We talk about something that is relevant to journalism "only" as context into which the practice of journalism is culturally embedded. Perhaps, we could avoid debate about the nature of ethics and morality if we would make use of the term "conventions" instead of "ethics."

Mindy McAdams (United States)

I'm not sure that I entirely agree or disagree with any of my colleagues here. That is, I agree on some counts and disagree on others.

Two things have changed in the past 10 to 20 years that affect how journalists and media consumers might think about the notion of objectivity. One of these changes is the concentration of media ownership and the absence of a strong partisan press in the United States. That is to say, we have a stark lack of diverse voices today in the mass media in North America. In some nations, there is more diversity. In others, there may be less diversity—but that is difficult to imagine.

(continued)

Exhibit 1.3 *(continued)*

The other change is the access to numerous other views of the world (and local matters as well) provided by the Internet, or more specifically, the Web. I am not saying that average media users all go out and seek diverse viewpoints as a regular habit. They do not. But if your local newspaper or TV news seems too one-sided (or perhaps too two-sided) to you, you have a wide range of other viewpoints to consider, if you care to look. So if you think the local newspaper is not telling the whole story, or has a particular bias, you can go online and find people who agree with you.

I believe this completely destroys the credibility of a stance of objectivity. . . . Readers and viewers and users do not believe that any journalist is really fair or balanced—perhaps they have never believed it. . . . So I think journalists would have more credibility if they did acknowledge that objectivity is an admirable goal, but not actually possible in reality. This may be like an alcoholic standing up in a meeting and admitting "I am an alcoholic." It may put journalism on the road to recovery.

Jan Schaffer (United States)

I would suggest that objectivity is a journalism convention that, like many other journalism conventions—fairness, balance, news judgment—is under siege these days. And perhaps it should be. It appears that aspirations towards "objectivity" are fueling the creation of journalism that is little more than stenography, parroting he said/she said statements—even when journalists know that the statements are totally false. Journalists are still far out of their comfort zone in calling a lie a lie. What might be more useful values for journalists are aspirations for telling fuller, wholer stories—multiple truths, not just one truth; for departing from conflict frames and striving for more explanatory reporting; and for giving readers and viewers the 5,000-foot view, not just the 50-foot view.

Personal Biographies

Stephen J.A. Ward is an associate professor of journalism ethics and acting director of the School of Journalism, University of British Columbia in Vancouver, Canada. He holds a doctorate in philosophy

(continued)

Exhibit 1.3 *(continued)*

from the University of Waterloo, Ontario. He has worked as a European correspondent for the Canadian Press news service, based in London, and as bureau chief in Vancouver. He is the author of *The Invention of Journalism Ethics: The Path to Objectivity and Beyond* published in 2005 by McGill-Queen's University Press in Montreal, Canada.

Christopher Harper has more than twenty years of journalism experience with the Associated Press in Chicago; *Newsweek* in Chicago, Washington, and Beirut; ABC News in Cairo and Rome; and ABC's *20/20* in New York. Since 1994, he has taught at New York University, Ithaca College, Adam Mickiewicz University in Poland, and Rostov State University in Russia. Harper is now an associate professor at Temple University. He is the author or editor of four books, two dealing primarily with digital journalism.

Thomas Hanitzsch teaches at the University of Zurich, Switzerland. He has taught journalism and media theory at Ilmenau University of Technology in Germany since 2002. He holds a recent PhD in media studies. He worked for German newspapers as a reporter, editor, and foreign correspondent in Southeast Asia and spent five years in Indonesia, where he also taught communications and journalism studies. He founded the Journalism Studies section of the International Communication Association in May 2004.

Mindy McAdams teaches online journalism at the University of Florida and spent seven months in Malaysia on a Fulbright grant in 2004–05. She is the author of *Flash Journalism: How to Create Multimedia News Packages* (2005). She has worked in both the online and print newsrooms of the *Washington Post*, for *Time* magazine, for a weekly business newspaper, and in book publishing.

Jan Schaffer is the director of J-Lab, the Institute for Interactive Journalism at the University of Maryland. Previously, she was the director of the Pew Center for Civic Journalism and, before that, an editor and reporter for twenty-two years at the *Philadelphia Inquirer*, where she earned part of a Pulitzer (and a six-month jail sentence). J-Lab administers the Knight-Batten Awards for Innovations in Journalism and New Voices, which funds community news ventures around the country.

Case Study: Political Blog

Suppose you are a former journalist and now publisher of the political blog Liberalamo.com. You pride yourself on being highly knowledgeable about politics, because you covered national politics for a major news organization and worked on political campaigns after leaving the newsroom. Your blog has gained a wide following and your readers rely on you to tell them all about the inner and outer workings of the national political scene.

In this hypothetical case, you are covering the efforts of an old friend, Bill Stevenson, to gain the Democratic nomination for president. You had long hoped that Stevenson, a first-term U.S. representative from Wisconsin, would launch a campaign for president since he shares your liberal views on foreign policy, health care, and other issues. You have openly supported him on your blog. He seems to be gaining momentum, partly because of your writing.

You have ignored rumors about his womanizing; you have no proof and do not seek to find any because what he does in his personal life does not matter to his candidacy, in your view. However, you have reported on another candidate's membership in a private country club that excluded nonwhites in the past, which you do consider relevant.

Now that Stevenson is on the primary ballot in most states, he will be a participant in a national debate next month. You have accepted an offer from his campaign staff to pay for your trip to the New York event.

Consider these situations and decide how you would handle them:

1. Stevenson gets the facts skewed on several answers, overreacts angrily to some of his opponents' answers, and by the end of the two hours is sweating profusely and seems completely unnerved. He seems to have trouble handling the pressure of that kind of spotlight. Do you feel an obligation to your readers to write about his missed answers and his apparent inability to handle a tough situation? Or since it is your blog and readers are not expecting an objective report, do you just accentuate the positive, especially since (a) you want him to be seen favorably and (b) you feel some obligation to his campaign, which paid for your trip because you are a supporter and blogger?
2. Another candidate, who went into the debate with a big lead

in the polls, was especially articulate and insightful on several issues. But in one convoluted answer, he seemed to say that he would support racial profiling in some circumstances. Do you nail him on that without asking him for a clarification of his views, basing your decision on the fact that many other viewers may have interpreted his remarks the same way?

3.   At the debate, you hear a lot of talk about Stevenson's womanizing. A young campaign aide tells you she is flattered by his advances even though he is married. Do you now feel an obligation to report on this aspect of his character? Or do you decide that you are only going to write about positive aspects of his candidacy and that readers who want other perspectives can probably find them from other sources?

4.   If other bloggers do raise the character issue, how would you respond?

5.   You have no qualms about having accepted money for the New York trip since you make no pretense of being objective and have openly supported Stevenson on your blog. Do you have an obligation to tell your readers who paid for your trip?

Notes

1. David T.Z. Mindich, *Just the Facts: How "Objectivity" Came to Define American Journalism* (New York: New York University Press, 1998), p. 149.

2. Ibid.

3. Mitchell Stephens, *A History of News* (Fort Worth: Harcourt Brace, 1997), p. 189.

4. Bill Kovach and Tom Rosenstiel, *The Elements of Journalism: What Newspeople Should Know and the Public Should Expect* (New York: Crown, 2001), p. 52.

5. Jill Geisler, "Blacked Out," *American Journalism Review,* May 2000, www.ajr. org/article.asp?id=360.

6. Kovach and Rosenstiel, *Elements of Journalism,* p. 53.

7. Ibid., p. 54.

8. Ibid., p. 51.

9. Ibid., p. 52.

10. Michael Schudson *The Power of News* (Cambridge: Harvard University Press, 1995), p. 9.

11. Mindich, *Just the Facts,* p. 65; Schudson, *Power of News,* pp. 67–88.

12. Schudson, *Power of News,* p. 67.

13. Mindich, *Just the Facts,* pp. 106–7.

14. Stephens, *History of News,* p. 245.

15. Schudson, *Power of News,* p. 78.

16. Robert Bremer, *From the Depths* (New York: New York University Press, 1956), p. 140.

17. Stephens, *History of News,* p. 245.

18. Mindich, *Just the Facts,* p. 65.

19. Kovach and Rosenstiel, *Elements of Journalism*, p. 99.

20. Schudson, *Power of News*, p. 69.

21. Stephens, *History of News*, p. 259.

22. Mindich, *Just the Facts*, p. 2.

23. Cecilia Friend, Donald Challenger, and Katherine C. McAdams, *Contemporary Editing,* 2nd ed. (New York: McGraw-Hill, 2005), p. 41.

24. Stephens, *History of News*, p. 258.

25. Ibid.

26. Schudson, *Power of News*, p. 8.

27. Mindich, *Just the Facts*, pp. 14, 134, 137.

28. Friend, Challenger, and McAdams, *Contemporary Editing*, pp. 193–198.

29. Mindich, *Just the Facts*, p. 2; Kovach and Rosenstiel, *Elements of Journalism*, p. 72.

30. Kovach and Rosenstiel, *Elements of Journalism*, p. 72.

31. Ibid.

32. Schudson, *Power of News*, p. 9; Stephens, *History of News*, p. 258; Mindich, *Just the Facts*, p. 138.

33. Chip Scanlan, "A Brief History of Newspaper Narrative," PoynterOnline, December 18, 2003, www.poynter.org/column.asp?id=52&aid=57899.

34. Friend, Challenger, and McAdams, *Contemporary Editing*, p. 194.

35. "The Future of Journalism," *Economist,* April 21, 2005, www.economist.com/business/displayStory.cfm?story_id=3896039.

36. Dan Gillmor, "What Professional and Citizen Journalists Can Learn from Each Other," Bayosphere.com, May 27, 2005, http://bayosphere.com/node/444.

37. Gillmor, "What Professional and Citizen Journalists Can Learn."

38. Kovach and Rosenstiel, *Elements of Journalism*, p. 78.

39. Gillmor, "What Professional and Citizen Journalists Can Learn."

40. Jonathan Dube, "Journalism = Community = Democracy," CyberJournalist, October 15, 2004, Cyberjournalist.com, www.cyberjournalist.net/news/001619.php.

41. K. Daniel Glover, "Journalists vs. Bloggers," Beltway Blogroll, excerpted from remarks at Heritage Foundation Roundtable, Washington, DC, July 8, 2005, http://beltwayblogroll.nationaljournal.com/archives/2005/07/journalists_vs.html.

42. Glover, "Journalists vs. Bloggers."

43. "CBS Ousts 4 for Bush Guard Story," CBS News, January 10, 2005, www.cbsnews.com/stories/2005/01/10/national/main665727.shtml.

44. Jonathan Klein, a former CBS News executive, video clip of appearance on the *O'Reilly Factor* and transcript in *Special Report with Brit Hume*, September 14, 2004, www.foxnews.com/story/0,2933,132494,00html.

45. Friend, Challenger, and McAdams, *Contemporary Editing*, p. 433.

46. Alex S. Jones, "Bloggers Are the Sizzle, Not the Steak," *Los Angeles Times*, July 18, 2004.

47. Dube, Jonathan, "Bloggers' Code of Ethics," CyberJournalist, April 15, 2003, www.cyberjournalist.net/news/000215.php.

48. Adam Cohen, "Editorial Observer; The Latest Rumbling in the Blogosphere: Questions About Ethics," *New York Times* online, May 8, 2005, www.nytimes.com/2005/05/08/opinion/08sun3.html?ex=1123300800&en=96d69423c3d28569&ei=5070&th&emc=th.

2

Newsrooms Go Online

Jane B. Singer

We have seen that newsroom ethics are a product of their time and place, subject to both transfer to and transformation by new media environments. This chapter provides a brief history and overview of the particular environment in which journalists work today, then explores one issue—the journalist's gatekeeping role—as an example of how that environment borrows, shapes, and calls into question norms and processes that are generally taken for granted in established newsrooms. Our consideration forces us to stop and ask just who is a journalist in this new media universe, anyway—and what, exactly, does such a person do?

Today, when we talk about online journalism, we generally mean content accessible through the World Wide Web, a graphics-based subset of the "network of networks" called the Internet. But the delivery of news content to a personal computer predates the Web by more than a decade, in the form of a variety of videotex projects sponsored by media companies in the late 1970s and early 1980s. We begin this chapter with a quick travel through time, from those early ventures through the explosion in computer-based news products after Web browsers became available in the 1990s; we then pause for an overview of online journalism today.

This book is essentially about ethics—the ethics of a particular occupational group called "journalists." But as this medium has evolved, it has become increasingly difficult to identify just who is and is not a journalist. As of this writing, approximately 1 billion people are using the Internet around the world; by the time you read this, the number will be even higher. And every one of them is capable of producing and disseminating content that can realistically be called "news." We suggest that this makes everyone a publisher, but it does not make everyone a journalist—and that the distinction lies in neither process nor product, but in the ethical guidelines to which journalists voluntarily adhere. This core definitional issue is a topic that we will return to in subsequent chapters, particularly when we look more closely at bloggers in Chapter 5. For now, in considering who is a journalist, we address the following questions:

- What might we identify as distinguishing characteristics of a journalist?
- Are the ethics of communication universal, or do the ethical choices made in publishing information, ideas, or opinions vary?

One widely used definition of a journalist revolves around the role of gatekeeper—a person whose judgment determines what information is and is not worthy to pass through a metaphorical gate for dissemination to the public. Such a role is grounded in the broad ethical norm of public service: The information that makes it through should in some way contribute to our ability to be free and self-governing citizens.[1] Yet in a networked world in which millions of people gather, organize, and publish timely information every hour of every day, there is no such gate. The idea that anyone can or even should guard one seems absurd[2] when virtually any bit of information, misinformation, or disinformation is just a Google search away.

- Does a journalist gate exist online? If so, how does it operate?

One of the advantages of traditional newsrooms is that they have multiple gatekeepers at various stages of the news production process. Reporters and editors at various levels provide a whole series of checks on information before it is disseminated.

- What happens to this idea of editorial oversight online, given not only the volume of available information but also the compounding pressures exerted by expanded competition and an emphasis on timeliness?

That last question will lead us into the next chapter, in which we explore the ethics of online information-gathering in more detail. For now, we start with a quick look at the forerunners of today's globally networked media.

A Brief History

In the United States, delivery of news and other information to people with computers in their homes dates to the late 1970s and early 1980s, when a handful of media companies went public with their experiments in something called "videotex." Videotex involved sending information from a central computer to an individual terminal over telephone lines, and the key advantages over print that its supporters suggested will sound familiar: speed, selectivity, the ability to personalize information, and the extent of available data.[3] Although similar systems in Europe were backed by national governments, notably departments providing mail and telephone services, those in the United States were developed and launched by corporations. They included television powerhouse CBS; newspaper chain owners Knight-Ridder and Times-Mirror; Dow Jones, publisher of the *Wall Street Journal*; and several financial magazines. About a dozen U.S. newspapers also explored electronic transmission through a service called CompuServe.[4]

The available technology in the 1980s, however, was not quite up to the task that these pioneers envisioned. Relatively few people had personal computers in their homes, and even fewer had modems that would enable digital information to reach them; both computers and modems were painfully slow at delivering and displaying content. Although the Internet existed as a civilian technology, having split from its military origins in 1983,[5] it was still a cumbersome text-based system used primarily by scientists and researchers and unknown to almost everyone else. Moreover, effective revenue models were elusive for videotex products' commercial backers, whose proprietary stand-alone networks were not connected to the fledgling Internet. By the end of the decade, many of the early services had been abandoned and others had morphed into something quite different, generally with few if any ties to existing news organizations. For example, the CBS experiment had evolved into the Prodigy Interactive Service, jointly owned by IBM and Sears; CompuServe had been bought by tax preparer H&R Block; and both were about to lose subscribers to a fast-growing start-up, America Online.

Meanwhile, those scientists and researchers connected to the Internet were realizing both the potential and the inadequacies of their interactive network—and beginning to address the latter. Two of their efforts were particularly important in bringing the medium into our lives. The first was the invention of a logical system for connecting something that existed in one place on the network to a different thing in a different place. In the late 1980s, Tim Berners-Lee, working in a particle physics lab in Switzerland, developed three technical keystones for sharing information in something he dubbed the World Wide Web. They were a language for encoding documents (HTML), a system for linking one document to another (http, a protocol for exchanging data among computers), and a document-naming system (URL, or universal resource locator) stemming from the World Wide Web.[6] A few years later, a group of undergraduate programmers working in a computer lab at the University of Illinois came up with a way to avoid tediously typing obscure text commands to navigate the network. They built Mosaic, a graphical user interface that let people simply click a mouse on a word or image to move from place to place. Mosaic was the first browser;[7] its commercial incarnation, Netscape Navigator, opened the doors of the Web wide to the world in 1994.

At the start of 1994, about twenty newspapers offered some sort of online product, mostly bulletin board services plus a handful of alliances with commercial online services such as Prodigy or America Online (AOL). By the end of that year, about a hundred online newspaper services were either operating or in development; the number climbed to about 300 by mid-1995[8]—and kept going. Advertising quickly followed; the first banner ads appeared on hotwired.com, the site of *Wired* magazine, in October 1994. Netscape was joined by Microsoft's Internet Explorer and then other Web browsers, as well. The easier it became to use the Internet and the Web, the more people started getting information online; the more people went online, the greater the opportunity for media companies and marketers to reach them there. Moreover, media executives quickly realized that an exclusive arrangement with a closed, proprietary service was unnecessarily limiting: They could create and maintain their own Web sites and reach the exponentially expanding online market no matter which Internet Service Provider users favored. Indeed, the explosive growth of the Web forced companies such as Prodigy to abandon the in-house information services they had been building for more than a decade in order to become what their erstwhile subscribers now wanted: a vehicle for fast, easy access to the global Internet.

A decade later, more than 1,500 daily U.S. newspapers—virtually all there are—have an associated Web site,[9] as do thousands of other media outlets around the world (not to mention countless numbers of bloggers and other "citizen journalists," whom we will discuss in Chapter 5). In addition to thousands of mainstream news sites, online journalism incorporates aggregator sites, such as Yahoo! News; myriad sites about news media and the media in general, offering journalism about journalism; and an exploding number of "share and discussion" sites offering diverse opportunities for interpersonal connection.[10] Although there are many variations in these online news operations, we can offer a few general ideas about what it is like to be an online journalist today.

Online Journalism and Its Audience Today

The second decade of Web-based journalism is similar to the first in some ways but increasingly different in others. Similarities include an overall emphasis on text rather than more visual forms of storytelling; an ongoing reliance on material from the parent medium, as well as on wire service feeds; and a continuing reluctance by publishers to staff online newsrooms at optimal levels. Differences include a turn toward profitability, at least for most newspaper-affiliated sites, and an increasing sophistication in taking advantage of some of the medium's attributes, notably to provide timely information.[11] Perhaps most striking is the fact that the Web seems to have become more central to news organizations' own view of what they do.[12] Many are taking greater advantage of technological capabilities; for instance, more than three-quarters of the nation's top hundred newspaper sites offered Really Simple Syndication (RSS) feeds (allowing users to have personalized context delivered directly to them) by mid-2006, and about a third offered podcasts (audio blogs). More and more media outlets are accommodating novel forms of journalism, too; for instance, eighty of those top hundred newspapers offer at least one, and often multiple, reporter blogs.[13]

A great deal of innovative online journalism has been produced in recent years, and awards contests to recognize the best of the best have sprouted, as well. Among others, there are the Webby awards from the International Academy of Digital Arts and Sciences, the Digital Edge awards from the Newspaper Association of America, the EPpys from *Editor & Publisher* magazine; and the Online Journalism Awards from the Online News Association (ONA), an organization formed in 1999 to serve journalists "whose principle livelihood involves gathering or producing news for digital presentation."[14]

The work honored by these organizations provides an idea of the contributions that online journalists are making at sites large and small, local and national. Recent winners in the ONA's "creative use of the medium" category—honoring achievement in combined use of multimedia, design, navigation, interactivity, and community—include a washingtonpost.com package on barriers between Israelis and Palestinians; a PBS Point of View package on the choices Americans make in what they eat, drink, and breathe (which also won a Webby); and a package titled "A Day in the Life of Our Schools" by DemocratandChronicle.com (Rochester, New York). Even the tradition-bound Pulitzer board agreed in late 2005 to consider online-only submissions for the most prestigious prizes in journalism; the 2006 Pulitzer Prize in Public Service awarded to the *New Orleans Times-Picayune* for its coverage of Hurricane Katrina highlighted not only the paper's staff reporting but also its Katrina-related blog.[15]

That said, much of what appears online is far less innovative. Most news organizations seem to be concentrating their limited Web resources on pieces with which they can make a big splash, producing outstanding special packages but relatively mundane day-to-day news coverage. So while online content is improving in quantity, timeliness, and technological sophistication, many news sites remain morgues for wire copy, secondhand material, and recycled stories from the morning paper or evening newscast.[16] In a review of predictions made in the mid-1990s about the potential for online news, long-time media observer Nora Paul suggests the promise has yet to be fully realized. For most of the news most of the time, the emphasis has been on fast and efficient delivery rather than the provision of comprehensive, in-depth coverage. The ability to link to background information and source documents all over the Web is fine, but it takes time to find and verify relevant material—and besides, who wants to send customers off to another site? The online news hole may indeed be bottomless, but journalists' time and resources for creating original content to fill it are still limited[17]—maybe even more limited than in traditional media formats, in fact, which generally employ far more journalists. A 2004 survey of Web sites affiliated with dominant newspapers in each state indicated an average staff size of fewer than a dozen full-time online editorial employees[18]—compared with hundreds in the newspapers' print divisions. A broader national survey of all U.S. newspaper-affiliated sites indicated that a median of five people were employed to oversee everything from content to sales, administration, and technology.[19]

When online journalists are good, however, they are very, very good—and, unlike the little girl with the curl in Longfellow's poem, even when they are bad, they are not so much horrid as merely mediocre. The interest in multimedia software such as Flash for creating new story forms is growing, with news organizations of almost every size experimenting with innovative presentations of information.[20] Online news is becoming a central source of information for major breaking news and for political information; in 2004, 63 million Americans went online for news or information about the elections and more than half said that what they found helped them decide how to vote.[21] Long-time new media observer John Pavlik, the chair of the Journalism and Media Studies program at Rutgers University, sees online journalism entering a new financially viable phase in which original content "is finally finding the beginnings of sustained economic support." In an e-mail to the authors, he wrote:

> In the early days of online journalism, there was essentially no business model. This made it extremely challenging for news organizations to make a lasting commitment to provide original reporting online, especially featuring interactive components. Now, as more online news organizations find financial support through the growth of online advertising and premium services, they are developing increased original online news coverage. The importance of this from an ethical perspective is it means online journalism can provide extensive coverage of important news events.

Advertising revenue is indeed picking up as the audience for online news grows. Readership of print newspapers has been declining steadily for forty years; only 40 percent of adult Americans now say they read the newspaper "yesterday." Even fewer, 28 percent, say they regularly watch the network nightly news, compared with more than 60 percent in 1993.[22] Meanwhile, about 70 percent of adult Americans now use the Internet; about 97 million of them go online for news, and steadily growing numbers do so "regularly." Overall, Americans' reliance on the Internet for news has doubled in the past few years.[23] Nor are young people the dominant online news consumers; as Internet news has gone more mainstream, its audience has aged. In 2006, as many people aged fifty to sixty-four were regularly getting news online as people in their late teens and early twenties, and the biggest online news audience of all was among thirty-somethings.[24]

However, while people are getting more and more news online with greater and greater regularity, they are not necessarily getting it from traditional news providers. By 2005, Yahoo! News had equaled and, in some months, overtaken longtime news leaders CNN.com and MSNBC.com as the most-used online news site; AOL News was not far behind—and ahead of the sites of traditional media companies such as the *New York Times, USA Today,* and ABC News.[25] As we discuss further below, journalists and the organizations they work for now share the role of news provider with many others.

One more audience trend is worth briefly noting here: the rapid and ongoing increase of broadband access, which makes compelling multimedia news ever more likely to be emphasized by news organizations. By early 2006, 84 million Americans had high-speed Internet access at home, a 40 percent jump in a single year. Growth has been especially strong among middle-income users and African-Americans. Moreover, people with broadband access at home are especially likely to post their own content to the Web rather than just read what journalists provide.[26]

In short, as the Project for Excellence in Journalism declared in its 2005 State of the News Media report: "The Web—and a converged multimedia news environment—seem more clearly than ever to be journalism's future."[27]

Within the newsroom, journalistic culture is evolving not only to adapt to new technologies but also to accommodate new organizational structures and, in particular, user expectations of input into the news-making process.[28] This book explores the way those changes are affecting the ethical choices journalists who work in these newsrooms face. Before we get there, though, we need to address a fundamental question that these and other changes raise. In the open, participatory world of online media, just who among the millions of active publishers is actually a journalist?

Who Is a Journalist?

Who can be considered a journalist has always been somewhat fuzzy. The occupation—which some call merely a craft and others elevate to the status of a profession—has no official definition and no formal requirements. In fact, members of the press have strenuously avoided such formalities, some fearing their existence would lead toward a reduction of autonomy and jeopardize the freedoms guaranteed in the First Amendment.

"Anyone can be a journalist and some may be, whether they like it or not. The question is whether their work constitutes journalism," says Tom Rosenstiel of the Project for Excellence in Journalism.[29] In *The Elements of Journalism*, Rosenstiel and colleague Bill Kovach emphasize that although First Amendment freedoms belong to everyone, the important issue is whether the work being done stems from "a respect for and adherence to the principles of truthfulness, an allegiance to citizens and community at large, and informing rather than manipulating—concepts that set journalism apart from other forms of communication."[30] Communication and journalism, they add, are not interchangeable terms. This view, however, is challenged by those who stress that the open architecture of the Internet and the flexibility of online publishing enable citizens to create their own journalism and thus fulfill the broader goal of strengthening democracy.[31] Exhibit 2.1 offers other takes on this controversial issue, particularly in the context of political coverage, from a variety of contributors of whom we asked: Can we—should we—define who is a journalist in a digital age? They, too, end up with Kovach and Rosenstiel's core principles.

What do journalists themselves think? Although there is an enormous diversity of self-perceptions among them, most journalists do see themselves as professionals, at least in the important sense that they feel loyalty to the ideals of a profession and a particular assortment of shared norms.[32] But sociological definitions of professions as occupational groups possessing special power and prestige do not quite fit the journalist.[33] Professions, for instance, share a core body of knowledge; virtually all lawyers have gone to law school (and passed a test about what they learned) and doctors to medical school. But large numbers of the nation's working journalists did not major in journalism or any other communications field, and a sizable minority have no college degree at all.[34] Journalists do not exercise oversight over other journalists' actions in the formal ways of other organizations; journalists cannot be "de-pressed" in the same way that clergy members can be defrocked or lawyers disbarred, for example.[35] Although journalists do have ethics codes, they are not bound to follow them as a doctor is bound by the Hippocratic oath. In fact, some media scholars argue that journalists should reject the notion of professionalism altogether. They say it implies homogeneity and standardization and thus potentially stifles the diversity that is the core strength of a free press.[36] And it reduces journalistic autonomy by forcing the subordination of individual ideals to those of a group or organization.[37]

Another approach is to focus on the process of journalism—the ways in which journalists "make news" through work routines, newsroom structures, and decisions about what should and should not go into a finite news product. Most of those routines, structures, and decisions are connected to—indeed, dictated by—the fact that journalism emanates from a newsroom, a place where journalists work together, located within a news organization, a collective enterprise structured to streamline (and, typically, profit from) that work. Control over the individual journalist comes from many directions, from subtle communication by peers about norms of acceptable behavior[38] to such institutional creations as beats and ways of both identifying and categorizing events in order to

Exhibit 2.1
Dialogues: Online Journalism Ethics:
Who Is a Journalist?

The question seems simple but turns out to be damnably difficult. We invited a group of smart people who have thought a lot about this topic to contribute to a blog associated with this book. Many chose to focus on coverage of the 2004 U.S. elections in considering who a journalist is. Here is just part of the discussion that ensued:

John Pavlik, chair of the Journalism and Media Studies program, Rutgers University: In the past, journalists were sometimes defined (in order to get press credentials in the United States) by the medium they worked for or were paid to publish/broadcast in. This definition no longer holds in the digital or online age. During the political party conventions in 2004, more than 30 "bloggers" were credentialed as journalists to cover the conventions. I'm reluctant to impose definitions on what a journalist is because it may constitute a form of censorship. I'd like to keep the notion of a journalist as open as possible in order to foster a robust discourse.

Ann Brill, dean of the School of Journalism and Mass Communications, University of Kansas: I agree that we've never had a good definition of "journalist" and it may be a moot point these days. The old gatekeeper function related to the hourglass idea of someone needing to decide what was important in an era of limited time during a broadcast or limited space in a newspaper. The new limitations, based on using the Web for information processing, are what users have time and motivation to access. So who decides what is important these days? I think recent elections have told us that traditional mass media communicators (aka journalists) may still see themselves as gatekeepers, but the audience has moved on to other sources. Perhaps we should replace the term "journalist" for, in the words of James Fenimore Cooper, "pathfinders."

Jan Schaffer, executive director for J-Lab, The Institute for Interactive Journalism, at the University of Maryland College of Journalism: I agree that the question of who is a journalist begs for a redefinition in a new media era. And judging from the coverage of the campaign, I'm not

(continued)

Exhibit 2.1 *(continued)*

sure that journalists, writ large, deserve the responsibility for "filtering out" what's important for public consumption. We are in an era when anyone can be a news producer. Journalists, hopefully, will no longer set themselves apart by a skills set, but rather by a mindset. To ferret out multiple truths, connect the dots, and cover the silences, not the noise.

Thorsten Quandt, project master in Communication Sciences at the University of Munich, Germany: The discussion on the definition of journalism in the age of the Internet . . . probably [is] one of the biggest problems in current journalism studies. I remember [an academic] convention where John Hartley challenged the audience with a programmatic idea: "Everybody is a journalist!" And Stephan Russ-Mohl answered: "Johnny Sixpack is as well a journalist as a miracle healer is a doctor." So who's right and who's wrong . . . ?

Chris Harper, associate professor of journalism, Temple University: There are a lot of Joe Sixpacks out there who had a far better clue about the issues in the U.S. presidential election than the pundits in Washington, the pollsters, and the analysts in academia. . . . The mainstream media were just awful. There is some hope, however, because of the way in which bloggers played a significant role in [the 2004] elections. I did a story in 1996 about online media and politics for *American Journalism Review,* and there was no one paying attention to digital journalists back then. In only a decade, there is a significant difference, particularly when it comes to journalists who have no affiliation with the mainstream press.

Ann Brill: The role of the different media, including the Internet, is being challenged by the changing media habits of different demographics. My students "read" *USA Today* and the campus paper. We have a program here that gets them four free newspapers every day, and my own observation during the elections was that there were the same amount of papers left in the box as any other time. . . . Students do have opinions, but they are generally not well-informed. I'm amazed at how many cite the *Daily Show* and Leno as their major sources of "news" about the candidates.

(continued)

Exhibit 2.1 *(continued)*

John Pavlik: I'd like to add a thought on "Jane" Sixpack, especially the wildcat blogger in the digital age of online journalism. I think adding the alternative perspective provided by the non-commercially affiliated blogger is a potentially wonderful addition to the diversity of voices in the online arena. Journalism can benefit greatly from hearing from individuals, even when not educated in the best traditions of journalism or affiliated with the best news organizations. In some cases, bloggers, such as those who were issued press passes to cover the conventions, did a splendid job of challenging conventional wisdom. This is all to the good. But where ethical problems can arise is when the question of acting responsibly comes into play. In some cases, media organizations trying to promote their own agendas or products can have staff pose as unaffiliated bloggers who are acting on their own, yet are really wolves in sheep clothing. This happened earlier this year when a major record label had its employees posting comments on music blogs as though they were just average fans, when in reality they were corporate lackeys. They were eventually sniffed out and the record labels were discredited. But then blogging and its potential good can be undermined.

Jonathan Dube, editorial director of CBC.ca and founder and publisher of CyberJournalist.net: I think the question of who is a journalist is an important one and not simply one we can avoid, as tempting as it may be in this increasingly complex media world. Among the reasons why this distinction is necessary is for legal questions such as who is entitled to protect their sources in court and who isn't; and for questions of who should be given press passes for access to events. It's important to keep in mind that the Web gives anybody the ability to be a publisher—but just because you are a publisher, that does not mean you are a journalist.

Rather than attempt to create a new definition, I'll point to the nine elements of journalism as outlined by Bill Kovach and Tom Rosenstiel in their book, *The Elements of Journalism:*

1. Journalism's first obligation is to the truth.
2. Its first loyalty is to citizens.
3. Its essence is a discipline of verification.
4. Its practitioners must maintain an independence from those they cover.

(continued)

Exhibit 2.1 *(continued)*

    5. It must serve as an independent monitor of power.
    6. It must provide a forum for public criticism and compromise.
    7. It must strive to make the significant interesting and relevant.
    8. It must keep the news comprehensive and proportional.
    9. Its practitioners must be allowed to exercise their personal
       conscience.

Note the last one. These elements by no means exclude bloggers—in fact, several of these (6 and 9 in particular) are very much what blogging is all about. But to be a journalist, one must practice all of these, including maintaining independence from those they cover, and most importantly, an obligation to the truth.

---

turn them into something disseminated as "news."[39] Importantly, such environments include not only reporters but also editors, whose job is to see to it that what a reporter has presented as news is accurate, appropriate, well-structured, and relevant to the audience.[40] Such a definition would seem to exclude bloggers, who typically work independently and autonomously—and whose "newsroom" is the Web itself.

The trouble is that the definition also excludes some people who we probably would agree are journalists. For television reporters, the increasing emphasis on live shots to enliven a newscast, arguably to the detriment of more meaningful coverage,[41] circumvents the role of the editor in broadcast news. Nor, thanks to technology, do journalists necessarily work anywhere near a newsroom. Laptop computers, cell phones, and other everyday tools of the trade serve reporters hundreds or even thousands of miles away, from those embedded with the military in war zones to statehouse reporters who live in the state capital during the legislative session.

At a more fundamental level, as well, technology challenges the notion of a journalist as someone engaged in a particular process. As we will discuss further in the next section, the journalist has always played the part of a gatekeeper, someone who chooses what merits inclusion in the day's news product and what does not.[42] This idea of the journalist as the person who decides what others need to know has become deeply ingrained over the years, particularly in connection with the idea of serving the information needs of a democratic society[43]—that is, giving people the information they need to be free and self-governing.[44] Through those decisions, the journalist actively shapes political reality, an agenda-setting function that lets citizens know which issues and ideas are important to think about.[45] In an online environment, though, such roles dissolve. An exploration of agenda-setting becomes a journey through a hall of mirrors in which an infinite number of participants simultaneously fill overlapping roles as sources, audiences, and information providers. The journalist has very little say in what any given individual will decide is important to think about; indeed, the key issue may well be what issues people tell the journalists they want to think about.[46] The traditional notion of a gatekeeper fractures, too; the journalist no longer has much if any control over what citizens will see, read, or hear.[47]

So ideas about professionalism and process, both of which have traditionally been used to distinguish the journalist from the nonjournalist, are problematic today. We would suggest instead that journalists in our current media environment are best defined not by who they are or even what they do, but by how and why they do it. What is definitive from our perspective is the journalist's ethics or norms, as well as the principles that underlie those norms. A label of "professionalism," therefore, works only to the extent that ethical guidelines set by that profession are followed—voluntarily, in the case of the journalist who, again, cannot be formally barred from (or initiated into) a profession whose autonomy is sanctified by the First Amendment. A consideration of process hinges on the extent to which ethical principles guide that process rather than on the news-making routines or structures themselves.

But are the ethics of communication universal, or do different principles take precedence for journalists and for nonjournalists? We will look at this question in more detail in Chapter 5, when we examine the ethics of bloggers, but for now, let us just say . . . yes and no to both options. There are overarching ethical norms for all human beings, such as the norm of treating other individuals with respect and of seeking to further the common good.[48] And there are overarching ethical norms of particular relevance to humans as communicators, such as commitments to truth[49] and to mutual accountability. But the ways in which those norms are articulated do vary according to a person's occupational role and the social context surrounding that role. Take truth, for instance. Journalists emphasize the process of verification as the optimal path to truth based on an Enlightenment philosophy of observable knowledge.[50] Bloggers emphasize transparency, notably the disclosure of contextual information about both themselves and their sources,[51] as well as open discourse with readers,[52] as routes to a truth based on collective knowledge. The person seeking to buy or sell an item on eBay may value honesty and integrity in a transactional context related to, but still different from, either truth-telling or accountability.

Online journalists, because they do their work in an environment that encompasses all these different sorts of communicators and more, face particular ethical challenges in seeking to define and distinguish themselves and what they do. Some have suggested that their best approach is to identify a set of "Net-native" editorial protocols that take the distinct demands of the medium into account in formulating professional ethics and guidelines.[53] Others say that the fundamentals of ethical journalism remain central and that existing codes, such as that of the Society of Professional Journalists, can lead to wise choices online as elsewhere.[54]

We think both views are correct; although they may seem to be mutually exclusive, they really are not. We believe journalists are journalists whatever the medium, so principles such as truth and independence are universally applicable. But at the same time, the online medium poses particular ethical challenges, rooted both in its technical structure and in the social norms that have taken shape around and because of that structure. Indeed, it is just those challenges that this book is devoted to addressing. We are ready now to turn to one example by way of introduction: challenges to one of the journalist's most basic and most easily understood role, the gatekeeper.

The Online Journalist as Gatekeeper

In a traditional media environment, one of the central roles of the journalist is that of gatekeeper, deciding what information is worth passing along to readers or viewers and what is not. Walter Lippmann was among the first to clearly articulate the role;[55] though he did not use the term, his idea of the press as "the beam of a searchlight that moves restlessly about, bringing one episode and then another out of darkness into vision" uses a different metaphor for basically the same idea. The editor, he said, must deal quickly and routinely with news accounts, each one of which "must be understood, put in relation to other bulletins also understood, and played up or played down according to its probable interest for the public, as the editor conceives it."[56] Three decades later, David Manning

White formalized the concept of the journalist as gatekeeper—the person who ensured, through selection of items for inclusion in or omission from the news product, "that the community shall hear as fact only those events which the newsman, as the representative of his culture, believes to be true."[57]

Perhaps no other journalistic function is so clearly challenged by the wide-open online environment. We will end this chapter by looking at how online journalists can continue to fulfill their ethical public service obligation as gatekeepers in a world without gates.

First, you may be wondering why this is an ethical issue at all; gatekeeping seems a straightforward metaphor for a routine editorial task. But the process involves more than the basic sorting of information. It involves power, and power carries an ethical mandate to wield it appropriately. The gatekeeping role gives the journalist the ability to construct public knowledge in a particular way and to ascribe particular importance to it—or not. It is a form of information control. Not everything passes through the gate, and what does is necessarily shaped by a process that includes not just selection and rejection of certain items but also such attributes as their display and timing.[58] Both the choices that the journalist must make and the potential effect of those choices on citizens turn the seemingly simple gatekeeping process into a matter of ethics.

But as we said earlier in this chapter, there is no gate in the online environment. Or perhaps more precisely, there is a gate—journalists still are selecting stories to put online and to display more or less prominently on their Web sites, much as they have traditionally selected stories for other media outlets with less space available for news—but anyone can simply go around it. In *Tuned Out,* a book exploring why news seems increasingly uninteresting and irrelevant to young Americans, David Mindich offers a wonderful photo of a lovely Georgian house, with a paved walkway leading to the front door and a gate (closed) at the end of the walkway. But the gate extends only across the narrow walkway; the lawn on either side is open to the sidewalk, without any barriers to deter curious passersby from wandering across it and up to the same front door—or around the side of the house.[59] So it is with the Internet: journalists may dutifully tend that gate, but the function has become an anachronism. Access to anything and everything is readily available, journalistic gate or no.

And yet we suggest that although the gatekeeping function indisputably changes in this new media environment, it does not disappear. Nor does it become less ethically important. Like many other aspects of journalism as it moves online, as we shall see throughout this book, gatekeeping simply becomes different.

The changes are obvious, and although they are multifaceted, we can group them into two broad categories. The first involves information itself. It is ubiquitous, it is virtually unlimited, and thanks to powerful search engines, almost all of it is nearly as easy to find as the information provided by CNN or *The New York Times*. For the first time in history, a single medium contains many billions of individual pieces of content, each universally accessible and each potentially connected to every other piece. The media product to which online journalists contribute is neither concrete nor discrete; it is merely a lone URL within a vast online universe.

The second broad category of change in the notion of gatekeeping involves the providers of that information. Less than a generation ago, almost all the information disseminated to a "mass" audience was produced and provided by journalists. Today, most of the information disseminated through the Internet—to an audience far more massive than even the largest single media outlet has ever reached—is produced and provided by people who are not journalists, at least not in the sense that they are employed by a news organization. And each of those individuals is his or her own personal gatekeeper, choosing what information to produce as well as what information to consume; indeed, the roles of producer and consumer have become wholly interchangeable.[60] The Internet is the first medium to make this fluidity possible. Moreover, it allows millions of individual producers/consumers to communicate directly with each other—and thus to obliterate the last vestiges of a traditional news gate.

If Lippmann lays the groundwork for the idea of the gatekeeper in a traditional media environment by stressing the importance of select information, his nemesis, John Dewey, offers a framework for understanding how that role has changed today. Dewey focuses on community and conversation as underpinnings of democracy; only when it is shared and discussed, he says, does information begin to realize its civic potential.[61] Contemporary observers also have emphasized the role of free and open discussion in the formation of public opinion, seeing conversation as the context in which knowledge can be understood.[62] As newspaper columnist turned grassroots journalist Dan Gillmor likes to say, traditional U.S. journalism is a lecture; Internet-enabled forms combine a conversation and a seminar.[63] The difference is profound.

And yet none of this means that the gatekeeping role itself, as interpreted and fulfilled by the journalist, is any less important than it has ever been. Arguably, in fact, it is more important than ever when information is unlimited and universal; the need for some means of assessing that information becomes urgent. What the enormous changes in the media environment mean is not that the role should be discarded but that it must be thought of, and carried out, differently. Here too, we can think of the challenge in terms of our two categories, the information and the producers/consumers of it.

A decade ago, at the start of the Internet era, media historian Michael Schudson imagined a world in which "governments, businesses, lobbyists, candidates, churches and social movements deliver information directly to citizens." As each person becomes a gatekeeper and goes about setting an individual information agenda, journalism is abolished. But not for long. People quickly realize that they need help in understanding events, in identifying what is most important, most relevant, most interesting. A professional press corps soon reappears.[64]

Such a press corps is readily recognizable today. Its gatekeeping task has morphed into something that is not new but is newly pressing. In this environment, gatekeeping is not a matter of keeping items out of circulation; it is a matter of vetting items for their veracity and of placing them within the broader context that is easily lost under the tidal wave of new "information."[65] Journalists' ethical obligation becomes helping citizens find and understand information they can trust; journalists in such an environment become not gatekeepers but sense-makers.[66] The emphasis shifts from regulating the quantity of information that enters public discourse to ensuring the quality of at least some of that information.[67]

Such a shift is not a dramatic change from the ethical conduct of journalism in any other environment; U.S. journalists overall put less emphasis on getting information out quickly than they did as little as ten years ago, as well as more emphasis on analyzing complex problems. Moreover, fewer journalists than at any point in the past thirty years believe that entertaining their audiences is an extremely important part of their job;[68] in a media environment in which comedians and even strippers double as "newscasters,"[69] journalists are wise to play to their own quite different strengths rather than try to compete on entertainment value.

In short, there is a growing sense that journalists must reconceptualize their role in relation to information. They are no longer able to determine what is or is not available. Instead, the medium offers them an opportunity to focus on helping citizens determine what is or is not truthful, valuable, and meaningful.

A related component of making sense of a glut of information involves the notion of newsroom checks and balances. Various editorial processes are designed to increase the likelihood that trustworthy information will be disseminated—truth as journalists define it, whatever the medium. A quality check of the information selected for inclusion in the news product is part of the editor's gatekeeping role, and such a check includes not just basic facts but also matters of fairness, balance, completeness, and other ethical norms of news. The demand for speed and other pressures of the online medium can put significant pressures on the online journalist, as discussed more thoroughly in the context of information gathering in the next chapter. But the process and the principles of producing news are every bit as worthwhile online as off.

We end this chapter with what we think is a dramatic change: from the journalist's former franchise as *the* gatekeeper to a role as simply *a* gatekeeper among multitudes. Again, the journalist is hardly the only one producing and disseminating information online; indeed, the overwhelming majority of online content does not come from a traditional journalist at all. If the journalistic adaptation in relation to information involves a shift from gatekeeping to sense-making, we suggest that the adaptation in relation to other information providers involves finding viable ways to include those others in the sense being made. Journalists should shift away from guarding the gate and toward sharing its upkeep.

Online journalists can do this more easily than their print or television counterparts because they work in a medium that facilitates participation. To date, evidence suggests that journalists in general have continued to rely on official sources in their news accounts[70] and although "citizen journalist" sites are becoming more popular, editors generally keep their content segregated from the information provided by the mainstream medium's online component. Axel Bruns terms these "gatewatching" sites; in contrast to traditional gatekeeping approaches, almost all incoming material is publicized and becomes an open source repository of content that appeals to special-interest communities, such as people in a particular geographic area.[71]

Clearly, there is a middle ground between ignoring these and other knowledgeable voices and turning the news product over to them completely. That middle ground lies in the ways that journalists open their historically restrictive gates surrounding who is privileged to speak through the media. Journalists can and should draw on a broad range of online information providers as sources for news and opinion. That is not to say such sources should not be vetted as journalists have always done; indeed, they should and arguably more thoroughly than ever. Nor is it to say that journalists should not exercise judgment in selecting to whom or what they accord the privilege that comes when they associate their name and that of their employer with a particular set of information; this chapter's case study will, we hope, steer you toward exactly such judgments.

But the interactive nature of the medium offers a prime opportunity to break away from restrictive conventions of sourcing in which only people holding particular badges of authority are allowed through the journalistic gate. Reliance on such sources, many of whom have their own agendas that do not necessarily coincide with the public interest,[72] has reached a point where trust in both the message and messenger is at dangerously low levels for the health of our society. Increasingly, people are tuning out altogether; in a democracy that depends on civic discourse, as various observers have stressed for nearly a century, the consequences are frightening. If journalists are indeed becoming sense-makers, then it is vital that the sense they make—and, in turn, that citizens who are themselves both consumers and producers of widely available information also make—be informed by more views and more voices than in the past.

These ideas bring us to the topic of online information-gathering practices. The journalistic gatekeeping function and its various modifications and permutations in an open, networked environment involve both reporting and editing. Let us now look more closely at the first of those, reporting or gathering information.

Case Study: News Director as Gatekeeper

(This case study involves an issue facing real journalists, but the specific circumstances, as well as the names used here, are fictional.)

Ashley Stephens is the online news director for NNN.com, the Web site affiliated with cable television's National News Network. "Trip N," as its staffers (and many users) call it, has been very successful in translating its "brand"—its reputation for strong live reporting, particularly of breaking news events—to the Web. NNN.com is consistently among the top five news sites in terms of usage, averaging more than 25 million unique visitors every month.

Stephens has been news director since late 2002, and one of her first decisions was to make the events in and around Iraq a showpiece for Trip N. "Whenever people want to know what's going on over there, this should be the place they think of checking first," she told her staff when she took the job. "I want NNN.com to *own* this story."

Her philosophy has been that if something happens that concerns Iraq, it belongs on NNN.com. She gave the multifaceted story its own permanent, prominent location on the home page; mandated that it be updated at least four times a day (corresponding to the morning, midday, late afternoon, and evening "dayparts" when usage tends to spike); and has consistently channeled resources into making it the most technologically innovative section of NNN.com.

It has proved to be a good call. Over the years, the site has won numerous prestigious awards for its combination of text, images, multimedia, and interactive features to tell the ongoing story of the war, its effects, and anything related to it. Both hit logs and user surveys indicate that the Iraq section is indeed a major reason why users regularly come to the Trip N site.

In short, Stephens set out to make NNN.com the nation's gateway to timely, credible, useful, and engaging information about Iraq. And she succeeded.

This morning on her way to work, she picked up the latest news on the radio. She learned about more bombings, another presidential speech on the necessary costs of victory, and that yet another group of angry young men claiming some nebulous connection to al Qaeda had kidnapped four American Red Cross workers and were threatening to execute them unless a set of equally nebulous demands was met immediately.

When she arrived in the newsroom, Stephens noticed several of her editors clustered around a computer terminal. She heard several of them gasp and glanced in their direction in time to see Ryan, the new intern, throw up . . . unfortunately, before making it to the nearest wastebasket.

Before she got her coat off, her senior foreign editor, who had been in the center of the group, was at the door of her office.

"Ashley, you need to see this video feed," he said. "FX News has already got it up on their site, and I just googled—it's all over the blogosphere. Should we run with it?"

Booting up her computer, Stephens glanced out the office window at a pale Ryan diligently scrubbing the carpet with a fistful of wet paper towels. As she had known it would be, the video was from Iraq. It showed the kidnappers mutilating and then beheading two of the Red Cross workers, a young woman and an older man, while the other two were forced to watch. As the masked kidnappers waved severed heads and bloody swords, Stephens fought back the compelling urge to follow Ryan's lead.

Trip N had staked its online name on all things Iraq. The story, including the video footage, was obviously news; moreover, it already was available on their chief competitor's news site as well as a no doubt rapidly expanding number of blogs. If the past was any guide, it would draw a lot of usage, too; video of the beheading of U.S. contractor Nicholas Berg in 2004 had been among the most-searched-for sites on the whole Internet for several weeks.

The foreign editor glanced at his watch. It was her call, and she had to make it now.

1. Should Trip N run this video on its Web site? Why or why not? Either way, what factors should go into Stephens's decision? Which of those factors are most compelling in making a decision?
2. What alternatives are available to Stephens? Whether she decides to run the video or not, there is a range of additional options, including related supplemental information, follow-up stories, explanations to users, and sources for additional reporting. List and briefly describe as many of those alternatives as you can. Which would you choose? How would you prioritize them— which would you do right away, which later? Why?
3. In a traditional news environment—television, say—few if any mainstream U.S. journalists would air this video. Acting as gatekeepers, most would decide that it was too disturbing and that the important aspects of the story could be conveyed in less nauseating ways. The vast majority of the public would therefore never see it. In an online news environment, however, anyone who wants to see it can do so easily. It will be talked about, and it will affect public opinion about the situation in Iraq—it will, that is, become part of the public discourse on this important topic regardless of what Stephens does. How, if at all, should this affect her decision about whether and how to use it herself?

Notes

1. Bill Kovach and Tom Rosenstiel, *The Elements of Journalism: What Newspeople Should Know and the Public Should Expect* (New York: Crown, 2001).

2. Bruce A. Williams and Michael X. Delli Carpini, "Unchained Reaction: The Collapse of Media Gatekeeping and the Clinton-Lewinsky Scandal," *Journalism: Theory, Practice and Criticism* 1 (April 2000): 61–85.

3. Efrem Sigel, *The Future of Videotex* (White Plains, NY: Knowledge Industry Publications, 1983).

4. David Carlson, "The Online Timeline," David Carlson's Virtual World, 2005, http://iml.jou.ufl.edu/carlson/1980s.shtml.

5. John V. Pavlik, *New Media Technology: Cultural and Commercial Perspectives*, 2nd ed. (Boston: Allyn and Bacon, 1998).

6. Robert Wright, "The Man Who Invented the Web," in *Online Journalism*, ed. Kathleen Wickham (Boulder, CO: Coursewise Publishing, 1998), pp. 5–9.

7. Pavlik, *New Media Technology*.

8. Steve Outing, "Join the Party! 300-Plus Newspapers Are Online," Stop the Presses, Editor & Publisher Online, August 21, 1995, http://web.archive.org/web/20000521022102/www.mediainfo.com/ephome/news/newshtm/stop/stop2.htm.

9. Jonathan Dube, "Number of Online Papers Grows," CyberJournalist.net, August 26, 2005, www.cyberjournalist.net/news/002826.php.

10. Mark Deuze, "Online Journalism: Modeling the First Generation of News Media on the World Wide Web," First Monday, October 10, 2001, www.firstmonday.org/issues/issue6_10/deuze/.

11. Project for Excellence in Journalism, "Online: Intro," *State of the News Media* 2005, www.stateofthemedia.org/2005/narrative_online_intro.asp?cat=1&media=3.

12. Project for Excellence in Journalism, "Online: Intro," *State of the News Media* 2006, www.stateofthemedia.org/2006/narrative_online_intro.asp?cat=1&media=4.

13. Erin Teeling, "The Use of the Internet by America's Newspapers," Bivings Report, August 1, 2006, www.bivingsreport.com/2006/the-use-of-the-internet-by-america's-newspapers/.

14. Online News Association, "The ONA Mission," 2005, http://journalist.org/about/archives/000012.php.

15. Seymour Topping, "Joseph Pulitzer and the Pulitzer Prizes" and "The Pulitzer Prize Winners, 2006: Public Service," Pulitzer Board, 2006, www.pulitzer.org/history.html, http://www.pulitzer.org/year/2006/public-service/works/timespicindex.html.

16. Project for Excellence, 2005.

17. Nora Paul, "'New News' Retrospective: Is Online News Reaching Its Potential?" *Online Journalism Review*, March 24, 2005, http://ojr.org/ojr/stories/050324paul.

18. Jane B. Singer, "Stepping Back from the Gate: Online Newspaper Editors and the Co-Production of Content in Campaign 2004," *Journalism & Mass Communication Quarterly* 83 (Summer 2006): 265–280.

19. Rob Runett, "Executive Summary: Newspapers' Online Operations: Performance Report 2004," Newspaper Association of America, November 2004, www.naa.org/Electronic-Publishing/Resources/Executive-Summary-Newspapers-Online-Operations-Performance-Report-2004.aspx.

20. Paul, "'New News' Retrospective."

21. Lee Rainie, Michael Cornfield, and John Horrigan, "The Internet and Campaign 2004," Pew Internet & American Life Project, March 6, 2005, www.pewinternet.org/PPF/r/150/report_display.asp.

22. Pew Research Center for the People and the Press, "Online Papers Modestly

Boost Newspaper Readership," July 30, 2006, http://people-press.org/reports/display.php3?ReportID=282.

23. Project for Excellence in Journalism, "Online: Audience," *State of the News Media 2006*, http://stateofthemedia.org/2006/narrative_online_audience.asp?cat=3&media=4.

24. Pew Research Center, "Online Papers."

25. Project for Excellence in Journalism, "Online: Ownership," *State of the News Media 2006*, http://stateofthemedia.org/2006/narrative_online_audience.asp?cat=5&media=4.

26. John Horrigan, "Home Broadband Adoption: 2006," Pew Internet & American Life Project, May 28, 2006, www.pewinternet.org/PPF/r/184/report_display.asp.

27. Project for Excellence, 2005.

28. Pablo J. Boczkowski, "Redefining the News Online," *Online Journalism Review*, 2004, http://ojr.org/ojr/workplace/1075928349.php; Jane B. Singer, "More Than Ink-Stained Wretches: The Resocialization of Print Journalists in Converged Newsrooms," *Journalism & Mass Communication Quarterly* 81 (Winter 2004): 838–856.

29. Tom Rosenstiel, "Who's a Journalist? Take Notes: You Might Be Surprised," *Boston Globe*, July 26, 2004, www.boston.com/news/nation/ articles/2004/07/26/whos_a_journalist_take_notes_you_might_be_surprised/.

30. Kovach and Rosenstiel, *Elements of Journalism*, p. 98.

31. Robert I. Berkman and Christopher A. Shumway, *Digital Dilemmas: Ethical Issues for Online Media Professionals* (Ames: Iowa State Press, 2003).

32. Philip Patterson and Lee Wilkins, *Media Ethics: Issues and Cases*, 5th ed. (New York: McGraw-Hill, 2005).

33. Margali Sarfetti Larson, *The Rise of Professionalism: A Sociological Analysis* (Berkeley: University of California Press, 1977); Jane B. Singer, "Who Are These Guys? The Online Challenge to the Notion of Journalistic Professionalism," *Journalism: Theory, Practice and Criticism* 4 (May 2003): 139–163.

34. David H. Weaver and G. Cleveland Wilhoit, *The American Journalist in the 1990s: U.S. News People at the End of an Era* (Mahwah, NJ: Lawrence Erlbaum, 1996).

35. John C. Merrill, "Merrill: Journalism Is Not a Profession," in *Media Debates: Issues in Mass Communication*, ed. Everette E. Dennis and John C. Merrill, 2nd ed. (White Plains, NY: Longman, 1996).

36. Theodore L. Glasser, "Professionalism and the Derision of Diversity: The Case of the Education of Journalists," *Journal of Communication* 42 (Spring 1992): 131–140.

37. John C. Merrill, *The Imperative of Freedom: A Philosophy of Journalistic Autonomy* (New York: Hastings House, 1974).

38. Warren Breed, "Social Control in the Newsroom: A Functional Analysis," *Social Forces* 33 (May 1955): 326–335.

39. Gaye Tuchman, *Making News: A Study in the Construction of Reality* (New York: Free Press, 1978).

40. Cecilia Friend, Donald Challenger, and Katherine C. McAdams, *Contemporary Editing*, 2nd ed. (New York: McGraw-Hill, 2005).

41. C.A. Tuggle and Suzanne Huffman, "Live Reporting in Television News: Breaking News or Black Holes?" *Journal of Broadcasting and Electronic Media* 45 (Spring 2001): 335–344.

42. David Manning White, "The 'Gate Keeper': A Case Study in the Selection of News," *Journalism Quarterly* 24 (Autumn 1950): 383–390.

43. Morris Janowitz, "Professional Models in Journalism: The Gatekeeper and the Advocate," *Journalism Quarterly* 52 (Winter 1975): 618–626, 662; Herbert J. Gans, *Democracy and the News* (Oxford: Oxford University Press, 2003).

44. Kovach and Rosenstiel, *Elements of Journalism*.

45. Maxwell E. McCombs and Donald L. Shaw, "The Agenda-Setting Function of Mass Media," *Public Opinion Quarterly* 36 (Summer 1972): 176–187.

46. Steven H. Chaffee and Miriam J. Metzger, "The End of Mass Communication?" *Mass Communication & Society* 4, no. 4 (2001): 365–379.

47. Jane B. Singer, "The Socially Responsible Existentialist: A Normative Emphasis for Journalists in a New Media Environment," *Journalism Studies* 7 (February 2006): 2–18.

48. Pontifical Council for Social Communications, "Ethics in Internet," February 28, 2002, www.vatican.va/roman_curia/pontifical_councils/pccs/documents/rc_pc_pccs_doc_20020228_ethics-internet_en.html.

49. Sissela Bok, *Lying: Moral Choice in Public and Private Life* (New York: Vintage Books, 1989).

50. Kovach and Rosenstiel, *Elements of Journalism*; Singer, "Socially Responsible."

51. Rebecca Blood, *The Weblog Handbook: Practical Advice on Creating and Maintaining Your Blog* (New York: Perseus, 2002), www.rebeccablood.net/handbook/excerpts/weblog_ethics.html.

52. Jonathan Dube, "A Blogger's Code of Ethics," CyberJournalist.net, April 15, 2003, www.cyberjournalist.net/news/000215.php.

53. Mark Deuze and Daphna Yeshua, "Online Journalists Face New Ethical Dilemmas: Lessons from The Netherlands," *Journal of Mass Media Ethics* 16, no. 4 (2001): 273–292.

54. Jay Black, "Journalism Nethics," *Convergence: The Journal of Research into New Media Technologies* 4 (Winter 1998): 10–17.

55. Berkman and Shumway, *Digital Dilemmas*.

56. Walter Lippmann, *Public Opinion* (New York: Free Press, 1922), pp. 352, 364.

57. White, "Gate Keeper," p. 390.

58. Pamela J. Shoemaker, *Gatekeeping* (Newbury Park, CA: Sage, 1991).

59. David T.Z. Mindich, *Tuned Out: Why Americans Under 40 Don't Follow the News* (New York: Oxford University Press, 2005).

60. Robert Burnett and P. David Marshall, *Web Theory: An Introduction* (New York: Routledge, 2003).

61. John Dewey, *The Public and Its Problems* (New York: Swallow Press, 1927).

62. James W. Carey, *Communication as Culture: Essays on Media and Society* (Boston: Unwin Hyman, 1989); Jürgen Habermas, *The Structural Transformation of the Public Sphere: An Inquiry into a Category of Bourgeois Society*, trans. Thomas Burger and Frederick Lawrence (Cambridge, MA: MIT Press, 1989).

63. Dan Gillmor, *We the Media: Grassroots Journalism by the People, for the People* (Sebastapol, CA: O'Reilly Media, 2004).

64. Michael Schudson, *The Power of News* (Cambridge, MA: Harvard University Press, 1995).

65. Singer, "Socially Responsible."

66. Tom Rosenstiel, "The Future of News: Sense-Making and Other Strategies for Survival," PoynterOnline, June 21, 2006, www.poynter.org/column.asp?id=34&aid=102671.

67. Jane B. Singer, "Still Guarding the Gate? The Newspaper Journalist's Role in an On-line World," *Convergence: The Journal of Research into New Media Technologies* 3 (Spring 1997): 72–89.

68. David H. Weaver, Randal Beam, Bonnie Brownlee, Paul Voakes, and G. Cleveland Wilhoit, *The American Journalist in the 21st Century: U.S. News People at the Dawn of a New Millennium* (Mahwah, NJ: Lawrence Erlbaum, 2006).

69. Mindich, *Tuned Out*.

70. Steven Livingston and W. Lance Bennett, "Gatekeeping, Indexing, and Live-Event News: Is Technology Altering the Construction of News?" *Political Communication* 20 (October/December 2003): 363–380.

71. Axel Bruns, "Gatewatching, Not Gatekeeping: Collaborative Online News," *Media International Australia* 107 (May 2003): 31–44.

72. Bryan Keefer, "Tsunami," *Columbia Journalism Review* (July/August 2004), http://cjr.org/issues/2004/4/keefer-tsunami.asp.

3

Gathering and Sharing Information

Cecilia Friend

Gathering and evaluating information has always been the essence of journalism's mission, and that mission has always had a distinct ethical dimension. Accuracy and credibility—the foundation of any news organization's unspoken but enduring contract with its audience—demand factual, reliable information and compelling evidence presented in a balanced way. While few working journalists and fewer scholars believe today that pure objectivity is possible, almost all would agree that hidden biases, covert manipulation, and disregard for factual truth are deeply unethical. And a new ethic may be emerging: Transparency, or opening up the *process* of news, is a growing practice that helps consumers better understand, and even participate in, the work journalists do.

The explosion in the number of Web sites and other online sources has been in one sense a gold mine for reporters, allowing them easy entry into worlds of information that once were either difficult or impossible to access: expert opinions, diverse and alternative points of view, little-known facts, and comprehensive statistical data. But the proliferation of Web information has come at a price. Ascertaining the authenticity and credibility of online information and sources can be fraught with difficulty. Few maps or models exist for deciding which traditional standards are applicable in the new media landscape. And the ethical and legal lines between private and public discourse, drawn with reasonable clarity in the realms of printed and spoken communication, are still emerging in the world of chat rooms, forums, and Listservs.

An oft-cited rule in newsrooms is to subject online sources—Web sites, blogs, forums, chat rooms, and so forth—to the same scrutiny and skepticism a reporter would bring to any unfamiliar source. That is certainly a valuable reminder, but as a general policy it may fall short because it conflates digital, print, and oral communication and the means by which journalists evaluate them. It says, in effect, that the same internal radar used to parse a police news release, elicit an expert opinion from a local professor, or interview a witness at a crime scene can be relied upon online as well. But can it? And, if so, under what conditions?

A news snippet, a poorly sourced or unattributed rumor, or a spectacular photo can circumnavigate the globe in minutes on the Web, reaching thousands or millions of people before it has been subjected to thorough reporting or even basic fact-checking. The credibility or even the identity of a Web source may be hard to verify. The rush to publish—to keep up with digital competitors—may make it impossible to balance a sensitive story by reaching sources with other points of view. Traditional newsroom checks and balances that uncover errors, biases, and blind spots may evaporate in the push to get stories online when the newsroom no longer works on a traditional deadline cycle.

When the source of information is a Weblog, reporters must evaluate both the information and the source, sometimes without knowing what partisan, ideological, or commercial affiliations the blogger may have. When the sources of information are e-mails, Web chat rooms, or other Web forums, reporters must consider not only whether such exchanges are public, but also how they can be accurately attributed and fairly gathered.

Such complex issues make the need for sufficient reflection and informed discussion crucial, yet the temptation to publish quickly online decreases the time available for deliberation, even as it erodes many of the traditional problem-solving models used in print and broadcast newsrooms. Nevertheless, journalists are as responsible for making sure the news is accurate today as they were in 1965, when Walter Lippmann said, "If there is one subject on which editors are the most responsible, it is in their judgment of the reliability of the source."[1]

This chapter explores the ethical dimensions of assessing, gathering, and using Web information in news stories. But it does not merely dwell on digital dangers. It also addresses important new ways in which the Web can make the news process *more* ethical—the growing practice of "transparency," or lifting the curtain on newsroom operations so that readers and viewers can better understand, comment on, and even participate in the work journalists do.

Accuracy and Verification

In the years since the advent of online journalism, it has become a truism that reporters and editors would have to relinquish their traditional role as gatekeepers of information in order to survive. With a nearly infinite number of news sources now available to everyone, the thinking went, the old model of a professional elite that decided which stories and viewpoints were worthy of attention was doomed. But as anyone who has searched a topic on the Web knows, only a fraction of the available information meets journalistic standards of accuracy and verification. Much of it is self-serving, partisan, dated, or poorly documented; even correct information is often several times removed from the original source. It has become apparent that the gatekeeper role needs to be modified, not abandoned, as Chapter 2 discusses.

Eric Ulken, a former producer for *Online Journalism Review* and now night managing editor at LATimes.com, says journalists must rely on their skills as information sleuths and synthesizers when sifting through masses of Web information. "In the age of information overload . . . journalists are most valuable as gatekeepers, carefully plucking the most interesting and accurate bits of information out of the ether and delivering them to viewers in an easily digested format," Ulken says. But journalists cannot read all the information accessed through Web searches. They must become expert searchers in addition to being expert reporters and producers. Ulken points out that searching the Web is unlike searching a database, which is structured and centrally organized: "The Internet is the opposite—unstructured and decentralized—making it both a useful repository for high-quality data and an information wasteland, teeming with lies and inaccuracies."[2]

Bruce Henderson, director of the New Media Center at the University of Colorado, says reporters often use the Internet as a "fishing expedition," casting a wide net into the Web and returning with "a lot of information that could be tuna, or dolphin, or worse." One initial, obvious way to evaluate information is to examine domain names as a first check on the credibility—or at least the bias—of certain information, Henderson says.[3]

Stephen C. Miller, assistant technology editor at the *New York Times,* has created a chart to do just that. The Miller Internet Data Integrity Scale is a guide to assist reporters in determining the relative merits of types of Web information using domain extensions. In Miller's hierarchy of trust, government data tops the list. A site with a .gov extension has data you may personally question, he says, but you can safely use and attribute it to a specific government entity or agency. University sites with an .edu extension, second on his scale, also get a high trust level, but with a crucial caveat: Colleges and universities often grant space on their Web sites to professors and students for personal Web pages, and the information on those pages may lack academic rigor or expertise. Even information posted by special interest groups, on sites with a .org extension, may be usable if reporters attribute the data, according to Miller. His fourth category, "other," covers everything else, including information published on commercial sites and personal pages with .com and .net extensions. Such sites need not be discounted entirely. Some of the information they offer may come from experts, authors, corporate officials, and consultants. But their credibility and the validity of their postings has to be checked out, and reporters must distinguish carefully among facts, opinions, and promotional claims. "While we are all caught up in terms like cyberspace . . . real people, not pixels, created the information. . . . Those people are no different from the ones we interview in person or over the phone," Miller says.[4]

Nora Paul, director of the Institute for New Media Studies at the University of Minnesota, also questions the perceived difference between gathering information from the Web and from traditional sources. "One of the things that always strikes me about Internet discussions is when things are framed as being Internet-created problems," Paul says. "In most cases, there are pre-Internet precedents for any of the ills that are now attributed to the Web."[5] Paul says online behavior should be informed by the best offline practices, and reporters should apply the same sort of rigor to questioning Web sources as they do for offline sources: Do these people know what they claim to know? How do they know it? And why are they telling me?

Mark Glaser, host of the PBS Weblog *MediaShift,* agrees that "to some extent, the horrors of the online world are just the horrors of the offline world in another format." On the other hand, he says, "the ability of one person to publish their thoughts to a global audience remains a unique online activity, difficult or impossible in broadcasting or print."[6] Such information might, for instance, take the form of war journals from individual soldiers and civilians in Iraq or postings from those able to maintain Web access during the Hurricane Katrina disaster on the Gulf Coast in 2005. Postings from such eyewitnesses are uniquely valuable to journalists, but they are not easy to verify independently or to place in a context useful to a wide audience.

This debate—do online sources require the same kinds of verification procedures as traditional sources, or do they demand something more?—returns us to a deeper question about the nature of the Web itself. Is it simply a new *tool for* communicating, or is it a new *way of* communicating? The implications of the question are clearer if we put it in a historical context. Is the Web something like the telephone, an advanced tool that made communication over distance immensely faster and more convenient? Or is the Web more like the printing press, a technology that fundamentally transformed society—and with it some of society's ethical values—through the spread of literacy, knowledge, and power?

That is an oversimplification, of course, and in any event we cannot know the answer yet. The printing press, after all, took centuries to fully reshape Western culture. But, as Glaser and others point out, we can already see some Web-related phenomena that seem to fall outside the parameters of traditional print and broadcast news. The wisest path at this point may be to understand the Web as *both* a tool and a transforming technology—a realm in which, as Paul points out, older journalistic standards are still critically important, but also a realm in which we must learn to recognize several new ethical wrinkles.

The Conversation Problem

A traditional interview is a dialogue, a live give-and-take in which much of the "information" resides not in the content of the exchange but in the cues that accompany it. Inflection, tone, pauses, pace, digressions, even breathing tell us a great deal about what is being said and help shape our attitude toward the speaker. In an e-mail, a Web posting, or even in instant messaging, a reporter has access to none of those nuances. In addition, follow-up questions and clarifications may not be part of the format. Sometimes, online exchanges can be little more than news releases disguised as interviews. Reporters should be reluctant to substitute written exchanges for real-time oral interviews unless necessary or unless the purpose is simply to collect background information or verify facts. And information from online exchanges should always be identified as such.

Exhibit 3.1
Evaluating Online Sites: Beyond the Suffix

The Miller Internet Data Integrity Scale gives journalists a foundation for evaluating Web sites—a hierarchy of suffixes from .gov to .org and beyond. Once you've considered the suffix, however, there are other issues to bear in mind. The following excerpt from Contemporary Editing *gives further guidance.*

Who's There?

A reputable site will tell you who operates or writes the material for the site, usually through an "about us" link displayed at the top or bottom of the home page. It will usually also give e-mail contact information. Many will link to personal home pages of key players. Such information helps journalists evaluate the expertise and likely point of view of the people behind the site. The *absence* of such information is a near-certain sign that the site is not trustworthy.

Who Says?

Credible Web sites, like all credible publications, explain where their information comes from. Academic sites may use formal end notes; other sites are likely to use some form of informal in-text credit or link. What matters is that the information can be traced to its original source.

What's the Slant?

Second- and third-hand information proliferates on the Web, as do various mixes of fact and opinion, bogus statistics and unreliable online "polls." Weblogs, for example, are great for finding out what people think but lousy for establishing the accuracy of information. Business sites, entertainment sites and many private sites are more likely to be promotional tools than to offer balanced views. Think about the site's purpose.

Where Are You?

A search beginning at a general-information site may lead through links to other Web pages. Be sure to note whether the new pages are part of

(continued)

Exhibit 3.1 *(continued)*

the original site. If not, ascertaining the credibility of the new site is just as important as it was with the previous one. A link between sites never means that they are equally credible. (Some, but not all, Web pages clearly distinguish between off-site and on-site links.)

Can You Back Up?

Searches often turn up pages deep within an extensive Web site. The page reached may have the information you want, but nothing that will help judge the reliability or ownership of the site itself. Move toward the front of the site by truncating the URL from right to left, eliminating the details of the extended address from one slash to the next until you find the ownership information. Or go straight to the home page by eliminating everything but the root URL that ends in .com, .edu, etc.

When Was the Last Update?

A discontinued site may still be available on the Web. When verifying facts that are time-sensitive, make certain the site is current. Most good sites include a "This site last updated on . . ." statement. If there is no such statement but the site seems otherwise reliable, find other evidence that it is current. Many blogs date every entry, for example. Or try checking the comments section to see if there are ongoing discussions.

What Does Your Gut Say?

Reporting and editing are above all critical thinking. A sloppy, un-grammatical or poorly researched news story makes readers question its reliability; a problem-plagued Web site should do the same. The reverse, however, is not always true. Don't automatically equate polish or high-tech gadgetry with accuracy. Many dubious organizations are smart enough to dress up biased, manipulative or plain false viewpoints in slick Web presentations.

Source: Excerpted from Cecilia Friend, Donald Challenger, and Katherine C. McAdams, *Contemporary Editing*, 2nd ed. (New York: McGraw-Hill, 2005).

The Design Problem

We are trained to associate a polished, visually appealing design and presentation with credibility. That is, in part, a legacy of the age of print. A strong, sophisticated visual identity in a newspaper or magazine suggests investment, professional care, and institutional voice—certainly no guarantee of reliability, but at least a sign that the publication has a long-term commitment to its mission and its readers. On the Web, however, a sophisticated design may require only a few hundred dollars' investment and a few hours or days of work. This is, in one sense, a remarkable and democratic leveling of the playing field; individuals and small groups of modest means can compete with the largest news organizations for the attention of viewers. On the other hand, it means that all manner of hate groups, conspiracy theorists, and other dubious sources can dress up their babble to look legitimate and professional. Reporters and editors must retrain themselves to disassociate design and content when online.

Reconciling News and Blogs

Despite these risks, the resources of the Internet represent an incredible leap forward for journalists once constrained by their Rolodexes, by geography, and even by the limits of a single medium. "We can see video showing what is really happening today in Sudan; we can read reports from other countries where the viewpoints differ from our own," says Mindy McAdams, who teaches online journalism at the University of Florida. "There is no downside that seriously overshadows this benefit. In this era of global media monopolies, the Internet is the only place left where the voice of the people might be heard."[7]

Those voices come to journalists from Web sites both in the United States and abroad, and also from the blogosphere, where Weblogs pose another level of ethical challenges. The blogosphere is a realm of unapologetic commentary and opinion, where ideology and attitude predominate and ranting—impassioned rhetoric, unrestrained by editors—is the lingua franca. Robert L. Berkman, author of *Digital Dilemmas: Ethical Issues for Online Media Professionals,* notes that bloggers shape their online identities largely in opposition to mainstream journalism. "In the blogosphere, 'objectivity' is an anti-value. The ethic is transparency," Berkman says. "Say what you believe in and your point of view and let the chips fall as they may. But unlike traditional journalists, bloggers who purport to be reporters are not obliged to follow any institutional or organizational code of ethics; they are lone rangers of a sort."[8]

Berkman cautions that as blogging achieves greater influence and more bloggers seek funding for their work, reporters must beware of bloggers who are surreptitiously working for a political or commercial organization but do not reveal those ties. In traditional newsrooms, conflicts of interest are serious ethical breaches and in some cases grounds for being fired. Bloggers, however, are not likely to fire themselves. The vast majority of bloggers display their political loyalties as a badge of honor, but claims of "transparency" may, in a few cases, veil vested interests that reporters can uncover only by careful investigation.

Blogging inverts a second core journalism ethic as well—the imperative that a news story be fully vetted and edited before it leaves the newsroom. Bloggers have replaced this "filter, then publish" standard with a "publish, then filter" model that emphasizes individual spontaneity and the ability of the blogging community to challenge inaccurate or covertly biased writing. The "publish, then filter" principle reflects bloggers' broadly libertarian orientation; it replaces the top-down hierarchy of the conventional newsroom with the blogosphere's network of equals. But it also makes a virtue of necessity. Because nearly all bloggers work alone, the editing function—insofar as there is one—must be assumed by the larger community.

Berkman says that to rely on bloggers' claims that inaccuracies and pretenders will always be "caught" by other bloggers who ferret out bogus information is unrealistic: "Perhaps that is true . . . but somehow I doubt it will always work."[9] Glaser acknowledges that relying on information from blogs, personal accounts, or nonnews Web sites presents journalists with ethical challenges that, while they may have precedents in print and broadcast, assume a new scope online: "When rumors run rampant on gossip sites, do newspaper sites and wire services report that? If videos of beheadings are some of the most popular content online—or represent the most searched-for sites—does that mean that broadcasters need to consider showing them to their audiences? And what happens when someone fakes a beheading and it spreads online as authentic, fooling even AP and Reuters?"[10]

Misinformation, Disinformation, and Rumors

Misinformation and rumors—the beheading hoax to which Glaser refers, the mistaken identification of Kobe Bryant's accuser in the NBA star's 2003 sexual assault case, the rumors surrounding President Bill Clinton's affair with White House intern Monica Lewinsky, and the charges and countercharges about John Kerry's and George W. Bush's Vietnam-era service during the 2004 presidential campaign—pose serious difficulties to traditional journalists who mine online sites for information.

Hoaxes and the spread of unfounded rumors are not unique to the Internet. But the Web might make it easier to fool reporters and editors. Keeping secret the identity of the accusers in sex assault cases, for example, has not always been possible, and publishing those names even has some journalistic adherents. But no one advocates the repercussions when the wrong name spreads around the Web—harassment or worse in the Kobe Bryant case. Those results, made possible through Web technology and culture, prove the need for additional verification in an era of increased speed of publication. (See Exhibits 3.2 and 3.3 on the Bryant case and the beheading hoax.)

The twenty-four-hour news cycle puts pressure on reporters and news organizations to get stories out quickly, especially when the information is already circulating in some form. Referring to the repeated rumors some news organizations put out as news stories during the Clinton-Lewinsky scandal, Michael Oreskes, then Washington bureau chief of the *New York Times* who is now executive editor of the *International Herald Tribune,* says, "The people who got it right were those who did their own work, who were careful about it, who followed the basic standards of sourcing and got their information from ultimate sources. The people who worried about what was 'out there,' to use that horrible phrase that justifies so many journalistic sins, the people who worried about getting beaten, rather than just trying to do it as well as they could as quickly as they could, they messed up."[11]

Another problem for reporters is not fully comprehending the nature of a Web site used as a source of information. Jonathan Katz, a former mainstream media reporter and editor turned media critic and Slashdot.com columnist, criticizes a *Wall Street Journal* article that quoted Friendster.com, a quasi-private Internet networking site, "where people write satirical personal ads about themselves and read profiles of their friends," as he describes it. The *Journal*'s January 23, 2004, article about Douglas Faneuil, the broker's assistant in the Martha Stewart trial, quoted a Friendster.com profile as background information. Katz writes, "I guess there are more stupid, less ethical ways to report, but I can't think of any. To access a Friendster profile first of all means that you are five degrees of separation or less from the person in question, which means the reporters are admitting that they, or one of their colleagues, have friends in common with the subject." Katz also points out that the information on Friendster is essentially private—not just anyone can access a profile. Another crucial detail about the site: "Everybody on Friendster lies. About everything. It's practically the point of the site." Katz cites posters who list their jobs as "ayatollah," "goldfish," or "perfessinal girlfriend." The *Journal* article quoted from a testimonial on the site, but Katz says that Friendster testimonies are often fake or written by fake users "who are actually bars, cities or the deceased." Katz asks, "Did this Friendster even know Faneuil? Can we know? Do we care? It's inanity like this that ruins Internet reporting for the rest of us."[12]

To resist the allure of easy Web information, reporters should hark back to a "discipline of verification," as Bill Kovach and Tom Rosenstiel call the search for accuracy. "How do you sift through the rumor, the gossip, the failed memory, the manipulative agendas, and try to capture something as accurately as possible, subject to revision in light of new information and perspective? . . . Every journalist operates by relying on some often highly personal method of testing and proving information—his own individual discipline of verification. . . . [but] the modern press culture generally is weakening the methodology of verification journalists have developed."[13]

Information as Commodity

Geneva Overholser, a media critic who holds the Curtis B. Hurley Chair in Public Affairs Reporting at the Missouri School of Journalism, told the Committee of Concerned Journalists that the Internet "affords journalists easy access to stories and quotes without doing their own investigating. . . . Facts have become a commodity, easily acquired, repackaged and repurposed. In the age of the 24-hour news cycle, journalists now spend more time looking for something to add to the existing news, usually interpretation, rather than trying to independently discover and verify new facts."[14]

The problem has only increased as Web news sites proliferate. Kovach and Rosenstiel say reporters risk becoming passive receivers rather than gatherers of information as they spend more time "trying to synthesize

Exhibit 3.2
The Kobe Bryant Case

Most mainstream news organizations have policies not to disclose the names of victims of sexual assault and rape. The reason for this practice stems from the ethical code that says journalists should try to minimize harm.[1] Society still stigmatizes victims of sexual assault, and the stigma becomes stronger in celebrity cases where accusers may be called gold diggers, publicity hounds, or worse. Keeping names private also encourages sexual assault victims to come forward instead of keeping quiet to avoid publicity.

Some journalists argue that shielding accusers while publicizing the names of the accused is unfair and may encourage false accusations. Others say that the way to overcome society's stigma is not to perpetuate it by withholding victims' names. But despite the dissenters, mainstream media have, for the most part, respected the tradition of withholding names. That tradition is a lot harder to maintain in an era of private Web sites where personal opinions reign and journalistic ethics are rarely invoked.

In 2003, a few days after Los Angeles Lakers basketball star Kobe Bryant was charged with sexually assaulting a Colorado woman, her name was posted online.[2] Soon after, her home address, phone number, e-mail address, and a link to a satellite photo of her neighborhood were available on the Web. Then came photos of her face superimposed on nude bodies. One site even got the photo wrong, posting the face of another nineteen-year-old with the same first name who went to the same high school.[3] Some Bryant fans defended revealing the accuser's name, saying Bryant was being falsely accused and they resented the tarnishing of his image that resulted. Tom Leykis, a nationally syndicated talk radio host who was among the first to reveal the woman's name on his show, told MSNBC that he did not understand why the victim of one crime should be treated differently than other victims, adding, "What about the stigma of Kobe Bryant being accused?"[4]

According to Lin Wood, the victim's lawyer, the postings resulted in "hundreds of threats" against the woman's life, two of which resulted in criminal charges.[5]

Nor were the mainstream media completely restrained. Much of the coverage was tawdry: the woman's friends were interviewed to gauge her

(continued)

Exhibit 3.2 *(continued)*

credibility, and the media reported that she had overdosed on drugs and been hospitalized and that she had auditioned for *American Idol.*

It was a hot story that drove media competition. That the name was circulating on the Web put pressure on mainstream media to reveal the name as well. Howard Kurtz, media writer for the *Washington Post,* commented on the media circus surrounding the case: "Inevitably, the question surfaces: If the 3,500 residents of Eagle, Colorado, know who this woman is, and if her life is being reported in such excruciating detail, what is the point of withholding her name?"[6] Most mainstream media, however, did resist the competitive pressures, at least until the criminal case ended in a settlement and the woman filed a civil lawsuit.

Lee Bailey, the radio host whose site first revealed the woman's name, said the decision to run her name was not easy. "I saw how Kobe was being excoriated," he said. "I wondered why this girl was being protected while he's being hung out to dry. In our system, you're supposed to be innocent until proven guilty. But not everyone was playing by the same set of rules." Bailey said the online world plays by a different set of rules: "There are no standards online—it's like the wild, wild West."[7]

Kurtz said that "when it comes to the Kobe Bryant story, it sometimes looks as though all of the media have crawled out of a dark, foul-smelling cave. Whatever the outcome . . . it's a slam dunk that the reputation of journalism will suffer."[8]

Notes:
    1. Society of Professional Journalists Code of Ethics.
    2. Mark Glaser, "Releasing Name of Bryant's Accuser Stirs Debate on Online Standards," Online Journalism.org, July 25, 2003, www.ojr.org/ojr/glaser/1059084839.php.
    3. Howard Kurtz, "Kobe Bryant Free-for-All Obscures a Serious Debate," washingtonpost.com, July 27, 2003, www. washingtonpost.com/ac2/wp-dyn/A51373-2003Jul26?language=printer.
    4. Ibid.
    5. Bob Steel, "Accuser's Attorney: Naming Endangers Client," PoynterOnline, October 15, 2004, www.poynter.org/content/content_view.asp?id=72917.
    6. Kurtz, "Kobe Bryant Free-for-All."
    7. Glaser, "Releasing Name of Bryant's Accuser."
    8. Kurtz, "Kobe Bryant Free-for-All."

Exhibit 3.3
Beheading Hoax

A story about a San Francisco man who was beheaded in Iraq turned out
to be a hoax, but not before it had been broadcast on two Arab-language
televisions stations and spread around the world by two premier international news agencies. The story that fooled the Associated Press and
Reuters in August 2004 was based on a grainy video made by three San
Francisco residents as an experiment to find out how quickly erroneous
information could be spread by the Internet.

The fifty-five-second video of the faked beheading of twenty-two-
year-old Benjamin Vanderford was made by him and two friends and
sent out over the Internet, according to *San Francisco Chronicle* reporters who interviewed two of the filmmakers, Robert Martin and Laurie
Kirchner, hours after the Associated Press story ran. The two told the
Chronicle that they never expected the faked video to be disseminated
so widely and they blamed the media for not checking the authenticity
of the clip before running with the story. "We never intended this to be
taken as real," Martin said.

The video was posted to Kazaa and Soulseek, two file-sharing sites,
in May. It spread to other online sites and, after appearing on Islamic-
Minbar.com, was picked up by the two news agencies and two television
stations in the Middle East. It then spread throughout the media.

The Associated Press usually includes a disclaimer when it runs stories
that are not independently verified. But the first four AP stories did not
include that information. The fifth story, sent out about ninety minutes
after the first, did include the caveat. Associated Press deputy managing
editor Tom Kent could not explain why the disclaimer initially had not
been included, but told the *San Francisco Chronicle* that the story had
been published before it could be verified "because in this case, everything was just happening fast and furious." He also said that the agency
relied on the Middle Eastern Web site Islamic-Minbar because it had
been reliable in the past.

But media watchers criticized the wire service for running the story
without verification. "Every reporter's safety valve is to put it in the
conditional, to use the words 'alleged' or 'reported,'" Ben Bagdikian, a
former journalism dean at University of California, Berkeley, told the
Chronicle. "Having said that, I think if we were in normal times and

(continued)

Exhibit 3.3 *(continued)*

someone heard of a beheading without very specific details and reasons, it would not be picked up by a responsible news service. But given the fact that there is a war in Iraq and there have been beheadings of foreign nationals in Iraq, it makes it plausible that another beheading happened. Still, you need to cite a source. You need to make more probes before it's put out on a news service."

Jonathan Dube of CyberJournalist.net, who writes for the Poynter Institute for Media Studies and American Press Institute, also sounded a cautionary note. "If you can't verify info, it's best not to publish until you can. If you choose to do so, be very explicit that the information wasn't independently verified," Dube wrote on CyberJournalist.net. Dube also warned against publishing something just because "everything was just happening fast."

One of the film's creators, twenty-year-old Laurie Kirchner, may have summed up the risk best when she told the *Chronicle*, "What is amazing is the power of the Internet. One person gets the file, they share it with someone else. It eventually ends up on some Arab TV station and is believed as the real thing."

Sources: Julian Guthrie and Bill Wallace, "Web Hoax Fools News Services: S.F. Man Fakes Beheading, Proves Need for Verification," *San Francisco Chronicle*, August 8, 2004, http://sfgate.com/cgi-bin/article.cgi?f=/c/a/2004/08/08/MNGBN83I3U1.DTL&hw=Web+hoax+fools+news+services&sn=001&sc=1000; Jonathan Dube, "Web Hoax Fools News Media," CyberJournalist.net, August 10, 2004, www.cyberjournalist.net/news/001541_print.php.

the ever-growing stream of data pouring in through the new portals of information." The simple solution: Reporters must do their own work.[15]

Rosenstiel and others also see the blogosphere and the trend toward partisan media as encouraging reporters to rely on "post-publication response and arguments to sort out truth." The new news forms are like "a free-flowing conversation with all the advantages and disadvantages that implies," Rosenstiel writes, "compared to the lecturing-at-you format of old media." Blogger activists, he predicts, will force traditional media to be more transparent about their sources and to hold themselves to higher levels of proof.[16]

The Pack Mentality

No good journalists would go to the library and check the best-seller list to research an issue, but that is essentially what they are encouraged to do online. The Web is, among other things, a massive, ongoing popularity contest. Search engines rank sites, in part, on the basis of how many other sites link to them and how often they are viewed. Visitor counters roll up hits. Quantity parades as quality. The popularity of a site may reflect a hard-won reputation for credibility and accuracy, or it may be a product of a pack mentality. Reporters and editors should make certain that information from even the most popular online sources is subject to scrutiny. They also should take the time to use multiple search engines and look beyond the first screen of results when doing research on the Web.

Berkman also cautions journalists against relying on Web popularity for hard information. "In the blogosphere, credibility is largely determined by 'popularity'—the more people link to you and cite you, the more influence you have and the more your words alone carry weight. This 'Google ranking' approach to conversation and knowledge, I think, has some very intriguing implications for researchers of all types. Right now we can look to see bloggers' outside affiliations (print publications, books, conference presentations, other offline peer review credentials), but soon bloggers will become influential *only* because of their popularity online. Does this then make them, de facto, a credible source?"[17]

Lionel Beehner, in "Lies, Damned Lies, and Google," criticizes reporters for using Web search results themselves as the basis for making judgments in trend stories or to prove a point. According to Beehner, research editor of the *New York Press,* the kinds of statistics Google and other search engines turn up are meaningless, but are used anyway by reporters who are "technologically smitten." While typing a key word into Google may be a simple, fast way of quantifying a trend, Beehner says, it is not only misguided, but inaccurate: "The writer can sit back and let the search engine's brainy algorithms do all the work—and then even pick up some tech-savvy bonus points, too. Google, and not polls or pie charts, has emerged as a journalist's best friend—and best source," but it is also a "telltale sign of sloppy reporting." Beehner says that top-tier publications are just as guilty of the technique as smaller media organizations, citing, among other examples, a story in the *New Yorker* that used Google to gauge the popularity of the diet drug Zantrex and a *Washington Post* story that based its observation that hating Britney

Spears had become a "rage" sweeping the nation on a Google search that turned up 9,000 hits for "Britney hater." Google may be an excellent starting place to gather background information, Beehner says, but it is neither a scientific nor a reliable tool to gauge a subject's impact. Its data can be "faulty, fleeting, and terribly inaccurate." Search engines often access blogs, message boards, and freshman term papers, and the hit counts "fluctuate faster than poll numbers in Iowa." One example Beehner cites is a Google search for Vermont governor and Democratic presidential hopeful Howard Dean in mid-January 2004 that netted 1,460,000 hits, according to a *Los Angeles Times* story. Dean's popularity subsequently plunged, yet a search of his name on February 10 yielded more than 2 million results—more than John Kerry, who later received the nomination—"proving Google's limitations at predicting primary results." According to Beehner, journalists should be sourcing hard statistics, not search-engine evidence, to bolster their stories.[18]

Source Transparency as a New Ethic

While thoroughly sourcing stories is an ethic of traditional journalism, sharing that research with audiences has been more common among bloggers than mainstream journalists. The technique is part of a new ethic of transparency that Berkman and Kovach and Rosenstiel say the blogosphere has fostered. It may be the only journalistic ethic that has moved from online to traditional newsrooms instead of the other way around.

Transparency, one source of bloggers' credibility, stems from bloggers' openness about their biases and from their extensive linking to documents, sources, and supporting evidence. Prominent bloggers also publish transcripts of interviews that they conduct or have been the subjects of, especially when their comments wind up as only small parts of mainstream news stories. Those practices, which give the audience a window into the journalistic process, are being recognized by many news organizations as ways to enhance their own credibility with audiences and regain readers' trust. Some reporters now put notes or interviews online, and some newsrooms provide behind-the-scenes looks at the news process. Experiments with other interactive techniques are being used by traditional news organizations to create closer relationships with readers. As Tim Porter, a former newspaper editor who now writes the blog First Draft, puts it, "The most important lesson mainstream journalists can learn from bloggers is that to gain trust from their readers they must put trust in their readers."[19]

Jeff Jarvis, the blogger behind BuzzMachine and former president of Advance.net who now directs the graduate interactive journalism program at the City University of New York, took that idea much farther in the United Kingdom's *Guardian.*

> No, blogging is not the cure for all ills, but it is an apt metaphor for how newsrooms should operate. Reporters should put what they know into a blogging tool when they know it, and editors can publish that anytime. They should link to other resource people who know more than they do or to wire stories that already report the basics. They should ask readers what they want to know before they report a story, and rely on readers to improve and correct stories after they are written. They should share notes and transcripts. They should reveal their process and prejudices to fulfill the open-source era's highest ethic   transparency. And they should shed their haughty, institutional persona and regain a human voice, facing the public they serve eye-to-eye.[20]

Transparency Instead of Objectivity?

Mary Hodder, a technology consultant and blogger, says that bloggers are upfront about their biases, speak from the heart, and use a personal voice while most mainstream journalists are constrained by an institutional objectivity. "I often read a reporter's story and wonder, What's their experience? Where are they coming from? What's the context? What do they really think?" Hodder says.[21]

Transparency works well in modes of writing that are primarily persuasive and confessional. The scaffolding does not obstruct the view; it is part of the view. The more personal voice that Jarvis and Hodder encourage mainstream journalists to adopt is a more "transparent" voice, but it is a less dispassionate one. Rhetorical transparency may compromise the values of objectivity and disinterest that most journalists have embraced for a century. Trying to achieve transparency throughout a newsroom raises other issues, stemming in part from organizational differences between mainstream journalism and blogging. Most bloggers work alone. To the degree that a blog is transparent, it need only reveal the blogger's biases, motives, methods, and sources. A daily news operation, even a small one, is exponentially more complex. A handful to dozens of people make decisions about what gets covered, how it gets covered, and how it gets played.

While few traditional journalists would disagree that transparency in the process of gathering, writing, and editing news is a positive step, jettisoning the traditional journalists' objective voice and ceding control over story content is not likely to happen, in the near term at least. Yet some news organizations are making an effort to be more transparent in the way they present their stories. Many reporters are linking to source materials and buttressing stories with raw data. Jarvis, Porter, and others suggest doing much more of that, in addition to giving audiences access to information that reporters gather but do not use in stories. Online versions of a story, for example, could include transcripts, audio or videos of complete interviews, and even e-mail addresses of those interviewed. Providing the uncensored, unedited material used to assemble a news story, opinion piece, or blog entry, these critics suggest, could alleviate allegations of misquoting, quote truncation, quoting out of context, or manipulation of interviews in the interests of a particular agenda.

Bringing Users into the Process

Even television, which has been perhaps the least transparent of media and least able to give viewers the opportunity to respond, has at least one high-level proponent of inviting viewers into the new process. Larry Kramer, president of CBS Digital Media, says the network is beginning to open up to viewers by explaining how it goes about its business. In September 2005, a year after the Dan Rather Memogate fiasco, CBS launched a Web site called Public Eye, where a team of CBS journalists explains and answers questions about news decisions. Its stated mission is "to bring transparency to the editorial operations of CBS News." The site, which uses a blog format, says it gives users "an unprecedented look inside the workings of CBS News."[22] Kramer suggests other online initiatives for CBS might be posting its "work product," such as an entire video interview from which the network used only thirty seconds for a news story. "There's no reason we can't allow our users to see the whole thirty-minute interview if they want," Kramer says. "The kind of restrictions that kept us from doing that before . . . was that there wasn't the bandwidth . . . [now] we can offer the user one level deeper into the news-gathering process, and show what used to be considered just work product. We remove our judgment in picking what was important for that interview, and let the readers decide for themselves. And there's absolutely no reason not to do it."[23]

The kind of openness Kramer is suggesting goes beyond making program transcripts available or using a question-and-answer format for print stories. It means sharing information that never made it into a program at all. Audiences, especially Web-savvy ones, may be interested in the ingredients of a news story. And providing detailed material for those who want more depth is a service that typically enhances the credibility of the reporter and the story. It also is a way reporters can use information that may be interesting but does not fit into the story because of space or time constraints or because the material fell outside the focus of the story.

Sharing All Information

Giving readers access to all source information, including entire interviews, is the kind of thing some bloggers have been doing for years. In 2003, Sheila Lennon, features and interactive producer at projo.com—the site of the *Providence Journal*—gave an interview to *New York Times* contributor David F. Gallagher for an article about journalist bloggers. Afterward, she posted the full text of the e-mail interview on her personal blog, The Reader. Gallagher, who only used one sentence of her comment in his story, was happy about the posting. "Your answers were great so I'm glad they're out there," Gallagher wrote in an e-mail to Lennon. Lennon later told *American Journalism Review,* "It seemed natural for me to publish 'the rest of the story' online for readers who might be interested. . . . It offers a chance for the reporter to use the words that wouldn't fit, for the source to say what he wishes had been published, for the reader to go as deep into the story as she desires."[24]

By 2004, the practice had become more common. Shayne Bowman and Chris Willis, coauthors of "We Media: How Audiences Are Changing the Future of News and Information," said in March 2004 that the media audience had found its voice. In their article "When Sources Become Media," they say bloggers and reporters now often expect sources to post their versions of interviews.[25]

One interaction between reporter and source highlights the way in which transparency and a willingness to go beyond the story can serve the truth better than a conventional correction. In August 2005, Professor Roger Pielke Sr. quit a Bush administration team researching global warming. *New York Times* reporter Andrew Revkin wrote that Pielke disagreed with the dominant view that global warming stems mainly from human activity. Pielke objected to that portrayal on his Web site and posted a "Summary for the Media," detailing why he resigned. Revkin then wrote an explanatory response, which he let Pielke also post. Pielke then posted his thanks for Revkin's comment, which he said cleared up the misunderstanding. Steve Outing, who wrote about the exchange in his blog on PoynterOnline, said, "I find this public exchange quite remarkable—though these days it's becoming more commonplace. The way we practice journalism has changed significantly when what in the past would have been a private exchange between an annoyed source and a reporter is part of the public record. This is the 'transparency' that we so often talk about as being a hallmark of journalism in the Internet era."[26]

Bowman and Willis concede that posting interviews and other kinds of public interactions with sources makes some journalists very uncomfortable: "But ultimately, this will lead to more transparency in the reporting process, which is good for everyone—journalists, sources and the audience."[27] Mainstream journalist turned blogger Jeff Jarvis makes a similar point about including audiences in the news process. "When you are not transparent, people will assume their definition of the worst. If you are transparent, you show the effort you put behind trying to serve them and you also give them the respect to include them in the process. That is a moral of weblogs. It's a moral the news business needs to figure out."[28] J.D. Lasica, another mainstream journalist turned blogger, also believes readers are interested in getting a look at how journalism is made and that the transparent aspect of blogs is part of what makes them so attractive: "By posting transcripts, exchanges with reporters and private emails, people get a much closer look at the guts of the research, writing and reporting that makes up the journalism process."[29]

Readers aren't the only ones who benefit from this type of transparency, says Jonathan Dube, publisher of CyberJournalist.net. Dube considers the U.S. Department of Defense's Web site (defenselink.mil) a "journalist's gold mine" of speeches, briefings, and transcripts of every media interview given by top defense officials. The site is a prime venue for what he calls "interview voyeurism—journalists can not only spy on the techniques of their colleagues, but pluck quotes for their own stories since the interviews are public record."[30]

Dan Gillmor, author *of We the Media: Grassroots Journalism by the People, for the People,* agrees. "We should link to source material as much as possible, bolstering what we tell people with close-to-the-ground facts and data," he argues. "To the extent that we make thoroughness, accuracy, fairness and transparency the pillars of journalism, we can go a long way toward the worthy goal of helping our audiences/collaborators."[31]

Opening Up Editorial Pages

Even editorial page editors are making efforts to remove the mystery from the workings of their departments. Some are posting interviews with political candidates online as a way to give voters a window into the endorsement process and the opportunity to see the candidates' complete answers. As long ago as 1996, the *Seattle Post-Intelligencer* broadcast its editorial board interview with gubernatorial candidates on TVW, Washington State's public affairs network, and the audio was posted on TVW's Web site. Since then, other papers also have experimented in posting audio or video clips of candidate interviews with editorial boards, including the *New York Times,* the *Washington Post,* the *San Francisco Chronicle,* the *Honolulu Star-Bulletin,* and the *Milwaukee Journal Sentinel.* And in 2005, the pioneering *Post-Intelligencer* went even farther, creating a virtual editorial board where users can post opinions on the newspaper's editorial before it is published. Mark Trahant, the *Post-Intelligencer* editorial page editor, said the paper considers readers' comments before the editors write the final version of the editorial, sometimes quoting in the paper someone's online comment or printing comments as an instant response. "I can imagine that we might even have to rethink our position occasionally," he said.[32]

The Los Angeles Times tried pushing the boundaries farther in 2005, opening up the editorial process by creating a "wikitorial" online where readers could add and edit content.[33] But it soon closed after some people inserted profanity and pornographic content into the editorial.[34] Under the headline "Where is the Wikitorial?" the *Times* told users, "Unfortunately, we have had to remove this feature, at least temporarily, because a few readers were flooding the site with inappropriate material. Thanks and apologies to the thousands of people who logged on in the right spirit."[35] Michael Newman, deputy editor of the editorial pages, later told a panel at the National Conference of Editorial Writers that the newspaper might try a similar format again, but give access only to a select group of people.[36]

Steve Outing says, "Too often the reading public perceives newspaper editorials as written as part of a secretive process by anonymous editors." Opening up the process "will help make the newspaper's editorials more 'human,' and the human writers of those editorials more accountable."[37]

Transparency as Ethical Principle

The Project for Excellence in Journalism, whose work resulted in Kovach and Rosenstiel's *The Elements of Journalism,* has embraced transparency as an ethical standard for the news process: "Be as transparent as possible about your reporting methods and motives."[38] Kovach and Rosenstiel call the rule of transparency "the most important single element in creating a better discipline of verification" and in signaling respect for the audience. Journalists should be not only truth seekers, but "truth presenters," being honest and truthful with their audiences about what they know and what they do not.[39]

While not specifically addressing the online issues discussed here, the authors say the principle of transparency allows the audience to judge the validity of the information, the process by which it was secured, and the motives and biases of the journalist providing it, which is the best protection against errors and deception by sources. The authors compare transparency in journalism to the principles that govern scientific method: "Explain how you learned something and why you believe it—so the audience can do the same. In science, the reliability of an experiment, or its objectivity, is defined by whether someone else could replicate the experiment. In journalism, only by explaining how we know what we know can we approximate this idea of people being able, if they were of a mind to, to replicate the reporting."

Case Study: Transparency and Verification

In this hypothetical case, Henry Horton, a veteran sports reporter for the *Ocean City Beacon* and Beacon Online, knew he was onto something. He had heard from a usually reliable source that Ocean College football players were secretly getting cash and other gifts from members of the booster club in direct violation of intercollegiate rules. Now he was reading what appeared to be confirmation on a popular fan blog. GridDude had posted several rants about star quarterback Jack Giocca's new SUV and how a wealthy booster had privately given him the money to buy it.

If true, the allegations could lead to heavy fines, suspensions, ineligibility, and loss of scholarships for the college's football program. The fallout could damage the athletic program and the reputation of the college itself for years to come.

Horton e-mailed GridDude, asking about the blog and the source of his information. GridDude, e-mailing back, identified himself as a former player who still had close ties to the team, but he would not give Horton his name or other personal information. "I deal in controversy on the blog, and fans around here take their sports seriously," GridDude wrote to Horton. "I don't need the drama of people hassling me at work or calling my house." Grid-Dude stated that the booster gifts to star players were common knowledge in the locker room. "I got a couple hundred bucks myself, back in the day," he wrote. "Nothing like this, though. Everyone on the team knows about it. And my girlfriend heard it from Giocca's girlfriend. Check around."

GridDude added that Horton had better hurry if he wanted to break the story. A national sports magazine and a reporter from network television already had contacted GridDude about the rumors. "I told them the same thing I'm telling you," he wrote.

The next day, a Friday, Horton worked the phones for hours, talking to about thirty coaches, college administrators, players, former players, and boosters. It was true that Giocca was cruising around campus in a new SUV, but the quarterback said he had earned a lot of money working two construction jobs over the summer. No one admitted to having any knowledge of secret gifts or payments to players—not that Horton expected them to. But several players sounded rattled and nervous, and they hung up quickly after refusing to comment.

Late Friday, Horton read on the college's Web site that the athletic director was calling a major news conference for Monday morning. Horton called the athletic director at home. The official said little that was not on the Web site, but he would not categorically deny that the news conference was related to an investigation of the football program.

Now racing the clock, Horton checked back on GridDude's blog. Several new posts attacked GridDude for trying to ruin the team with libelous charges, but other new contributors who seemed to have inside knowledge backed up the allegations. Two claimed to be current players, and they named several other stars besides Giocca who they said were involved. One insisted he had seen envelopes of cash actually handed to players from car windows outside the sports complex. However, like GridDude, all the new accusers refused to use their real names. They said they had too much to lose.

Horton wished he had more information, but he also felt that he must get the story to readers before the Monday news conference. And he knew that the magazine and the TV newsroom working on the story could scoop him if he waited. He went to his editors Saturday morning and made his case to publish the story in the Sunday edition. The editors were reluctant at first. But Horton told them that he had multiple sources, including an eyewitness and a former player who claimed to have received cash himself. He pointed out that the athletic director had danced around the investigation question instead of denying it. And it helped when Horton hinted that the *Beacon* would be beating a national magazine on a blockbuster story. He got the go-ahead.

- Would you have pushed to publish the story? If so, defend that position to your editor. If not, why not?
- Are there changes you could make to the story that would make it more ethical and credible, given the information you have?
- What if you found out that players making accusations on the Grid-Dude blog had personal feuds with Giocca or other players accused of taking cash or gifts? How would that change your decision to publish?
- What if you found out that GridDude or other bloggers involved were not who they claimed to be? How would that change your decision?
- What if you found out at the last minute that the athletic director's upcoming news conference was not related to your story at all?

Notes

1. Walter Lippmann, *Public Opinion* (New York: Free Press, 1965), p. 226.
2. Erik Ulken, Dialogues: Online Journalism Ethics, October 2004, http://jethics-dialogues.blogspot.com.
3. Bruce Henderson, Dialogues: Online Journalism Ethics, October 2004, http://jethicsdialogues.blogspot.com.
4. Miller Internet Data Integrity Scale (tip sheet used at IRE/NICAR seminars), www.notrain-nogain.org/Tech/MIDIS_handout.pdf.
5. Nora Paul, Dialogues: Online Journalism Ethics, October 2004, http://jethics-dialogues.blogspot.com.
6. Mark Glaser, "On the Wild, Woolly Internet, Old Ethics Rules Do Apply," *Online Journalism Review,* August 10, 2004, http://ojr.org/ojr/ethics/1092186782.php.
7. Ibid.
8. Robert L. Berkman, Dialogues: Online Journalism Ethics, October 2004, http://jethicsdialogues.blogspot.com.
9. Ibid.
10. Glaser, "On the Wild, Woolly Internet."
11. Bill Kovach and Tom Rosenstiel, *The Elements of Journalism: What Newspeople Should Know and the Public Should Expect* (New York: Crown, 2001), p. 85.

12. Jim Romenesko, Romenesko Letters, PoynterOnline, February 3, 2004, www. poynter.org/column.asp?id=45&aid=60380.

13. Kovach and Rosenstiel, *Elements of Journalism*, p. 71.

14. Ibid., p. 75.

15. Ibid., pp. 76, 84.

16. Rick Edmonds, "Report on State of the Media 2005: New Roles for News," PoynterOnline, March 12, 2005, www.poynter.org/content/content_view.asp?id= 79676.

17. Berkman, Dialogues.

18. Lionel Beehner, "Lies, Damned Lies, and Google," Mediabistro.com, February 18, 2004, www.mediabistro.com/articles/cache/a1217.asp.

19. Tim Porter, "Transparency and Trust," First Draft, August 12, 2004, www.timporter. com/firstdraft/archives/000345.html.

20. Jeff Jarvis, "Hacks Must Get with the Program," *Guardian*, August 8, 2005, www. guardian.co.uk/online/news/0,12597,1544871,00.html.

21. Porter, "Transparency and Trust."

22. Dick Meyer, Editorial Director, CBSNews.com, "About Public Eye," www. cbsnews.com/stories/2005/08/30/publiceye/main805566.shtml.

23. Henig, "Larry Kramer."

24. Barb Palser, "Sources Who Publish Transcripts of Their Interviews? It's Becoming More Common," Every Last Word, *American Journalism Review*, January/February 2003, www.ajr.org/Article.asp?id=2754.

25. Shayne Bowman and Chris Willis, "When Sources Become Media," Hypergene MediaBlog, March 16, 2004, www.hypergene.net/blog/weblog.php?id=P172 .

26. Roger Pielke, "Summary for the Media," Climate Science, August 25, 2005, http://climatesci.atmos.colostate.edu/?p=38; Andrew C. Revkin, Climate Science, August 26, 2005, http://climatesci.atmos.colostate.edu/?p=37; Andrew Revkin, "Panelist Who Dissents on Climate Change Quits," the *New York Times*, August 23, 2005; Steve Outing, "The Source Strikes Back," PoynterOnline, August 26, 2005, www.poynter. org/content/content_view.asp?id=87827.

27. Bowman and Willis, "When Sources Become Media."

28. Ibid.

29. Ibid.

30. Palser, "Sources Who Publich Transcripts."

31. Dan Gillmor, "The End of Objectivity," January 20, 2005, http://dangillmor. typepad.com/dan_gillmor_on_grassroots/2005/01/the_end_of_obje.html.

32. Cyberjournalist.net, "The P-I's Virtual Editorial Board," August 16, 2005, www. cyberjournalist.net/news/002827.php.

33. A wiki is a Web application that allows users to add content, as on an Internet forum, but also allows anyone to edit the content. The term *wiki* also refers to the collaborative software used to create such a Web site. Definition retrieved from http://en.wikipedia. org/wiki/wiki.

34. Steve Outing, "More Wikis in LATimes.com Future?" September 19, 2005, www. poynter.org/column.asp?id=31&aid=89210.

35. www.latimes.com/news/opinion/editorials/la-wiki-splash,0,1349109.htmlstory.

36. www.ncew.org/web/2005/08_Portland_program_highlights_1.aspx.

37. Outing, "More Wikis in LATimes.com Future?"

38. Project for Excellence in Journalism, www.journalism.org/resources/principles; Kovach and Rosenstiel, *Elements of Journalism*, p. 80.

39. Kovach and Rosenstiel, *Elements of Journalism*, p. 80.

4

Ethics and the Law

Jane B. Singer

Some of the ethical issues facing online journalists also have legal implications. Although, in general, the same laws apply online as offline, the application of those laws can be tricky. Moreover, technology generally changes much faster than the law. The constantly evolving, open, networked, global nature of the Internet creates new permutations of old issues.

Some of these issues straddle a blurry line between ethics and the law. Privacy is one example, and we begin the chapter by exploring the explosive topic of online privacy in the context of journalists' use of the Internet. Journalists now rely on the Internet for most aspects of information gathering, from generating story ideas to locating background materials to communicating with sources. For reporters, online privacy issues revolve largely around the question of where to draw the line between a private conversation and a public arena—raising concerns about deception, another ethical issue with legal ramifications that we consider in the first part of this chapter. For example:

- Most content published on the Web is, legally, just that—published, and thus fair game for a reporter under standard conditions of fair use and attribution. But the Internet is more than the Web; it includes a range of other interpersonal communication forms, including newsgroups, listservs, forums, and chat rooms. The people engaged in these online conversations typically have little or no experience talking with journalists—or suspicion that a journalist might be monitoring, and may even publish, what they post online. Should journalists use what people say in such quasi-public online venues?

- Undercover reporting generally is a dubious practice unless extremely important information that the public needs to know can be obtained no other way. But journalists easily can "lurk" in online gathering places without anyone else realizing they are there; just as easily, they can participate in online discussions without disclosing that they are reporters. When and how should journalists reveal their professional identity to online conversation partners?

For media companies, the privacy issues are larger, encompassing their relationship with the public as consumers of a journalistic product. Questions involving the ethical responsibilities they owe their users require difficult business decisions, in a medium in which a solid business model is still evolving.

- What sorts of information about their users do media Web sites collect, what do they do with it—and what should they tell their users about their practices?
- What limits on the uses of such information are legally required, and what additional limits are ethically desirable for media companies?

The chapter then turns to additional issues that have both ethical and legal implications but seem to us to be more clearly about matters of law. Of course, the field of communication law is vast, and its application online is evolving continuously and rapidly. Court rulings issued by the time you read this book will update and potentially even refute what we have written here. But we think two additional issues will be the source of ongoing controversy for some time to come. One is that although traditional media are governed by the laws of the states and nations in which they operate, the Internet is not geographically limited. Under which laws, then, do online journalists work? We use copyright law as a framework for examining this question.

The second issue involves that surprisingly difficult question, which we raised in Chapter 2 and consider again in Chapter 5: "Who is a journalist?" In the United States, journalists historically have enjoyed protections and perquisites not routinely accorded other citizens. What legal or ethical precepts related to information gathering and dissemination might we consider universal, and how might they be applied online? A look at shield laws helps us explore these questions.

Privacy and Deception: Can You Hide Your Prying Eyes?

Changes in media technology led to legal recognition of a right to privacy in the United States only a little more than a century ago. In an 1890 *Harvard Law Review* article, two prominent Boston lawyers, annoyed at what they saw as intrusive and offensive media coverage of their social lives, called for legal protection of the "right to be let alone." "Instantaneous photographs and newspaper enterprise have invaded the sacred precincts of privacy and domestic life," wrote Samuel Warren and Louis Brandeis, a future U.S. Supreme Court justice. "Numerous mechanical devices threaten to make good the prediction that 'what is whispered in the closet shall be proclaimed from the house-tops.'" They argued that the dignity of the individual, which various other laws recognized, accorded people the right not to have intimate information about them published by a callous and powerful press.[1] Warren and Brandeis urged society to recognize that some information about individuals, including both words and images, should be sacrosanct.[2]

Gradually, U.S. courts began to issue rulings supporting that premise, though the rulings have been neither consistent nor uncontested. Today, the legal right to privacy encompasses four areas:

- Intrusion, or the unwarranted violation of a person's physical solitude. For instance, a journalist's use of a telephoto lens to capture the private moments of an unsuspecting subject can constitute intrusion.
- Publicity of embarrassing private facts, the kind of things that Warren and Brandeis had in mind. Public complaints about privacy invasion typically involve a perception that journalists use their freedom to rummage, often irresponsibly and unnecessarily, through the private lives of others.
- Placement of a person in a false light, which involves publishing distortions that leave an erroneous impression. An example is use of a newspaper file photo in which an identifiable individual is used to illustrate a current story that has nothing to do with that individual.
- Appropriation, or the use of a person's name, picture, or likeness without permission, usually for commercial gain. The least ambiguous area of privacy law, appropriation is designed to protect public and private figures from having their personal identities exploited for someone else's benefit.[3]

Although the same laws apply online as offline, the Internet and other digital technologies can make privacy concerns especially acute. Cookies and other computer programs, many of them invisible to users, that capture information about every Web site they visit, how long they spend there, and which links they click are inherently intrusive technologies. Embarrassing information and misleading distortions can be published by anyone and disseminated globally in an instant. Click-and-paste capabilities, as well as such image manipulation tools as PhotoShop, make appropriation exceptionally easy.

The legal right to privacy is important for journalists. But the ethical need for privacy is at least as crucial. As media ethics scholar Lee Wilkins points out in the accompanying sidebar (Exhibit 4.1), everyone needs a private space, safe from the observation of others, in which to develop a sense of self and an understanding of who we are. In addition, society needs privacy as a shield against the power of the state as protection from government influence, manipulation, or control. Privacy, then, is a "necessary component of a democracy upon which many of its values, such as freedom, individual dignity, and autonomy, rest."[4] Ethicists urge journalists to respect the privacy rights of those on whom they report by being especially careful not to intrude unduly when gathering information.[5] Only an overriding public need, the Society of Professional Journalists code warns, can justify privacy intrusions.

But for journalists, knowing just where the ethical line is between private and public information can be extremely difficult, particularly because law and ethics in this area do not necessarily point toward the same decision. Indeed, legal rights sometimes directly conflict with ethical responsibilities. The First Amendment grants U.S. journalists the right to publish things that they might ethically choose not to publish. For instance, there is no law prohibiting the publication of a rape victim's name, yet most news organizations choose to withhold it; journalists also commonly withhold the names of accident victims until families have been notified even though those names are part of police reports.

Moreover, the public is ambiguous about privacy, scarfing up details about juicy crimes and philandering celebrities at the same time it decries media excesses in obtaining and providing that information. Although the law generally supports making information available to the public, that public thinks that media coverage of private lives, even those of public officials, is excessive and unfair.[6] People do not seem to feel they have a universal "right to know," which journalists love to cite at every opportunity

Exhibit 4.1
Privacy Primer

Lee Wilkins, an award-winning professor in the School of Journalism and the Truman School of Public Affairs at the University of Missouri, is a leading expert on media ethics. She is the coauthor of The Moral Media, *a book about how professional communicators make ethical decisions, and of a popular college ethics text,* Media Ethics: Issues and Cases. *Wilkins, a former newspaper reporter and editor, currently is coeditor of the* Journal of Mass Media Ethics. *Here are her thoughts about privacy online. She provided these thoughts about online privacy on a blog associated with this book in October 2004.*

Let me say a couple of things about privacy in general, from the philosophical perspective. In ethics terms, privacy is not what is considered a prima facie right—in other words, it's a right that can be "trumped" by other rights or obligations. For example, most of us would like our medical records to be kept private, but if we were in the emergency room having a heart attack, I believe reasonable people would agree that we would like even a doctor we did not know to have access to our medical history. In this case, our right to life has essentially overwhelmed whatever privacy we would like to maintain under more normal circumstances. So privacy always has to be considered in a context.

Second, from a philosophical as opposed to a legal sense, privacy is about two things—human dignity and control. Part of the psychological work we do to make ourselves people needs privacy. So it's essential to the process of becoming and remaining human. One way that brainwashing works is to deprive people of a sense of privacy—psychological breakdown can result if people don't have some sense of a "private self."

Privacy also assumes control over information and the context in which information is understood. Here's an example. There are things you would tell your best friend—things that might not be very flattering—because your best friend has a wellspring of context about you. Your best friend also probably likes you and is willing to accept you even if you have flaws. So information that might not be very flattering is understood in a generous way. But imagine if the same thing became a headline in a traditional newspaper. Strangers would read it, and they, lacking the context of your best friend, might interpret it somewhat differently and probably more negatively.

(continued)

Exhibit 4.1 *(continued)*

Third, privacy isn't secrecy. In fact, there are few secrets anyone but hermits keep. Think about rape. If you or a friend is raped, there are lots of people who know about it—the doctors who treated you, family or friends that you tell, the police. Your rape is not a secret. But it is private—because you have chosen to tell a limited circle of people. Journalists actually help you in this regard; news organizations seldom publish the names of rape victims without obtaining their permission first. Of course, there have been notorious exceptions to this general professional rule—but the fact that they are notorious provides some indication of the lack of ethical justification for these news decisions.

Fourth, it's hard to get your privacy back once you've lost it. In fact, in some ways the loss is irreparable. So thinking about privacy really requires that journalists provide reasons for what they do that other people—their readers, attorneys, the clergy—would find understandable. In ethics language, we need justification that goes beyond "everyone else printed it" or "the U.S. Supreme Court says I can do it." In my view, relying on legal precedent is a very poor way to guide thinking about this issue.

All this is really prefatory, because the Web provides journalists (and others) with ways to invade privacy on a worldwide scale. Some of those ways appear novel—for example, is lurking in a chat room the same thing as hiding in the bathroom to overhear conversations during a break in a public meeting . . . or leaving your tape recorder running when you leave that same room?

When phrased this way, it's fairly obvious that things in the "virtual" world have their real-life counterparts. Most journalists don't hide in bathrooms to get stories—because hiding in the bathroom means we can't ask follow-up questions or seek multiple and other points of view (in my case, from the people in the men's bathroom.) So lurking and then quoting without first identifying yourself seems, to me, to be a pretty easy call. There's not really a good justification for it—and there are a lot of "facts" essential to readers and viewers that one might miss by hiding behind the closed door or the Web.

but which, as ethicists point out, appears nowhere in the Constitution[7] and applies, at best, only in a limited way related to open government.[8] The framework of moral values that most people hold is not necessarily in line with most journalists' normative commitment to full disclosure—even in areas that journalists generally do not see as problematic.[9]

The journalist, then, faces two general areas of ethical concern related to privacy: in gathering information and in publishing it. Particularly for the first of those, the Internet poses unique challenges.

Online Information Gathering

Much of the information that journalists gather online does not raise ethical issues significantly different from similar information gathered in more traditional ways. Companies publish the same material on their Web sites as they do in printed press releases or annual reports. Government documents and public record databases available online are the same ones obtainable at city hall, in the state capital, or in Washington, DC. Even your address and a map to your house are available in the local phone book, albeit without the turn-by-turn instructions that online mapping programs provide. It is more convenient and easier—maybe disconcertingly so, when the map leads straight to your door—to obtain such information online, but its availability and use pose few if any ethical issues for journalists.

When we move beyond Web sites and into the world of online interpersonal communication, however, things become murkier. Take e-mail, for starters. Electronic mail has become a vital online tool for journalists, who use it extensively to communicate with sources, from making initial contact to conducting full-fledged interviews.[10] Yet e-mail has failed to replace the telephone as the dominant interviewing tool for most journalists. Although it offers some advantages—direct access to difficult-to-reach sources; written quotes that can be especially helpful on complicated or technical stories; and, of course, the joy of avoiding telephone tag—journalists also perceive significant disadvantages. E-mail interviews limit or eliminate the ability to engage in give-and-take with a source, to ask spontaneous follow-up questions, and to get the important nonverbal cues that face-to-face or even phone interviews can provide. For that matter, reporters cannot even be sure the person from whom they want a response is actually the one writing the e-mail.[11] Many journalists are skeptical of the validity of what they are told through e-mail.

E-mail, however, still is just one form of digital communication. Millions of other conversations are taking place online every hour of every day. The Internet is open, participatory, interactive, and easy to use, and ordinary online users readily share their opinions, ideas, thoughts, and insights on any and every topic. It is tempting to think of these conversations as comparable to a late-night bull session in a college dorm room or a lively discussion with colleagues in the local coffeehouse, with the wonderful enhancement of being open to participants from around the world. And so they are. But unlike those face-to-face conversations, the online ones are conducted in writing (and, increasingly, in audio and video formats) rather than verbally. That is, they are published.

The conversations take a variety of forms, including discussion groups, listservs, forums, chat rooms, and social networking sites such as Facebook or MySpace. They vary in structure and accessibility, as summarized in Exhibit 4.2, but in general, their publication means these conversations are legally available to others, including journalists. Even listservs with a codified set of usage guidelines can do little to punish violators other than barring them from the list. So journalists' use of what people say in informal online conversations is a matter of ethics rather than law. Ethically, should journalists repeat portions of these conversations to others? Such use raises questions about loyalty—the journalist's duty to sources and to the public.

Let us start with a journalist's loyalty or duty to a source, in this case the online conversationalist. The key ethical issue here involves disclosure, of both presence and intent. The least problematic way for journalists to use such online conversation venues is to post their own message identifying themselves and stating their desire to talk with someone about the topic of interest; volunteers then can be interviewed individually, separate from the public conversation.[12] Somewhat more problematic is listening in on conversations without disclosing one's presence—called "lurking" online—in order to pick up ideas ("What are people saying about this topic?") or identify potential sources ("Who is saying something especially interesting?"). Critics might call this eavesdropping. But proponents would call it good reporting. Investigative Reporters and Editors is among the respected professional groups that urge reporters to use discussion groups and listservs for just such purposes of locating knowledgeable sources.[13] Ethically, such a practice is not significantly different from keeping one's eyes and ears open on a beat; good journalists always are attuned to "buzz" of all kinds, and the Internet is the quintessential buzz machine.

The real issue here involves what the journalist does with the overheard (or, in this case, overseen) conversations. Using them as leads, whether to a story idea or a source, is one thing. But if those conversations find their way into a reporter's story without their author's knowledge or consent,

Exhibit 4.2
Online Conversations

Online conversations take various forms. Here are a few common ones:

- Discussion groups are like online bulletin boards and generally are open to all comers. Indeed, search engines enable anyone to instantly find a conversation on any topic; from there, jumping in is a keystroke away.
- Listservs, on the other hand, generally require subscription (almost always free) through e-mail. These are self-regulating online communities with their own sets of guidelines for members, but they generally are open to anyone who asks to subscribe.
- Forums are a cross between the two. Like discussion groups, they are accessible through the Web and thus generally open to anyone to read; like listservs, they typically are subject to someone's oversight, and many require registration before you can contribute to them. Many companies and news organizations sponsor forums, either moderated or unmoderated, and invite comments on issues, stories, or products.
- Chat rooms provide places for people to communicate by publishing messages to others in the same "room" (or "channel") in real time. Many chat functions have given way to instant messaging programs, which enable real-time conversations among people on one another's contact or buddy lists.
- Social network sites connect college students, friends, business partners, or other groups of individuals together using a variety of tools. Typically, an initial set of founders sends out messages inviting members of their own personal networks to join the site. New members repeat the process, and the total number of members and links grows, creating rapidly expanding social connections.

Source: Kathleen A. Hansen and Nora Paul, *Behind the Message: Information Strategies for Communicators* (Boston: Pearson Education, 2004); *Wikipedia* (2005), s.v. Chat room, Chat, Instant messenger, http://en.wikipedia.org/wiki/Chat_room, . . . /Online_chat, . . . /Instant_messenger . . . /Social_networking.

the ethical problems have multiplied. Both lurking and engaging other users in online conversation without letting others know that the journalist is there as a reporter—that is, intends to use people's comments in a story—are comparable to undercover reporting. The lack of disclosure means the journalist is using deceptive information-gathering practices; the deception involves hiding the journalist's presence, intent, or both.

Such deception may sometimes be justified, just as it is offline. Harvard philosopher Sissela Bok, in her seminal work titled *Lying,* warns that although deception always erodes trust, deception sometimes is warranted. The decision to lie demands a rational choice that weighs, among other things, potential good and potential harm, as well as a willingness to be publicly accountable for both the deception and the rationale for deceiving.[14] Building on this framework, media ethicist Edmund Lambeth says deception in pursuit of a story may be permissible as a last resort, when the problem in question is significant, pervasive, and systemic, and when it demands an urgent solution that can be achieved only through media attention.[15] That is a difficult bar to meet; in effect, it discourages the practice of deception unless there is a compelling public service need—and no other viable way to serve it. The vast majority of conversations among ordinary online users will fail to meet such a test.

So journalists wanting to use online conversations face ethical issues involving both deception and privacy: Users have a reasonable expectation that information from or about them will not be published without their knowledge and consent. But what if journalists identify themselves and get the online conversationalist's permission to quote from the discussion group or chat room? The issues of privacy and of deception are addressed, so there should be no problem, right? Wrong. True, the journalist has been loyal to the source. But now the problem is loyalty to the public.

Kovach and Rosenstiel remind us that journalism's first loyalty is to citizens; indeed, just about any consideration of professional ethics puts a premium on a commitment to public service. They also remind us that the essence of journalism is what they call a "discipline of verification."[16] Journalists separate what they do from the work of entertainers, novelists, and propagandists with the implicit promise to their audience that they have not made up anything that they have included in their report. This loyalty to the public, and its enactment through truth-telling, should guide Journalists in their use of information, wherever it is obtained.

But how does a journalist know that the person who sounds so knowledgeable in a discussion group is not, in fact, an entertainer, novelist, propagandist, or someone else with a self-serving motive or love of a good yarn? The only way is by exercising that "discipline of verification": checking out both the person and the information through independent, trustworthy sources. That cannot be done from within the online conversational space, where identities are perpetually open to invention and reinvention. It has to happen through other channels—including but not limited to one-on-one communication between source and journalist, where the credentials of each can be adequately verified.

A now-famous *New Yorker* cartoon back in 1993 showed a dog sitting in front of a computer and explaining to his canine companion, "On the Internet, nobody knows you're a dog."[17] But the public counts on the journalist to distinguish the curs from the credible sources. Merely passing along something said online is no better than using an anonymous source without a compelling reason to do so. Like the anonymous source, the guy dominating the online discussion group may be lying or slanting the information; the chat room regular may be a mouthpiece for some other person or organization–or she may simply not know what she is talking about. She may even turn out to be a twelve-year-old child. The journalist has an ethical duty to the public to find out.

One caveat to close this section on privacy and deception related to online information gathering: There may be times when the journalist will indeed decide to protect the privacy and even the anonymity of a source found online—just as there are times when the anonymity of offline sources should be protected. In fact, the sorts of online conversation areas considered here are precisely the places where journalists may be able to find people with expertise about sensitive topics—a debilitating disease, for instance—who may be hard to locate in other ways.[18] In such cases, there may be good reasons not to reveal such a source's "real" identity. How can you tell if you have such a case? Media ethicist Louis Day suggests careful consideration of the appropriate balance among three principles: respect for individual dignity, minimization of harm, and social utility. Journalists must decide what information is essential or at least useful to the audience in understanding the message being communicated, as well as the degree to which their sources deserve privacy under the specific circumstances involved.[19] Public officials accused of wrongdoing, for instance, would deserve less privacy than the man in an online AIDS support group who agrees to share his story with a reporter.

The *Washington Post,* which has dealt with more than its share of anonymous sources in the nation's capital over the years, has a policy urging reporters to grant requests for anonymity only with reluctance and only when "we can give our readers better, fuller information by allowing sources to remain unnamed than if we insist on naming them." In particular, the *Post* emphasizes the loyalty it owes the public: "When we use an unnamed source, we are asking our readers to take an extra step to trust the credibility of the information we are providing. We must be certain in our own minds that the benefit to readers is worth the cost in credibility. . . . We must strive to tell our readers as much as we can about why our unnamed sources deserve our confidence. Our obligation is to serve readers, not sources."[20] The same policy should apply to the online world as the offline one.

Media Sites and Their Users

Although this book focuses on online journalists, privacy is a highly contentious issue for the companies that employ them, as well. Offline, media companies make their money primarily from some combination of advertising and subscriptions: Advertisers pay the media company to gain access to consumers, and consumers pay the media company to gain access to content—including the ads. The Internet began as an open, noncommercial space; as it has become increasingly commercialized over the past decade, users have generally resisted paying for what started out free. Some specialized information sites, notably financial news leader *The Wall Street Journal* and niche media sites such as Broadcasting and Cable, offering "essential" information for a particular audience, have been successful at getting people to pay. But many online news executives doubt that a subscription model for general news sites can be viable.[21]

Instead, two primary revenue models have emerged, both based on the idea that personal data are a form of online currency with significant economic value. One model involves collecting personal information about users in exchange for allowing them access to a site's content and services.[22] For media sites, this generally means requiring users to fill out an online registration form in order to get past the home page. When users register, the news site stores a cookie on their computer's hard drive; when they return to the site, it remembers who they are and opens the door.[23] Publishers increasingly see registration as a business necessity, and for large U.S. newspapers in particular, mandatory registration has emerged as an industry norm. Supporters say requiring registration produces better data for site development; it also facilitates the creation of targeted on-screen advertising and lists for e-mail marketing,[24] which nonsupporters know less than fondly as spam.

The second revenue model involves gathering information about how people use the online medium and aggregating it into profiles for use by marketers; the information allows advertisers to predict user interests and purchasing habits so they can deliver targeted sales pitches.[25] Instead of "unique visitors," "page views," or other Internet jargon that confounds advertisers, sales reps can explain the power of their site in terms of loyal customers, reach, and frequency, terms every marketer understands. Online publishers say the ability to target advertising is key to their profitability[26]—and sizable majorities of major newspaper sites are profitable. On the other hand, less than 25 percent of local television news sites—virtually none of which requires users to register—made a profit as of 2004.[27] Overall, advertising on all media sites was estimated to have topped $12.5 billion at the mid-2000s mark, with an increase of 30 percent from 2004 to 2005 alone.[28]

So converting information about users into bait for advertisers clearly is profitable for media companies. Is it ethical? That depends, and the answer rests largely on whether users know what will be done with information they provide and are able to make a rational judgment based on that knowledge. One potential problem is that those registering and using a site may be children; although registration forms typically ask for a year of birth, any child old enough to count can figure out what year to enter to magically turn eighteen. Children claiming to be adults will be targeted by advertisers just like the grown-ups that they are pretending to be.

If children using the Internet are honest about their ages, information about them will be protected by relatively tough privacy laws. The Children's Online Privacy Protection Act (COPPA) of 1998 requires Web site operators to get parents' permission before collecting personal information from children; the type of parental consent required depends on how the information will be used. If only those collecting the information will use it, simple e-mail consent from a parent is sufficient. If the information is intended to be shared with marketers, more detailed, verified permission is required. And there are more stringent rules for providers of sites designed for children under age thirteen than for teens.[29]

Nonetheless, sites aimed at children remain chock-full of advertising and marketing messages; kids under twelve, after all, have more than $40 billion in personal spending power and influence family purchases to the tune of an estimated $500 billion.[30]

For sites aimed at adults, including most mainstream media sites, the privacy requirements are less stringent. In the 1990s, the Federal Trade Commission (FTC) outlined a set of Fair Information Practice Principles, which include notice, choice, access, and security. First, consumers need to be notified of a site's practices before any personal information is collected; without notice, the user cannot make an informed decision about providing that information. Second, users should have a choice about how personal information collected from them is used beyond what is necessary to complete a requested transaction, such as displaying linked information. Such secondary uses can be internal, such as placing the user on a list to receive company e-mail, or external, such as transferring information to third parties. There are various ways to provide such choices. The most common are "opt-in" procedures, which assume the users do not approve the collection or sale of personal information and thus must give explicit permission for it to occur, and "opt-out" procedures, which assume the users do approve such secondary use and will take the initiative to contact the company if they want the data-collection practice to stop. The third principle refers to the users' ability both to access collected information about themselves and to contest its accuracy and completeness. And finally, the FTC says that Web sites should take "reasonable steps" to ensure that information collected is accurate and secure.[31]

All that said, the U.S. government has largely made privacy a matter of self-regulation for media and other companies doing business online —meaning that aside from protections for children, much of what media sites do with information about their users is a matter of business ethics. The extent to which companies adhere to the FTC's principles is open to question and interpretation; certainly, widespread reports of identity theft and rampant use of spyware do little to support the premise or the promise that companies are adequately safeguarding information collected online. Most media sites do have privacy policies accessible from their home pages. Many, however, are written in boilerplate legalese that makes them difficult to read.[32] A study earlier this decade found that a majority of media Web sites failed to let users know what they were doing with the data they collected,[33] an ethically problematic finding given that news organizations often demand, in the name of public service, transparency and accountability from government and industry.[34]

Journalists are among the select groups of people in our society for whom it is ethically acceptable to do occasional harm in service to the greater public good; although professional journalists seek to minimize harm, their primary ethical obligation is to inform the public by seeking and reporting truth, even painful truth.[35] Media companies as business enterprises, on the other hand, are not among that select group. The ethical question, then, boils down to whether the collection of information about users causes harm.

Marketers, of course, say no: People both want and need information about goods and services available to them, and targeted advertising, they argue, is simply a way to deliver that information efficiently. Media companies add that someone has to pay for the expensive process of gathering and disseminating the news; if we do not want that someone to be either us or a government "sponsor," that leaves a commercial press system financially supported by advertisers. And what makes the Web an attractive advertising vehicle is precisely its ability to target prospective consumers in ways that traditional media cannot match.

All true. But people seeing an ad in a newspaper or on a television news program do not have to disclose personal information about themselves in exchange for the sales pitch. Online users do—sometimes inadvertently and even unknowingly. Merely publishing a privacy policy seems an inadequate remedy in light of the amount of harm that can ensue. Relatively few people ever read such policies;[36] even fewer are likely to understand the legal jargon they typically contain. And there often is little middle ground between not using the site at all, thus missing the news and other valuable information the site contains, and accepting that either the media companies themselves or unspecified "third parties," or both, can do whatever they like with whatever information about users they can get.

Frankly, this business practice seems ethically unacceptable. Since U.S. law gives media companies nearly free rein in their dealings with advertisers, it is up to those companies to act in a way that supports the public service commitment they profess to uphold in their news coverage. Displaying privacy policies more prominently and making them easier to understand are easy steps. But more is required.

We urge the online news industry to adopt a unified stance that requires advertisers to abide by standards of ethical use of information about online users and to safeguard that information from other, potentially unscrupulous "third parties." That, in turn, means media companies must provide an editorial product strong enough to attract legitimate advertisers who will be happy to reach users whoever they may be and wherever else they may go online—that is, without the need to collect personal information about them. A strong online editorial product requires money—a news budget substantial enough to enable online journalists to consistently provide the sort of coverage that stretches both their creative abilities and the medium's technical ones.

Local Statutes, Global Medium

Most of our laws, including most of those directly relevant to working journalists, are limited by geography. They are enacted, implemented, and enforced within the borders of a physical place, such as a city, state, or nation. Under our system of federalism, courts have the authority to determine the legality of things that occur within their jurisdiction; that generally means a person must have done something within the geographical boundaries of a state, say, in order to be sued there.[37] But the Internet, of course, is a global medium. What if jurisdiction is determined by the location where someone downloads content rather than the location where it was published or uploaded? Whose rules apply then?

There are relatively few international laws, mostly in the areas of human rights and commerce, and even those must be adopted by individual nations. As it happens, journalists are directly affected by one of the few international commerce laws, that of copyright. In this country, copyright protection is granted in the original U.S. Constitution. The protection has been extended repeatedly since the eighteenth century, most recently in 1998, when Congress passed the Sonny Bono Copyright Term Extension Act; works for hire—including most journalistic work—now are copyrighted by their publisher for a whopping ninety-five years.[38] Also in 1998, the United States ratified two international agreements intended to strengthen copyright protections worldwide and, in particular, to provide legal ammunition to fight piracy of computer software, music, and other intellectual property. Under the auspices of a special United Nations agency called the World Intellectual Property Organization, the treaties include provisions that enable copyright owners to prevent the unauthorized posting or transmission of copyrighted works through the Internet.[39] Enforcement, of course, is another matter.

For online journalists, copyright law poses a number of issues. The right to link from one site to another, fundamental to both the structure and the utility of the Web, has been challenged in court in an assortment of creative ways. Legal battles over links have ranged from a war between two tiny newspapers in the Shetland Islands of Scotland (one accused the other of infringement for linking to its stories and replicating its headlines to do so) to a case in which several of the largest media companies in America, including the *Washington Post* and CNN, sued a small Arizona enterprise for using framing technology to essentially repackage their news. "Deep links," in which a site's home page (and the ads it contains) are bypassed by linking to a page deep within a Web site, also have been challenged in court. So has the use of "metatags," keywords embedded in the code used to build Web pages, to promise customers more than the sites delivered—a copyright issue when an Asian site used the words "playmate" and "playboy" in its tags. Playboy Enterprises Inc. won that case on trademark infringement grounds.[40] And copyright law has played a role in legal disputes involving freelancers; the U.S. Supreme Court ruled in 2002 that *The New York Times* infringed on authors' copyright when it converted stories from the newspaper into digital databases without permission, saying the release agreement signed by the authors did not cover new technologies.[41]

New forms of online content, particularly those generated by users, raise additional copyright issues. In July 2006, for instance, the video-sharing site YouTube was sued by a Los Angeles news videographer for violating copyright of footage shot during the 1992 riots in that city. You-Tube declared the suit "without merit," and as we write, the case is still open. But as *Online Journalism Review* contributor Mack Reed points out, "the Web has made the unauthorized propagation of information, copyrighted or not, instantaneous and virtually irreversible."[42] The fight over peer-to-peer file-sharing services such as Napster earlier in this decade made that clear. So has the growth in popularity of Internet-friendly legal arrangements such as those proposed by Creative Commons, a nonprofit organization based at Stanford University that issues licenses allowing the creators of original work to specify how it can be used. Options that vary from those available under traditional copyright law include allowing unlimited use as long as proper credit is given to the originating source and allowing works to be copied or performed as written but not reproduced in derivative forms.[43] By the time you read this, other creative approaches to copyright will no doubt have gained attention.

The online legal issues facing journalists are complex, and copyright is just one example, one where the national law is clear and laws among nations are relatively consistent, at that. Whole books are devoted to Internet law, but we want to focus here on one particular wrinkle: the fact that most laws are *not* consistent from place to place.

Take privacy, for instance, which we have just been discussing. Privacy law—actually a series of congressional acts and court rulings, since, unlike copyright, privacy is not explicitly covered in the Constitution—is primarily national in scope. There are legal limits to what others can know about us, and the laws are periodically updated to deal with new technologies that facilitate obtaining such information. But laws in this country generally favor openness of information—openness to journalists and, as we have seen, to commercial enterprises, as well. Compared with the laws in many other democracies, our personal privacy laws are relatively weak. When it comes to commercial use of personal information, the United States tends to rely on industry self-regulation. The European Union, in contrast, sees privacy of personal data as a human rights issue, and the state has been much more actively involved in regulating the collection and use of such data.[44]

The openness of personal information for potential use by journalists derives in part from our most famous national communications law, the First Amendment. Our protections of free speech and a free press are unique in their scope, even among democracies. Hate speech, for instance, which is generally legal in the United States, is illegal in France, Germany, Sweden, Canada, and other nations; in 2002, the Council of Europe adopted a measure criminalizing Internet hate speech, including links to pages containing offensive content.[45] Hate speech already was a crime under a human rights act called the International Convention on the Elimination of All Forms of Racial Discrimination, to which the United States is a signatory, and other nations have criticized the United States and Internet services based within this country for permitting "cyberhate."[46] Yet unless it constitutes a direct threat—and both individuals and groups using the Internet to threaten ethnic or minority groups have been successfully prosecuted—limiting hate speech is generally defined as unlawful censorship in this country.[47] Most such limitations, then, must be voluntary—that is, they must be rooted in ethics rather than law. In reality, that means the rest of us generally have to put up with online hate speech—or, better, avoid it altogether.

A Closer Look: Libel Law

Journalists, though, are not in the business of disseminating hate speech. For them, one of the most troubling issues related to the global nature of the Internet has been the area of libel law. In this country, liability is a matter of state law, though the criteria for determining whether a published statement is libelous are fairly uniform from state to state. To win a libel suit, plaintiffs must prove that defamatory language—damaging to their reputation or causing other personal harm, such as emotional distress—was used and that they were identified by the defamatory statement. The defamation must have been disseminated or published as a result of negligence or recklessness; that is, the publisher must have been at fault. And the plaintiff must establish that what was published was false; truth, however much it hurts, is legally protected.[48]

Fault has been an area of contention in libel cases involving online information providers. In particular, there was some legal confusion in the early 1990s about just who was the "publisher" of content in online bulletin boards and thus responsible for that content if it proved libelous. In a 1991 libel case involving CompuServe, the court said the service provider was analogous to a bookstore, library, or newsstand; it could hardly be expected to know the contents of a message posted online if it had no editorial involvement with that content. But a few years later, another court went in the opposite direction. It ruled that Prodigy Services Company, which promoted itself as a family-oriented computer network that screened online postings for appropriateness, did exercise sufficient editorial control over its bulletin boards to make it a publisher rather than just a distributor. Some clarity came in 1996 with passage of the Telecommunications Act, a mammoth act that overhauled U.S. communications policy. It includes a provision immunizing Internet service providers, or ISPs, from being held liable for information provided by others over their networks.[49]

In the current decade, controversy over the application of libel law online has shifted to the global nature of the Internet, involving cases more directly affecting journalists. Dow Jones, publisher of the *Wall Street Journal* and *Barron's* magazine, has been at the center of two such cases. In 2000, an article in both the print and online versions of *Barron's* connected a wealthy Australian businessman with money-laundering operations in the United States and Australia. The man sued in his home state of Victoria, Australia, where libel laws relating to privileges, burdens of proof, and public figures make a libel case easier to win than in the United States. But where was the online article published? Dow Jones said it was New Jersey, where the publisher placed the article on the Internet. The plaintiff said it was Australia, where the article was downloaded and his reputation harmed. The case reached the highest court in Australia, which decided that publication occurs where the alleged damage to reputation takes place.[50]

According to the court ruling, "If people wish to do business in, or indeed travel to, or live in, or utilize the infrastructure of different countries, they can hardly expect to be absolved from compliance with the laws of those countries. The fact that publication might occur everywhere does not mean that it occurs nowhere."[51] "The Internet is such a new and different medium of human communication that it demands a radical reconceptualisation of the applicable common law, specifically with respect to the tort of defamation," Justice Michael Kirby wrote.[52] Dow Jones settled the case two years later, paying the plaintiff $440,000 in fees and damages.

In 2005, Dow Jones won a ruling when appeals court judges in London threw out a libel suit against the *Wall Street Journal*'s online publication because only five people in England had read the allegedly defamatory item, which purported to link the plaintiff to funding for suspected terrorist leader Osama bin Laden years earlier. That court ruled that online publishers could not be sued in the English courts unless there had been a "substantial" publication in England.[53] Although media representatives welcomed the decision, it did not really address the jurisdiction issue involving the location of an online publication.

As media law expert Constance Davis (see Exhibit 4.3) explains, the cases highlight the fact that libel law is seen differently in the United States than in most other countries. For more than forty years, since the landmark *New York Times v. Sullivan* case, U.S. courts have considered libel in a First Amendment context, she says. That is, libel suits can be a tool for squelching information—such as an open discussion of civil rights, the issue at the core of that 1964 case—and the courts have remained, in general, committed to protecting free speech. As a result, the bar for winning a libel suit in the United States is exceptionally high; proving all the components outlined above is a difficult task for any plaintiff. About 90 percent of the libel complaints filed in this country are dropped, dismissed, or settled before trial. Media companies that do go to court are likely to lose libel cases at the trial level but have a fifty-

fifty chance of having the loss converted to a win on appeal,[54] where First Amendment issues are more likely to prevail.

But the Internet raises the possibility that plaintiffs can bring their libel suits in countries where the bar is much lower. In fact, they can pick the nation whose laws best suit their needs, called "forum shopping." Davis cites the example of Richard Perle, a former member of the Pentagon's Defense Policy Board, who was unhappy with a story published in the *New Yorker* in 2002 and available in the magazine's online version. Perle vowed to bring a libel suit—and to file it in England, where libel laws are more favorable to plaintiffs. Although he ultimately did not, online publishers have every reason to be concerned. "While judges in other countries may be claiming that publishers should be aware of the different libel laws in any country in which story subjects might reside, U.S. publishers may very well find that chilling," Davis said. "It is probable that companies will continue to publish as they have before, going ahead with stories once they have been adequately verified. But it will not be surprising if some news companies choose not to upload to the Web some of their controversial stories that deal with citizens of other countries."[55]

In summary, the fact that online publications are accessible everywhere makes it very difficult to predict where suits will be brought and thus under what legal standards. Within the United States, courts have ruled in at least two separate cases that libel plaintiffs in one state cannot sue local media outlets in another state merely because their Web sites are accessible everywhere; legal jurisdiction remains in the state where the physical product, such as the newspaper, is published and the primary audience located.[56] But the real concern for U.S. journalists is having to worry about compliance with laws in any of 190 different countries, some of which harshly punish unpopular writings or those critical of the government.

The Australian court's precedent is seen as dangerous because, as former newspaper columnist and grassroots journalism advocate Dan Gillmor says, it encourages "powerful and paranoid people" to use local laws designed to stifle unwelcome news or opinions. "If we all have to temper our speech to fit the restrictions of the worst abusers of liberty," he writes, "no one will say anything worth hearing." Although some legal experts have suggested the Internet jurisdiction question ultimately may demand an international solution, perhaps in the form of a global code or treaty, such a treaty could well require compromises the U.S. media will

Exhibit 4.3
Law and Ethics

Constance Davis has one foot in the world of academia and the other in the journalism profession. She holds a doctorate in mass communication and is an expert in media law, particularly cyberlaw, which she has taught at a number of prestigious Midwestern universities. She also is a newspaper veteran who has done everything from editing a small weekly to serving as managing editor over a 175-person newsroom. As a journalist, Davis was heavily involved in freedom of information and public access issues. Here are her thoughts on a few of the legal and ethical issues facing online journalists, as well as issues related to blogs (covered in the next chapter), in response to questions posed by the authors.

Q: What ethical considerations are involved when journalists use public online discussion areas for reporting purposes? Should they alert the other participants that they are there and identify themselves as journalists—even if that instantly changes the nature of the conversation? Should journalists participate at all? Do "lurking" journalists have any obligations to make their presence known?

A: On the one hand, lurking online might be no different from eavesdropping at an event or in a particular setting and using that information. But what you do with the information you gather is another question. Would you write a story in the offline world based on information you gathered only through eavesdropping? Do you know the people who were talking and whether they have an ax to grind or are credible? Would you expect readers to view that as credible information if you did not gather names and other information from those sources? Probably not. While lurking might allow you to get a sense of what is being said about a particular topic, it might be a less-than-credible source of information in the eyes of your readers.

In the offline world, you let sources know who you are before you gather information. Admittedly, many sources speak differently when they know they are speaking to a reporter, and reporters who announce that they are reporters lurking in a chat room will likely find that the other participants leave. On the other hand, reporters need to be very careful about the kind of information they choose to publish. If they

(continued)

Exhibit 4.3 *(continued)*

do decide to lurk, perhaps they could gather information, then alert the participants that they have done so for a story. They should provide an e-mail address where participants could contact them with specific questions or concerns. And reporters might be able to get names of real people to go with a story.

Q: In contrast to discussion groups, listservs use e-mail to communicate among those who have signed up to join the list. Does the quasi-private nature of the communication space change the answers to the questions above?

A: Using listserv information may be safer. Some listservs may set up rules that what is said on the list stays on the list. Participants in other listservs know that information they discuss may very well be forwarded to others and they do not have that expectation of privacy. It is important to understand the nature of the listserv.

However, reporters should consider contacting listserv participants whose information they might want to use and allowing them to discuss it further. When we do face-to-face interviews, we may give our sources time to deliberate over their response and we may read back quotations to make sure we understood them correctly. If we misspeak at times (and we all do), it is likely that people also "mis-write." They leave out an important word that changes the meaning of a sentence. Not guilty becomes guilty. Reporters should still check with the source to see if that is what he or she really meant to say.

Q: Should journalists set up their own Web sites? What ethical constraints should govern them? Could media organizations forbid a journalist from setting up Web sites or participating in blogs?

A: Journalism organizations may be revisiting their ethics policies in light of the growth of blogs. If a news organization allows employee blogs, it will have to decide whether such blogs will be associated with the organization's Web site or whether they can be purely personal blogs in which journalists might voice opinions, including opinions criticizing the news organizations. Some news organizations allow reporters to have blogs on the organization's Web site; the reporters are encouraged to provide background or other information that might not have made it into a published story.

(continued)

Exhibit 4.3 *(continued)*

It is important to remember, though, that information published online is public. Some professors and editors routinely tell students and staffers that they should never put into an e-mail anything they do not want to have placed into evidence in a court of law. The same advice can be given to reporters who blog, with or without the consent of their employers. Remember that public-figure libel plaintiffs are required to demonstrate the reporter's actual malice. Reporters will need to be careful about what they say about their sources because information from a blog could be admissible as evidence of actual malice.

In this same vein, reporters should be aware that e-mails to and from public officials may be part of the public record. Even if a reporter intends an e-mail to be a private message, the public record laws in that state might require it to be a public record. And in most states, anyone can seek those public records.

Q: Do journalists give up certain civil liberties in order to be effective as professionals? Which liberties are most vulnerable? Does the wide-open nature of the Internet make any difference in balancing individual rights and professional responsibilities?

A: Journalists should not have to give up civil liberties in order to be effective. News organizations should make clear what their expectations of journalists are. If the organization has a clear policy that forbids employees from establishing blogs or participating in online discussion forums, employees can decide whether that is a policy they like and will abide by or whether it is a policy they want to challenge.

The journalist who wants to use public online forums to pursue an agenda that allows him or her to criticize the news organization or to spread rumors about people in the news should not be too surprised if management frowns upon that activity—just as it would be in the offline world.

Although the nature of journalism seems to be changing, journalists should take seriously the concept of striving for fairness, balance and accuracy in their stories. Journalists who post to discussion forums that can be accessed by the public really do need to be careful in what they say in those forums. Electronic copies can live for a very long time.

not want to accept. Because most of the world's libel laws are harsher on the media than ours, negotiating with other countries might mean giving up protections. Indeed, one previous attempt to negotiate such a treaty in 2001 was abandoned because no consensus on the issue of libel and other tort actions could be reached.[57]

We will discuss bloggers more fully in the next chapter, but before we leave the subject of libel, a couple of points are relevant here. It seems clear that as the one-to-many mass communication model is replaced by one in which millions of people can "publish" whatever they like from their own living rooms, libel laws that historically have focused on the press are increasingly outdated forms of protection for both free expression and personal reputation. Although both courts and Congress have moved to protect ISPs, the law of defamation remains relatively unchanged for individuals: Those who publish something online can expect to be held accountable for it.[58]

Although libel suits involving bloggers have been rare, bloggers would not seem to qualify as protected ISPs. Legal experts agree that the standard for liability is just the same whether the defamatory statement is made in a blog posting or in some other media form. And while pure opinion generally is not considered libelous (because it cannot be proved either true or false), a blogger cannot escape liability simply by labeling an otherwise factual statement as "my opinion," especially if the implication is that the opinion is based on undisclosed facts known to the writer.[59] As Davis points out in the accompanying sidebar, reporters who participate in blogs also need to be careful what they say about their sources because such postings could be admissible evidence of actual malice, one of the additional burdens of proof that a public figure or official must meet to win a libel suit.

Shield Laws: Who Is a Journalist?

The question of just who is a journalist recurs throughout this book. Of course, national laws do apply to everyone in a nation; the First Amendment grants all American citizens the right to speak freely, not just journalists. But even within the United States, there are variations from state to state in laws designed to apply specifically to journalists. Who, exactly, that would be is a matter of legal dispute in at least one area—that of shield laws.

In 2005, when *New York Times* reporter Judith Miller was convicted of contempt of court and eventually sent to jail for refusing to divulge the name of a confidential source, many individual journalists, journalism organizations, and even some members of Congress renewed long-standing calls for a national shield law. As of this writing, thirty-one states and the District of Columbia have a law protecting the identities of confidential sources (and most of the rest have court precedents that serve a similar purpose), but the laws are inconsistent and do not apply to federal courts. Advocates say a federal shield law is needed to safeguard journalists' ability to find out information the public needs, which sometimes can be obtained only by promising confidentiality to whistle-blowers. As one supporter of a national law writes, "As more and more newsgatherers work on the national stage—through television, books, and the Internet—the lack of a national newsgatherers' privilege is more and more problematic. Without a national privilege, these newsgatherers are subject to different and contradictory standards, with little guidance as to which standard might apply in a particular case."[60]

Bills were introduced in both the U.S. House and Senate in 2006 (revising earlier bills proposed but never voted on in 2005) to create such a national law. The Senate version would cover all journalists, which it defines as people who, "for financial gain or livelihood," are engaged in gathering, writing or publishing news or information for a news organization. The bill specifically includes Internet news services as such an organization, along with any other "professional medium or agency which has as one of its regular functions the processing and researching of news or information intended for dissemination to the public." The House bill, on the other hand, covers publishers, broadcasters, and wire services and those who work for them, including freelancers, but not those who publish solely on the Web.[61]

If such a bill passes (at the time of this writing, a new proposal from the 110th Congress was being awaited), it would set a precedent. Not one of the state statutes specifically mentions the Internet. Some are clearly limited to traditional print and broadcast reporters; others are worded broadly enough that they probably would be interpreted to cover online journalists. For example, the statute in North Carolina—the most recent state to enact a shield law, in 1999—covers "persons, companies, or other entities engaged in the business of gathering or disseminating news."[62] But no state court rulings to date have directly addressed the issue of whether shield laws cover online journalists. And just as libel laws vary from nation to nation and thus raise issues of jurisdiction for a global medium, shield laws vary from state to state and raise the same issues.[63]

Legal experts are divided over just how inclusive laws designed to protect journalists should be. "So many divergent groups of persons could be called journalists that the protection of the privilege would be dissolved," writes Laurence Alexander, a University of Florida professor. "Application of the journalist's privilege to a variety of social communicators would require universal acceptance of an excessively broad perspective of our traditional notions of the press. Such expansion runs counter to the fundamental notions of a privilege, which should be maintained for a select, well-defined group to the exclusion of all others." Alexander proposes defining a journalist as "any person who is engaged in gathering news for public presentation or dissemination by the news media," in turn defined as "newspapers, magazines, television and radio stations, online news services, or any other regularly published news outlet used for the public dissemination of news."[64] By such a definition, then, journalists working for established online news outlets would be protected, but independent folks such as bloggers would not.

In contrast, Eugene Volokh, a law professor at UCLA who also is a popular blogger, says the rules "should be the same for old media and new, professional and amateur. Any journalist's privilege should extend to every journalist."[65] Linda Berger, a former Associated Press reporter who is now a professor at the Thomas Jefferson School of Law in San Diego, proposes a functional definition that focuses on the process of gathering and disseminating information necessary for self-governance. She says shield laws should protect anyone "engaged in journalism," which means being "involved in a process that is intended to generate and disseminate truthful information to the public on a regular basis." Berger emphasizes that journalism is identifiable by its practitioners' commitment to the "discipline of verification" that Kovach and Rosenstiel have outlined. "By turning to the profession for a definition of what it means to be engaged in journalism," she says, "we may be able to preserve the journalist's privilege and accommodate the 'unmedia' without undermining journalism's values."[66]

So far, state legislatures have been reluctant to take such a position or, for that matter, to define journalists and journalism at all. Somewhat similar issues, for example, arise with the publication of errors and efforts to correct or retract them. The corrections law in Wisconsin, for instance, says that before proceeding with a libel suit, the person who was defamed must issue a written demand for a retraction to give the publisher a "reasonable opportunity" to set the record straight. The statute specifically mentions "any newspaper, magazine, or periodical"—and that's it. When a case involving information published online in the mid-1990s came before the Wisconsin Court of Appeals, the court said the law did not cover the Internet: "Applying the present libel laws to cyberspace or computer networks entails rewriting statutes that were written to manage physical, printed objects," which was a job for the legislature, not the court.[67] The lawsuit therefore could proceed without any prior request for a retraction.[68]

A decade later, few legislatures have taken up the challenge. Although most states do have a retraction statute, most are worded too narrowly to cover something published online. One legal expert estimates two-thirds of the state statutes would have to be amended to protect Internet communication. In the meantime, both the legal and the ethical thing for online publishers to do is to scrupulously follow their state's corrections law as if they were covered by it, promptly posting corrections and retractions in a place as conspicuous as the content being corrected.[69]

Actually, the question of just how online journalists should handle online corrections is itself controversial. Some advocate simply deleting anything that is wrong and replacing it, so that all accessible versions of a story are correct. Others leave old versions intact but append corrections to them, with a note informing users of what has been done.[70] Still another option, favored in particular by bloggers, is to use a strikethrough so that users will instantly notice that a change has been made but still be able to see what was corrected.[71] In short, the law related to corrections is unclear in its application to online journalists, and the optimal way of adhering to the ethical principle to "be accountable" by admitting mistakes and promptly correcting them, as the SPJ code urges, is no less murky. Perhaps as a result, in the early years of the twenty-first century, many media sites—including the two most heavily used news sites in the nation, MSNBC.com and CNN.com—either failed to articulate and publish a corrections policy for their users to see or simply had no such policy at all.[72]

To end this legal consideration of just who is a journalist on a somewhat positive note, however, we can note at least one area in which online journalists seem to be gaining acceptance. Until recently, it was difficult for Internet news providers to gain access to events for which their counterparts in traditional media routinely were credentialed. From the Grammy Awards to the NCAA basketball championships, from International Monetary Fund meetings to Capitol Hill, online journalists were denied press passes and thus access through much of the 1990s.[73] The proliferation of online journalism has placed press offices for all sorts of organizations in the position of trying to decide who should, and should not, be treated as a journalist. It can be, as we have seen, a difficult call.

The rules for credentialing print journalists seeking admission to the congressional press galleries, for instance, state that an applicant must demonstrate that "his or her principal income is obtained from news correspondence intended for publication in newspapers entitled to second-class mailing privileges."[74] Although such rules have not officially changed, they are increasingly honored in the breach; dozens of online writers are credentialed to cover Congress, from those affiliated with such mainstream publications as the *Washington Post* to reporters for Web-only ventures such as CancerPage.com and AllAfrica.com. Indeed, most press offices now recognize that the Internet, even sites that do not have an offline component, is a legitimate news medium. As recently as the 2002 Winter Olympics in Utah, Sportsline.com's reporters had to prove their legitimacy. But a Sportsline managing editor says, "the Olympics was one of the last problem areas we had. We pretty much have zero problems now with credentials."[75]

Even bloggers have gained access to the press gallery, with more than three dozen of them credentialed to cover the 2004 Democratic convention in Boston and nearly as many the GOP convention in New York a month later. And then there was one James Guckert, a conservative online writer who somehow gained coveted access to the White House briefing room—maybe a reporter, kind of a blogger, definitely a man who had offered his services online as a $200-an-hour male escort. Who, indeed, is a journalist these days?

Which brings us to those legions of people who are creating blogs, wikis, and other forms of what has variously been called amateur journalism, citizen journalism, grassroots journalism, or participatory journalism. Legally, as we have seen, many but not all of the same rules apply to these folks as to journalists working for the online branches of traditional news media. This chapter has offered examples of the ways in which laws governing journalism vary. Ethics are, at some level, universal, based on core concepts of human dignity and the common good. However, professions such as journalism explicitly codify a particular set of ethics: They take universal principles and lay out their applications for their own members. What happens when membership is no longer easy to define? The next chapter considers the ethics of blogging, which rests heavily on this question.

Case Study: Deception Justified?

(This case study involves an actual series of events involving real people.)

Many residents of Spokane, Washington, loved their outspoken mayor. Jim West was a conservative Republican with a strong anti–gay rights record. A veteran of twenty years in public office, including seventeen in the state legislature and a stint as state senate majority leader, the fifty-five-year-old mayor was popular locally for his efforts to bolster economic development, expand technology, and improve the roads.

Then in 2004, while working on a story about victims of sexual abuse, a reporter for the *Spokane Spokesman-Review* got a shocking and un-expected tip: A source suggested he talk with an eighteen-year-old man who had told friends he had met Mayor West online and had a date with him—a date that led to consensual sex. The reporter tracked down the young man, who confirmed the story. He said he had met an older man, who claimed to be West but used the screen name Cobra82nd, on the Gay.com Web site. The man offered the teen gifts and perks. But the teen had not recognized the mayor and had no proof of his identity; even the online correspondence had long since vanished into the ether.

The reporter and his colleagues kept digging. They turned up a second young man with a similar story—and a similar lack of proof. What to do now?

"We had multiple choices," said *Spokesman-Review* editor Steven Smith. "We could just go ask the mayor. Not very smart. A simple denial and then he drops off the Web site and we're done. We could ask the young man to go back in . . . which he did once. But the communication was inconclusive. And he didn't want any more contact with Cobra82nd. We could find another young man, a real person, but that seemed ethically suspect, maybe more so."

Smith made a decision. The paper would hire a consultant, someone skilled in using the Internet to track people down. His assignment: Go into Gay.com and ascertain the identity of Cobra82nd. Ideally, he would do this by lurking, without chatting with anyone, and by tracking computer and Internet Protocol (IP) information. But Gay.com turned out to have effective firewalls, filters built to prevent third-party tracking. Smith and his editors decided they had only one remaining option. The consultant would go to the site as a regular individual and see what happened.

So he did. He presented himself online as a seventeen-year-old with a birthday coming up. He dropped in on some chat rooms using that persona. And he waited. Before too long, Smith said, Cobra82nd (who also went by the name RightBiGuy) made contact, initiating sex talk with the supposed young man.

"The conversations happened in the way the mayor has done this before," Smith said. "We initiated no new or unusual behavior from him. And they built trust."

After the consultant told West he had turned eighteen, the mayor offered him gifts, ranging from an autographed Seahawks football to an introduction to Microsoft magnate Bill Gates, and an internship at City Hall. In early April 2005, West revealed his identity, and the two arranged to meet at a Spokane golf course. In fact, the mayor arranged the meeting through America Online's Instant Messenger, outside the Gay.com firewalls, thus revealing his IP address.

It took several more weeks to fully nail down the story and to interview everyone involved, including the mayor. A series of stories published in the *Spokesman-Review* on May 5, 2005, laid out the details of the mayor's activities not just in recent months but over the past quarter-century. In a note to readers, editor Smith wrote, "Through the use of public records, court documents, first-person accounts and a forensic computer expert, the newspaper has uncovered evidence that West has led a secret life for more than 25 years. Beyond the serious allegations of sexual abuse, West had been using his position in the Legislature to block gay-rights legislation. And he has been trolling the Internet for young lovers while serving as mayor of Spokane, offering gifts and favors."

On the same day, in both a public statement and an e-mail to city employees, West admitted visiting a gay chat line and having relations with adult men; he denied other allegations contained in the stories. The mayor asked employees to pray for him and to remember that "our primary job is to provide the best service possible to our citizens."

He also declared his intention to serve out his term as mayor of Spokane.

1. Was the newspaper justified in hiring a consultant to investigate the mayor's online activities?

2. Once the consultant determined that he could find out very little because of Gay.com's firewall, was the newspaper justified in having him pose online as a teenage boy in the hope of luring the mayor into an assignation? Review the criteria offered by Sissela Bok and Edmund Lambeth for determining when deception is justified, outlined on page 89. Does this case meet those public service criteria? Why or why not?

3. The American Society of Newspaper Editors statement of principles, originally adopted nearly a century ago, states, "The American press was made free not just to inform or just to serve as a forum for debate but also to bring an independent scrutiny to bear on the forces of power in the society, including the conduct of official power at all levels of government." Does this story serve that function, or does the way in which the information was obtained cross an unacceptable line?

4. Steve Smith, the editor of the *Spokesman-Review,* spent a great deal of time after the articles about West were published answering questions from the public and from other media entities about the story and the newspaper's ethical decisions along the way. What effect, if any, do you think this "transparency" might have on public assessment and/or acceptance of the story and the newspaper?

Source Notes for Case Study:

Spokane *Spokesman-Review* package on the Jim West investigation:

Bill Mortin, "West Tied to Sex Abuse in '70s, Using Office to Lure Young Men," SpokesmanReview.com, May 5, 2005, www.spokesmanreview.com/jimwest/.
Steven Smith, "Stories Result of 3-Year Investigation," SpokesmanReview.com, May 5, 2005, www.spokesmanreview.com/jimwest/story.asp?id=050505_editors_note.

Interview with Steve Smith:

Jay Rosen, "Spokane Mayor Sex Scandal: Would You Give Paper an Award?" PressThink, May 11, 2005, http://journalism.nyu.edu/pubzone/weblogs/pressthink/2005/05/11/steve_smith.html.

Additional coverage:

Associated Press, "Embattled Gay Spokane Mayor Opts Out of Public Events," July 5, 2005, www.washblade.com/thelatest/thelatest.cfm?blog_id=1455.

Notes

1. Kent R. Middleton, William E. Lee, and Bill F. Chamberlin, *The Law of Public Communication* (Boston: Allyn & Bacon, 2003), pp. 160–161.

2. Donald M. Gillmor, Jerome A. Barron, Todd F. Simon, and Herbert A. Terry, *Mass Communication Law: Cases and Comment,* 5th ed. (St. Paul, MN: West Publishing, 1990).

3. Louis Alvin Day, *Ethics in Media Communications: Cases and Controversies,* 3rd ed. (Belmont, CA: Wadsworth/Thomson Learning, 2000).

4. Philip Patterson and Lee Wilkins, *Media Ethics: Issues and Cases,* 5th ed. (Boston: McGraw Hill, 2005).

5. Louis Hodges, "The Journalist and Privacy," *Journal of Mass Media Ethics* 9, no. 4 (1994): 197–212.

6. Daniel Riffe, "Public Opinion About News Coverage of Leaders' Private Lives," *Journal of Mass Media Ethics* 18, no. 2 (2003): 98–110.

7. John C. Merrill, *The Imperative of Freedom: A Philosophy of Journalistic Autonomy* (New York: Hastings House, 1974).

8. Patterson and Wilkins, *Media Ethics.*

9. Matthew Kieran, David E. Morrison, and Michael Svennevig, "Privacy, the Public and Journalism: Towards an Analytic Framework," *Journalism: Theory, Practice and Criticism* 1 (August 2000): 145–169.

10. Bruce Garrison, "Newspaper Journalists Use E-mail to Gather News," *Newspaper Research Journal* 25 (Spring 2004): 58–69.

11. Russell Frank, "You've Got Quotes!" *Quill* (October 1999): 18–22; Kathleen A. Hansen and Nora Paul, *Behind the Message: Information Strategies for Communicators* (Boston: Pearson Education, 2004).

12. Hansen and Paul, *Behind the Message.*

13. NICAR 'Net Tour, "Finding and Cultivating Sources: Newsgroup and Listserv Postings," 2004, www.ire.org/training/nettour/sources.html.

14. Sissela Bok, *Lying: Moral Choice in Public and Private Life* (New York: Vintage Books, 1989).

15. Edmund B. Lambeth, *Committed Journalism: An Ethic for the Profession,* 2nd ed. (Bloomington: Indiana University Press, 1992).

16. Bill Kovach and Tom Rosenstiel, *The Elements of Journalism: What Newspeople Should Know and the Public Should Expect* (New York: Crown, 2001), p. 71.

17. Peter Steiner, "On the Internet, Nobody Knows You're a Dog" (cartoon), *New Yorker,* July 5, 1993, p. 61.

18. Hansen and Paul, *Behind the Message.*

19. Day, *Ethics in Media Communications.*

20. Poynter Ethics Journal, "*The Washington Post*'s Policies on Sources, Quotations, Attribution, and Datelines," PoynterOnline, February 20, 2004, www.poynter.org/column.asp?id=53&aid=61244.

21. Project for Excellence in Journalism, "Online: Economics," *The State of the News Media* 2005, www.stateofthemedia.org/2005/narrative_online_economics.asp?cat=4&media=3.

22. Robert I. Berkman and Christopher A. Shumway, *Digital Dilemmas: Ethical Issues for Online Media Professionals* (Ames: Iowa State Press, 2003).

23. J.D. Lasica, "Getting to Know You," *Online Journalism Review,* June 27, 2002, www.ojr.org/ojr/lasica/1025227718.php.

24. Peter Krasilovsky, "Success Stories Help to Cure Industry's Registration Phobia," Newspaper Association of America, March 2003, www.naa.org/home/digitaledge/content/management/connections-2003-success-stories-help-cure-registration-phobia.aspx.

25. Berkman and Shumway, Digital Dilemmas.

26. Rob Runett, "The Value of User Data," *Presstime,* 2003. www.naa.org/sitecore/content/Home/PRESSTIME/2003/June/PressTimeContent/The-Value-of-User-Data.aspx.

27. Project for Excellence in Journalism, "Online: Economics," *The State of the News Media 2006,* http://stateofthemedia.org/2006/narrative_online_economics.asp?cat=4&media=4.

28. Ibid.

29. Jan Samoriski, *Issues in Cyberspace: Communication, Technology, Law and Society on the Internet Frontier* (Boston: Allyn & Bacon, 2002).

30. New American Dream, "Facts About Marketing to Children" (n.d.), www.newdream.org/kids/facts.php.

31. Federal Trade Commission, "Fair Information Practice Principles," Privacy Online: A Report to Congress (June 1998), www.ftc.gov/reports/privacy3/fairinfo.htm; Berkman and Shumway, *Digital Dilemmas.*

32. Berkman and Shumway, *Digital Dilemmas.*

33. Larry Pryor, "Who Gives a Damn About Privacy?" *Online Journalism Review,* June 13, 2001, www.ojr.org/ojr/ethics/1017956617.php

34. Berkman and Shumway, *Digital Dilemmas.*

35. Jay Black, Bob Steele, and Ralph Barney, *Doing Ethics in Journalism: A Handbook with Case Studies,* 3rd ed. (Boston: Allyn & Bacon, 1999).

36. Keith Regan, "Does Anyone Read Online Privacy Policies?" *E-Commerce Times,* June 15, 2001, www.ecommercetimes.com/story/11303.html.

37. Michael Overing, "Defining Jurisdiction on the Internet," *Online Journalism Review,* September 26, 2002, www.ojr.org/ojr/law/1033079518.php.

38. Samoriski, *Issues in Cyberspace.*

39. Middleton, Lee, and Chamberlin, *Law of Public Communication.*

40. Mark Sableman, "Link Law: The Emerging Law of Internet Hyperlinks," *Communication Law & Policy* 4 (Autumn 1999): 557–601; Samoriski, *Issues in Cyberspace..*

41. Michael Overing, "The Tasini Ruling: What the Future Holds," *Online Journalism Review*, April 2, 2002, www.ojr.org:80/ojr/law/1017780534.php.

42. Mack Reed, "Publishers vs. YouTube: Does Either Side Win?" *Online Journalism Review,* July 20, 2006, www.ojr.org/ojr/stories/060720reed.

43. Linda Seebach, "Send 'Free' to Work: Creative Commons Brings Copyrights into the Digital Age," *Online Journalism Review,* January 20, 2005, www.ojr.org/ojr/stories/050120seebach/index.cfm. See also Creative Commons, http://creativecommons.org.

44. Duncan H. Brown and Jeffrey Layne Blevins, "The Safe-Harbor Agreement Between the United States and Europe: A Missed Opportunity to Balance the Interests of E-Commerce and Privacy Online?" *Journal of Broadcasting & Electronic Media* 46 (December 2002): 565–585.

45. Anna Nguyen, "Recent Developments in Internet Law: Council of Europe Criminalizes Internet Hate Speech," *Silha Bulletin* 8 (Winter 2003), www.silha.umn.edu/winter2003.htm.

46. Laura Leets, "Responses to Internet Hate Sites: Is Speech Too Free in Cyberspace?" *Communication Law & Policy* 6 (Spring 2001): 287–317.

47. Samoriski, *Issues in Cyberspace.*

48. Middleton, Lee, and Chamberlin, *Law of Public Communication.*

49. Samoriski, *Issues in Cyberspace.*

50. Wendy Tannenbaum, "Questions of Internet Jurisdiction Spin Web of Confusion for Online Publishers," Reporters Committee for Freedom of the Press, 2003, www.rcfp.org/news/mag/27–1/lib-interjur.html.

51. Wikipedia, "Gutnick v. Dow Jones," 2005, http://en.wikipedia.org/wiki/Gutnick_v._Dow_Jones

52. Kirsten Murphy, "Recent Developments in Defamation Law: Dow Jones & Company Inc. v. Gutnick," *Silha Bulletin* 8 (winter 2003). www.silha.umn.edu/winter2003.htm.

53. Clare Dyer, "Wall St. Journal's Online Libel Win Brings 'Much-Needed Clarity,'" *Guardian,* February 4, 2005, www.guardian.co.uk/business/story/0,3604,1405498,00.html.

54. Middleton, Lee, and Chamberlin, *Law of Public Communication.*

55. Constance Davis, Dialogues: Online Journalism Ethics, October 2004, http://jethicsdialogues.blogspot.com.

56. Tannenbaum, "Questions of Internet Jurisdiction."

57. Ibid.

58. Samoriski, *Issues in Cyberspace.*

59. Sam Byassee, "Bloggers Are Liable for Libel Suits," *Online Journalism Review,* February 19, 2004, www.ojr.org/ojr/law/1077151572.php.

60. Douglas Lee, "Shield Laws: Overview," First Amendment Center, 2005, www.firstamendmentcenter.org/Press/topic.aspx?topic=shield_laws.

61. Reporters Committee for Freedom of the Press, "Federal Shield Law Efforts," 2006, http://rcfp.org/shields_and_subpoenas.html#shield.

62. Laurence B. Alexander, "Looking Out for the Watchdogs: A Legislative Proposal Limiting the Newsgathering Privilege to Journalists in the Greatest Need of Protection for Sources and Information," 20 *Yale Law & Policy Review* 97 (2002).

63. Mark Thompson, "States' Shield Laws Might Not Cover Online Journalists," *Online Journalism Review,* June 16, 2004, www.ojr.org/ojr/law/1086825172.php.

64. Alexander, "Looking Out for the Watchdogs."

65. Eugene Volokh, "You Can Blog, but You Can't Hide," *New York Times,* December 2, 2004, p. A39.

66. Linda L. Berger, "Shielding the Unmedia: Using the Process of Journalism to Protect the Journalist's Privilege in an Infinite Universe of Publication," 39 *Houston Law Review* 1371 (2003): 1411, 1416. Kovach and Rosenstiel, *Elements of Journalism,* pp. 70–93.

67. Mark Thompson, "New Media Often Takes Back Seat to Old Media on Press Credentials," *Online Journalism Review,* April 22, 2004, www.ojr.org/ojr/workplace/1075604186.php.

68. Samoriski, *Issues in Cyberspace.*

69. Mark Thompson, "Law Offers Internet Publishers Scant Guidance on Libel," *Online Journalism Review,* June 16, 2004, www.ojr.org/ojr/law/1087423868.php.

70. Mark Thompson. "To Fix or Not to Fix: Online Corrections Policies Vary Widely," *Online Journalism Review,* July 28, 2004, www.ojr.org/ojr/workplace/1091056600.php.

71. Berkman and Shumway, *Digital Dilemmas.*

72. M. David Arant and Janna Quitney Anderson, "Online Media Ethics: A Survey of U.S. Daily Newspaper Editors" (paper presented to the Newspaper Division of the Association for Education in Journalism and Mass Communication, Phoenix, August 2000); Mark Glaser, "Newspaper Sites Are Slow to Fix Their Online Corrections Policies," *Online Journalism Review,* August 19, 2003, www.ojr.org/ojr/glaser/1061336081.php.

73. Julie Panna, "I'm in Online News–Why Can't I Get One of These?" *Quill* (September 2000): 12–17.

74. United States Senate Daily Press Gallery (n.d.), www.senate.gov/galleries/daily/rules.htm.

75. Thompson, "New Media Often Takes Back Seat."

5

Bloggers and Other "Participatory Journalists"

Jane B. Singer

Although the Internet has always thrived as a sort of free vanity press (a publisher who charges authors to print their books, as opposed to the usual system in which authors are paid for their work), the explosion of self-expression is largely a twenty-first-century phenomenon. In the past two years, the number of "amateur," "citizen," "participatory," or "grassroots" journalists—that is, ordinary folks who publish regularly online—has soared. By 2006, the Pew Internet & American Life Project reported, more than 12 million American adults had created their own blog and more than a third of Internet users—57 million people—said they read them.[1] Dave Sifry of the blog search engine Technorati, which tracks more than 50 million blogs, reports that the blogosphere is doubling in size every 200 days, with about 175,000 new blogs being created every day.[2] Popular blogs are updated frequently, often multiple times a day, and attract thousands of readers; millions of other blogs are personal affairs, of interest only to a "nanoaudience" composed of the blogger's family, friends, or fellow students.[3]

Other new forms of content creation are rapidly gaining popularity, as well. Wikipedia, an online encyclopedia with more than 1.3 million English-language entries, all of them user-generated and user-edited, claims about 48,000 regular contributors and more than 2 million registered users; as of summer 2006, the site was growing by about 8,000 articles a day. Wikipedias are available in 230 different languages, from Polish to Portuguese, Hebrew to Hungarian, Chechen to Cheyenne.[4] In late 2004, Wikipedia added a "Wikinews" component, "the free news source that you can write"; by mid-2006, Wikinews sites offering about

25,000 articles from more than 1,200 active contributors were available in twenty languages in addition to English.[5] More than 6 million American adults have tried podcasting, a feature that allows people to create audio (and, increasingly, video) segments for the Web that others can download.[6] And a growing number of sites, some affiliated with mainstream media, are providing space for "citizen journalism," contributions from users that they, rather than the journalists, see as newsworthy. (Not sure what all these things are? You are not alone; the Pew project reassures us that millions of Americans are unfamiliar with this terminology. Exhibit 5.1 offers help.)

Millions of people are using the Internet to express their ideas and opinions in a joyous—and raucous—celebration of free speech, facilitated by a medium that extends that freedom both within and among societies. Although this chapter focuses primarily on bloggers, the ethical issues apply to all the other participants in this vast, unfettered conversation, as well.

- Are the ethics of communication universal or do the ethical choices involved in publishing information, ideas, or opinions vary depending on whether a person is a professional journalist or an amateur one? Do different principles take precedence? Do blogs raise issues for their creators that traditional journalists typically do not encounter, or are ethical challenges merely matters of degree?
- Journalists and bloggers both value truth—but they get to it in very different ways. Are their approaches complementary or contradictory? Is one more valuable than the other?
- Bloggers have taken on a self-appointed role as "watchdogs of the watchdogs," carefully and continuously monitoring what journalists report and how they report it—and calling attention to perceived problems such as hypocrisy, bias, inaccuracy, and inattention to potentially big stories. Is such a role useful to journalists or threatening to their autonomy or merely annoying? What, if anything, can journalists learn from such criticism—and what can they do with what they learn?

Media organizations have joined the blogosphere, as well. Hundreds of professional journalists, both columnists and reporters, maintain blogs connected to their employers' Web sites. A few media organizations have begun to experiment with wikis and podcasts, too. Others are opening

Exhibit 5.1
Glossary

People love to generate jargon about online publishing almost as much as they love to generate the published material itself. Here is a quick glossary. All these definitions are taken—appropriately, we think—from Wikipedia, an online encyclopedia created and edited by its users. Wikipedia is available at http://en.wikipedia.org.

- Blog: A Web-based publication of periodically posted items, normally in reverse chronological order. The format varies from simple bullet lists of hyperlinks to article summaries to complete stories with user-generated comments. Blog entries are usually date- and time-stamped, with the newest post at the top and comments below it. Blogs range in scope from individual diaries to arms of political campaigns, media programs, and corporations. They range in scale from the work of one occasional author to the collaboration of a community of writers.
- Blogosphere: The totality of Weblogs or blog-related Web sites.
- Blogroll: A blog's collection of links to yet other blogs. Criteria for inclusion vary with the blogger, from matters of common interest to personal favorites.
- Blogstorm (or blog swarm): A large amount of activity, information, and opinion erupting around a particular subject or controversy in the blogosphere.
- Citizen journalism: Also known as "participatory journalism," citizen journalism involves ordinary people playing an active role in collecting, reporting, analyzing, and disseminating information —activities that previously were the domain of professional reporters. In *We Media: How Audiences Are Shaping the Future of News and Information,* Shayne Bowman and Chris Willis say, "The intent of this participation is to provide independent, reliable, accurate, wide-ranging, and relevant information that a democracy requires."
- Mainstream media (MSM): What journalists traditionally work for. To bloggers, MSM is generally a derogatory term.
- Podcasting: A method of publishing files via the Internet, allowing users to subscribe to a feed to receive new files automatically; unlike traditional broadcasting, podcasting has neither a mass audience

(continued)

Exhibit 5.1 *(continued)*

nor a fixed delivery time. Podcasts originally were intended largely as a way to download audio files onto a portable player, although any digital device with audio-playing software can play a podcast. The same technique also can deliver video files.

- RSS: A system of content distribution and republication widely used by blogs and podcasts, as well as a large and rapidly growing number of news sites. RSS is short for Really Simple Syndication (as well as Rich Site Summary). There are lots of permutations and technological twists, but RSS is commonly used to provide short content descriptions along with links to headlines, complete stories, multimedia files, full sites, or whatever else is desired.
- Wiki: With a capital W or a lowercase w? Not sure? Here's the difference: A lowercase wiki (which is probably the one you mean) is a web application that allows users to contribute content. Anyone can add, anyone can edit. An uppercase Wiki, as well as WikiWikiWeb, refers specifically to the Portland Pattern Repository, the first wiki ever created. Either way, the name is based on the Hawaiian pidgin term *wiki wiki,* meaning "quick" or "informal."

up their online space for user contributions, moving beyond forums and bulletin boards to news sections entirely created by users. Many ethical questions accompany these moves.

- What professional principles lend themselves especially well to such formats—and which create potential conflicts?
- Should journalists offer their opinions through such formats—and if so, should they offer them instead of or in addition to more traditional aspects of their jobs? How might such publications change journalists' relationships with sources or with the public?
- Should editors have any oversight over journalists' blogs? Should publishers or owners of media companies?
- Should newsrooms sponsor places online for users to offer their own blogs or other forms of information? If so, what if any responsibility does the news organization have to ensure the information is accurate and fair? How should it deal with material that may be offensive, threatening, or potentially libelous?

Let us start by trying to define just what a blogger does—and whether it constitutes journalism.

Are Bloggers Journalists?

We are going to set aside for now the people who provide an easy answer to this question: the reporters, editors, and columnists who maintain their own blogs, either independently or under the auspices of their media employer. We will deal with them later in this chapter because they raise a whole set of ethical issues of their own.

One way to approach the question of whether bloggers are journalists is to figure out what makes someone a journalist in the first place. But as we suggest throughout this book and explored in some detail in Chapter 2, coming up with a working definition is not easy. We have seen that definitions based on professionalism, process, and practice are all problematic.

Indeed, both bloggers and journalists continue to wrestle with this issue of what, if anything, separates them, not infrequently descending into mutual name-calling along the way. Some journalists who appreciate the role bloggers can play still do not want them considered journalists; many bloggers flat-out reject the term and what it stands for. "It's just the latest manifestation of the vanity press," says Steve Lovelady, managing editor of *Columbia Journalism Review*'s online *CJR Daily.* "Most of them don't consider themselves journalists."[7] Nor should anyone else consider them that way, some observers say. "They're certainly not committed to being objective. They thrive on rumor and innuendo," says journalism professor Tom McPhail. Bloggers "should be put in a different category, like 'pretend' journalists."[8]

But others, including some journalists, argue that what bloggers do is real—and valuable. For instance, the *Washington Post*'s Thomas Edsall, who has reported on politics and government for more than thirty-five years, says political bloggers can serve as an antidote to journalistic group think: "We in journalism—there's an orthodoxy to our thinking. You can come up with an idea and you know it's sort of *verbotten,* or they're gonna say, 'Oh, that's only worth ten inches,' and they're gonna put you inside the paper. It's not worth the fight. The blogs can sort of break the ice and make it clear that there is something pretty strange or pretty unique or pretty interesting or pretty *awful* about something."[9]

Many bloggers do have backgrounds as journalists, and they are among the most passionate about the benefits of blogging. Long-time journalist and media executive Jeff Jarvis frequently discusses these issues in his popular BuzzMachine blog. "Journalism is institutional, impersonal, and dispassionate; blogs are human, personal, and passionate. Institutions take pledges because they have become separated from the people they serve," Jarvis says. "At the end of the day, I don't want to see blogs turn into an institution, or try to, for then they wouldn't be blogs anymore."[10]

The debate over whether bloggers are, can be, or should be journalists is not likely to end anytime soon. An ethical perspective may help add clarity. Although broad ethical approaches such as those outlined in our introduction can be valuable in all human interactions, the journalist has always had a special set of obligations tied to a commitment to provide citizens the information they need to be free and self-governing.[11] The fact that those citizens can choose from a vast array of different information does not change the commitment or the obligations. Unlike those with institutionally defined social roles and ethics, such as lawyers, journalists have been left to their own devices in deciding what actions are ethical and in publicly enacting them.[12] According to the Society of Professional Journalists (SPJ), the ethical principles that journalists have laid out as guidance toward an optimal way of doing their work are to seek truth and report it, to minimize harm, to act independently, and to be accountable.[13] Do these principles apply equally well to bloggers?

Bloggers and Journalistic Principles

We will start with a topic we touched on in Chapter 2: a commitment to truth, foremost among the journalist's obligations.[14] As it happens, both bloggers and journalists are committed to truth, but they have quite different ideas about how best to attain it. Journalists hold an Enlightenment view of truth as something rationally arrived at through well-tested methods. They understand truth as something that can be seen or heard, either by themselves or another reliable source, and that can then be verified. Despite challenges to the gatekeeping role discussed earlier in this book, they do consider themselves gatekeepers, collecting and vetting information as best they can before disseminating it—or not.[15] The news product then offers as truth the information that has survived the rigorous scrutiny (ideally) of this journalistic process. The essence of journalism is this process of verification.[16]

Bloggers have an entirely different view. They do not see truth as resting on the decisions of one individual or group of individuals within a news organization or anywhere else. Nor do they see truth as having to do with attempts at objectivity. Instead, bloggers see truth as emerging from shared, collective knowledge—from an electronically enabled marketplace of ideas.[17] A blog, one researcher points out, "depends upon a different model of its authority, establishing itself as a site of multiple knowledge and of breadth of knowledge of the world." Knowledge is seen as evolving through connections rather than as contained within one entity such as a newspaper or newscast.[18]

Bloggers and other Web users who contribute to wikis, podcasts, and other participatory media forms see themselves as the opposite of gatekeepers. On the contrary, they offer a space for all comers to post what they know or think, to receive a hearing, and to have their ideas publicly debated, modified, expanded, or refuted. Truth for the blogger is created collectively rather than hierarchically. Information is not vetted before its dissemination but instead through the process of disseminating multiple views, with truth, in the bloggers' view, as the end result of the discussion.[19]

Both bloggers and journalists, then, "seek truth and report it," but in fundamentally different ways and with significant implications for notions such as credibility, which for journalists often rests primarily with the reputation of their media organization but must be earned by each individual blogger.[20] Online, reputations are based not on claims of objectivity but on "a synthesis of consistency, accuracy, and frequent comparison by the reader," say Chris Willis and Shayne Bowman in their online book, *We Media.* They quote well-known author and Internet veteran Howard Rheingold, who suggests that the standards for credible information are the same regardless of who publishes it: "People who are dedicated to establishing a reputation for getting the story right and getting it first don't necessarily have to work for the *Washington Post* or *The New York Times.*"[21]

Fair enough, though it also is true that while journalists at the *Post* or the *Times* face consequences if they publish lies—think infamous plagiarist Jayson Blair—bloggers do not. Bloggers' ethics are almost wholly personal; they can choose to provide a platform for the collective pursuit of truth, or they can publish whatever outrageous nonsense strikes their fancy. Either way, they will still be blogging tomorrow (if they feel like it). The ethics of the traditional journalist are both personal and social. The additional safeguard of being part of an occupational group that values the responsible pursuit of the truth is important.

Is there common ethical ground here? Yes, and not just because the Internet is big enough for both blogging and traditional journalism to coexist. Ironically, journalists are part of a functioning collective to an arguably greater extent than the freewheeling bloggers—the collective of the newsroom and the profession at large. Moreover, some observers believe the two forms are inevitably converging and that "bloggers vs. journalists is over."[22] To its detractors, traditional journalism has long treated the news as a lecture: Journalists and the media organizations they worked for proclaimed what the news was, and the audience could either take it or leave it—but not affect it much one way or the other. But journalist-turned-blogger-turned-citizen-journalist-activist Dan Gillmor predicts (in a book whose chapters were initially published on his blog, where feedback was invited and incorporated), "Tomorrow's news reporting and production will be more of a conversation, or a seminar." The shift will force journalists, newsmakers, and, in particular, the "former audience" to adapt. "Blogs and any other modern media are feedback systems," Gillmor writes. "They work in something close to real time and capture—in the best sense of the word—the multitude of ideas and realities each of us can offer. On the Internet, we are defined by what we know and share."[23]

We will return at the end of this chapter to this idea of common ground between bloggers and journalists, but we first turn to the other guiding principles of journalism. For journalists, the most controversial of these has been accountability. The current version of the SPJ code of ethics was adopted only after two years of debate, much of it about the nature and extent of journalists' responsibilities to the public.[24] Eventually, it was agreed that journalists are accountable to their audiences and to each other. Related responsibilities include clarifying and explaining news coverage, inviting dialogue with the public about journalistic conduct, encouraging the public to voice grievances about the news media, and admitting and promptly correcting mistakes.[25] The controversy primarily involved the perception that accountability conflicted with journalists' long and legally protected history of cantankerous independence, and the eventual inclusion of the principle in the professional code initially had minimal impact on journalists' behavior.[26]

However, journalists today downplay the idea of accountability less than they did only a few years ago. It would be simplistic to credit bloggers for the change. A host of interrelated events and trends account for the expanded efforts of the media to both examine and explain themselves. These include, among economic pressures and other commercial influences, a string of public embarrassments at major news organizations; highly visible moves toward expanded accountability by industry leaders, such as the management shake-up and addition of an ombudsman at *The New York Times;* a desire to separate "journalism" from the increasingly entertainment-oriented "news media"; and loudly persistent calls by industry observers, from trade publications to media think tanks to academics, for journalists to do better. Add the cumulative effects of an almost uniformly antagonistic White House administration and an increasingly hostile public; more than half of Americans say they do not trust journalists to tell the truth, for instance,[27] and more than a third see them as outright immoral.[28]

Still, it would be a mistake to exclude from the equation the pressure for greater accountability exerted by bloggers. Although they ultimately are answerable only to themselves, bloggers do move the notion of accountability—which they (and others) term "transparency" and label the "golden rule of the blogosphere"[29]— to the foreground in at least two ways. One is by constantly monitoring journalists' work, a topic we will explore later in this chapter. The other is by their own publishing practices, which include, ideally, disclosure of the principles they hold, the processes they follow, and the people they are.[30] Mary Hodder, a product manager at blog search engine Technorati, emphasizes that bloggers are transparent in both their motive and their process. They are upfront about their biases and subjective approach; moreover, they have greater autonomy to speak from the heart than journalists, who are constrained by institutional norms of objectivity and distance from any given subject. And blogs are characterized by their extensive use of links to documents, sources, news articles, and other sorts of evidence that bloggers use to buttress their own views and, ultimately, to establish their own authority.[31] Indeed, the two work together: Bloggers tell readers who they are and what they find interesting or important, then invite those readers to see for themselves if they agree. "To be interesting, the blog must have a discernible human voice," says blogger and veteran journalist Sheila Lennon of projo.com, a Web site affiliated with the *Providence Journal* (Rhode Island). "A blog with just links is a portal."[32]

Bloggers also are relatively good at admitting, and correcting, their own mistakes. For one thing, their embrace of interactivity means they are likely to hear from readers—or other bloggers, often one and the same people—when they have made an error. Most bloggers quickly post corrections, displayed as prominently—that is, as the top item in the blog, at least temporarily—as the original mistake. In contrast, newspaper corrections typically are relegated to a special area on an inside page.[33] And television news executives tend to ignore complaints entirely unless they arrive on a libel lawyer's letterhead.[34]

On other ethical standards, bloggers fare less well in comparison with journalists who practice what the profession preaches. As might be expected for communicators who wear their views on their sleeves, independence has been a sticky issue for bloggers. For starters, unlike most journalists, most bloggers have other jobs that pay the bills. Sometimes, those jobs create what journalists would decry as conflicts of interest. For example, Markos Moulitsas, who operates the popular Daily Kos political blog, is a Democratic activist who worked for the Howard Dean campaign in 2003, raised money for Democratic candidates in 2004, and posted comments in support of candidates for whom he was working as a paid consultant.[35] In fact, critics say, bloggers rarely disclose whether they are receiving money from the people or causes they write about.[36] In some cases, they may actually have been recruited to post positive comments about a particular product or service; at least one Internet marketing firm, USWeb.com, has offered to pay bloggers $5 per post for favorable comments about clients along with a link to the client's site.[37]

Advertising has raised related problems for bloggers, who simultaneously serve the dual and sometimes conflicting roles of editor and publisher. As blogs have gained both popularity and visibility through their prominent display on popular search engines such as Google, advertisers have taken notice; by 2005, nearly two-thirds of marketers were telling Forrester Research that they were interested in advertising on blogs.[38] But the traditional wall between editorial content and advertising is often (though not always) lower on a blog than in the newspaper. Wonkette, a witty Washington blog, has posted weekly "shout-outs" to advertisers, including some who are politically partisan.[39] Gawker Media, which operates several popular blogs, accepted $25,000 a month from Sony in exchange for sole sponsorship of its Lifehacker blog about personal gadgetry software. Inevitably, commercial entities also have begun offering direct payments or freebies in an attempt to get popular bloggers to write about them. For instance, a company called Marqui, which sells communication management services for automating Web sites, paid twenty bloggers to increase awareness of its brand by mentioning the company in a post at least once a week.[40] And the list goes on.

To be fair, bloggers as a community have been quick to criticize such blatant marketing ploys. Marqui's program, for instance, was denounced as a threat to "turn the blogosphere into a graffiti-laden slum."[41] When Dr Pepper recruited a group of young bloggers to write about its new Raging Cow milk drink, the company drew widespread condemnation from bloggers, who ridiculed the move as greedy corporate exploitation of the form. In 2004, Mazda was similarly lambasted for creating a fake blog including videos by a fictional twenty-two-year-old blogger;[42] Still, it seems inevitable that marketers will continue to explore the potential of blogs in ways that go beyond easily distinguishable banner ads; indeed, the ability to insinuate marketing messages into an ongoing conversation among actively engaged participants is likely to prove irresistible. And public relations firms are close behind marketers in taking advantage of the blog form. In announcing a new service called "Blogger Relations," for example, a company called Issue Dynamics Inc. pointed out that blogs "provide an opportunity to reach so-called 'influentials'—those members of society responsible for influencing mass opinion within their personal and professional circles." Its service promised to allow organizations to "maximize outreach and influence public perception within the blogosphere."[43]

The fourth principle included in the SPJ ethics code involves minimizing harm. Although this principle can clash with that of truth-telling, the two are not mutually exclusive. Journalists need to be concerned about the consequences of their actions and to weigh those consequences against the significance of the truth they are pursuing, as well as to look for alternative routes to that truth that may be more humane.[44] As we saw in the last chapter, the concept of harm to privacy and to personal reputation also has legal ramifications, and the application of those laws to bloggers and other "citizen journalists" is still evolving.

In the meantime, the minimization of harm does not seem to be a high priority in the blogosphere, though of course individual bloggers make individual choices about what to post and what to withhold. In general, however, the idea of collectively derived truth steers bloggers away from restraint. If the group will correct bad or erroneous ideas anyway, what is the harm in expressing them? On the contrary, this marketplace of ideas approach suggests that the best, if not the only corrective for such information is to give it as wide a hearing as possible and to allow the presumably wiser collective to prevail. However, there is no guarantee that the collective will indeed refute the harmful information rather than simply piling on, and considerable harm can be done in the interim to the person who is the subject of the original post.[45] This is especially problematic given the "echo chamber" nature of the blogosphere, in which a single post may be linked to or reiterated by hundreds of other bloggers.

For instance, bloggers like to cite their political triumphs in the 2004 presidential campaign, from Howard Dean's rise from obscurity through skillful use of the medium to the "outing" of the faulty CBS News story about President George W. Bush's National Guard service. But there were potentially harmful blogger exploits, too, from the bogus Drudge Report story about John Kerry's affair with an intern in February 2004 to the slew of blogs that posted Election Day exit polls showing Kerry well ahead of Bush.[46] In the first case, the error was corrected—after several days in which journalists (not bloggers) hounded potential sources, including the intern's family, and during which the story permeated not only the Internet but other media outlets, as well. As for the exit polls, it is difficult to say whether they caused harm and if so, how much; it is certain, however, that many American voters thought the election was decided by mid-afternoon—in favor of the eventual loser.

Examples of harm at a more personal level can be found with virtually any scroll through your favorite blogs. Bloggers are nothing if not blunt in their assessments of virtually everyone and everything, including each other. They seem to see this outspokenness as a form of free speech. An interesting study by a doctoral student in North Carolina in 2004 explored how bloggers' ethics stacked up against traditional ethical approaches to stakeholders, duties, and values. "Minimizing harm" was not a top priority for any of the bloggers in this small-scale study; a majority cited "freedom of expression" as their strongest value.[47]

Is any harm done to the individuals who may be maligned by something a blogger posts? You will have to ask the person who is the subject of discussion—or consider how you would feel if it were you. Harm that rises to the level of libel becomes a legal issue to be dealt with in court. But at a broad social level, the Poynter Institute's Bob Steele offers this caution: "If bloggers create rumors that cause harm, that's a disservice. It leads to erosion of trust for other forms of information, it can lead to badly informed opinions, it can produce misguided actions by some, it can cause problems for people's reputations, it can in some ways erode the fabric of a civil society."[48]

Bloggers' Ethics

So the direct application of journalists' ethics to bloggers is difficult, given differences in what they do and their underlying philosophies of doing it. How about a set of ethics just for bloggers?

In some ways, the notion is counter to the idea or ideal of bloggers as freewheeling commentators. Begin to organize them or codify their behavior even informally, some say, and the whole unfettered beauty of a form that thrives on innovation and individuality starts to fade. Even so, proponents have offered various proposals intended to help bloggers gain credibility. In this section, we will summarize a few of them. All, of course, have been debated and critiqued by the blogging community.

Among the most widely cited are the ethical guidelines proposed by Jonathan Dube of CyberJournalist net. Dube draws extensively on the SPJ code we have just been discussing. He argues that although blogging is a more casual form of publishing than journalism, it is still publishing, and bloggers therefore have ethical obligations to readers, to the people they write about, and to society in general.

Dube suggests three broad principles and, like the SPJ code, specific guidelines for meeting them. The principle "Minimize harm" provides guidelines that are virtually identical to those offered by SPJ, underscoring the need for bloggers to treat those whom they write about with respect. Under "Be accountable," Dube incorporates journalistic approaches to both accountability and independence while also emphasizing the bloggers' obligation for disclosure. For example, under this guideline, bloggers are urged to "explain each Weblog's mission and invite dialogue with the public over its content and the bloggers' conduct" and to "be wary of sources offering information for favors. When accepting such information, disclose the favors." The third guideline, "Be honest and fair," borrows from several of the journalistic principles, particularly that of truth-telling. Dube urges bloggers, among other things, to "identify and link to sources whenever feasible. The public is entitled to as much information as possible on sources' reliability." Bloggers also should clearly differentiate the types of information available on their blog: "Distinguish between advocacy, commentary, and factual information. Even advocacy writing and commentary should not misrepresent fact or context," he urges. And "distinguish factual information and commentary from advertising and shun hybrids that blur the lines between the two."[49]

Another widely discussed set of ethical guidelines is offered by blogging pioneer Rebecca Blood, whose 2002 book, *The Weblog Handbook,* was one of the first to systematically explain blogs and explore their connections to the media and the larger culture. In her book, Blood suggests that "the blog's greatest strength—its uncensored, unmediated, uncontrolled voice—is also its greatest weakness." Although media organizations and the journalists who work for them are far from perfect, they do have a vested interest in upholding certain standards in order to retain both audience and advertisers. In contrast, she says, the lack of gatekeepers and bloggers' relative freedom from any consequences of publishing may compromise their integrity and thus their value. She offers a set of six principles, each of which incorporates the notion of transparency.[50] A condensed version of Blood's "Weblog Ethics" is provided in Exhibit 5.2.

Scholar Martin Kuhn draws on both of these proposals, as well as on philosophical approaches to ethics such as those outlined in the introductory chapter, in formulating his own proposed code of blogging ethics. In addition to transparency, his code incorporates notions of truthfulness, accountability, and minimization of harm. In addition, he calls on bloggers to actively promote such online attributes as free expression, interactivity (for instance, through regular postings both on their own and others' blogs), and community formation and enrichment (for instance, through links to other blogs as well as responses to readers).[51]

Blogger and online journalist J.D. Lasica emphasizes transparency and disclosure as central to a "loose-knit set of general tenets" for bloggers. Actions, motives, and financial considerations all should be shared with readers, he emphasizes. Beyond that, his guidelines are simple. Bloggers should follow their passions, blogging about topics they care about deeply. They should be honest, writing what they believe. They should trust readers to form their own judgments and conclusions. And, remembering that "reputation is the principal currency of cyberspace," they should safeguard their independence and integrity in order to maintain readers' trust.[52]

Online Journalism Review (OJR) offers a more formal set of guidelines, in the form of advice for "writers, bloggers, and others getting started in journalism." *OJR,* which posts its guidelines in the form of a wiki to which anyone can contribute, also emphasizes the importance of

Exhibit 5.2
Weblog Ethics

From The Weblog Handbook: Practical Advice on Creating and Maintaining Your Blog *by Rebecca Blood. Blood writes on the Internet's impact on business, media, and society on her Weblog, Rebecca's Pocket, and has also written important essays on the history and development of blogging.*

1. Publish as fact only that which you believe to be true.

If your statement is speculation, say so. If you have reason to believe that something is not true, either don't post it or note your reservations. When you make an assertion, do so in good faith; state it as fact only if, to the best of your knowledge, it is so.

2. If material exists online, link to it when you reference it.

Linking to referenced material allows readers to judge for themselves the accuracy and insightfulness of your statements. Referencing material but selectively linking only that with which you agree is manipulative. Online readers deserve, as much as possible, access to all of the facts—the Web, used this way, empowers readers to become active, not passive, consumers of information. Further, linking to source material is the very means by which we are creating a vast, new, collective network of information and knowledge.

On the rare occasion when a writer wishes to reference but not drive traffic to a site she considers to be morally reprehensible (for example, a hate site), she should type out (but not link) the name or URL of the offending site and state the reasons for her decision. This will give motivated readers the information they need to find the site in order to make their own judgments. This strategy allows the writer to preserve her own transparency (and thus her integrity) while simultaneously declining to lend support to a cause she finds contemptible.

3. Publicly correct any misinformation.

If you find that you have linked to a story that was untrue, make a note of it and link to a more accurate report. If one of your own statements proves to be inaccurate, note your misstatement and the truth. Ideally,

(continued)

Exhibit 5.2 *(continued)*

these corrections would appear in the most current version of your weblog and as an added note to the original entry. . . .

4. Write each entry as if it could not be changed; add to, but do not rewrite or delete, any entry.

Post deliberately. If you invest each entry with intent, you will ensure your personal and professional integrity.

Changing or deleting entries destroys the integrity of the network. The Web is designed to be connected; indeed, the weblog permalink is an invitation for others to link. Anyone who comments on or cites a document on the Web relies on that document (or entry) to remain unchanged. . . .

The network of shared knowledge we are building will never be more than a novelty unless we protect its integrity by creating permanent records of our publications. . . . History can be rewritten, but it cannot be undone. . . .

The only exception to this rule is when you inadvertently reveal personal information about someone else. If you discover that you have violated a confidence or made an acquaintance uncomfortable by mentioning him, it is only fair to remove the offending entry altogether, but note that you have done so.

5. Disclose any conflict of interest.

Most webloggers are quite transparent about their jobs and professional interests. It is the computer programmer's expertise that gives her commentary special weight when she analyzes a magazine article about the merits of the latest operating system. Since weblog audiences are built on trust, it is to every weblogger's benefit to disclose any monetary (or other potentially conflicting) interests when appropriate. . . . Quickly note any potential conflict of interest and then say your piece; your readers will have all the information they need to assess your commentary.

(continued)

Exhibit 5.2 *(continued)*

6. Note questionable and biased sources.

When a serious article comes from a highly biased or questionable source, the weblogger has a responsibility to clearly note the nature of the site on which it was found.

In their foraging, webloggers occasionally find interesting, well-written articles on sites that are maintained by highly biased organizations or by seemingly fanatical individuals. Readers need to know whether an article on the medical ramifications of first trimester abortion comes from a site that is pro-life, pro-choice, or strongly opposed to medical intervention of all kinds. A thoughtful summation of the Israeli-Palestinian conflict may be worth reading whether it is written by a member of the Palestine Liberation Organization (PLO) or a Zionist—but readers have the right to be alerted to the source.

It is reasonable to expect that expert foragers have the knowledge and motivation to assess the nature of these sources; it is not reasonable to assume that all readers do. Readers depend on weblogs, to some extent, for guidance in navigating the Web. To present an article from a source that is a little nutty or has a strong agenda is fine; not to acknowledge the nature of that source is unethical, since readers don't have the information they need to fully evaluate the article's merits.

If you are afraid that your readers will discount the article entirely based on its context, consider why you are linking it at all. If you strongly feel the piece has merit, say why and let it stand on its own, but be clear about its source. Your readers may cease to trust you if they discover even once that you disguised—or didn't make clear—the source of an article they might have evaluated differently had they been given all the facts.

Source: Copyright © 2002 by Rebecca Blood. Reprinted by permission of Basic Books, a member of Perseus Books Group.

disclosure: "Tell your readers how you got your information, and what factors influenced your decision to publish it. If you have a personal or professional connection to people or groups you're writing about, describe it. Your readers deserve to know what has influenced the way you reported or wrote a story." Any commercial ties also should be made clear: "Don't hide whom you work for, or where the money to support your site comes from." *OJR* admonishes bloggers and other writers to stay away from plagiarism and from conflicts of interest, such as acceptance of gifts or money for coverage. And it stresses the importance of verification, accuracy, truth, and honesty. "Check out your information before you print it," the guidelines urge. "Find facts, not just others' opinions, to support your comments." Honesty is essential for credibility, *OJR* says: "Be honest with your readers and transparent about your work. If people wonder for a moment about your honesty or your motives, you've lost credibility with them. Don't let them do that. Answer those questions even before readers ask."[53]

Are you seeing a pattern here? Those who have thought through what ethical guidelines for bloggers might look like are finding that they look a whole lot like ethical guidelines for journalists. The bloggers perhaps put greater emphasis on transparency, but the journalists got there first with the controversial addition of accountability to their code back in 1996. And bloggers are finding that their credibility comes down to honesty, accuracy, and an avoidance of conflicts of interest. They may lean more toward offering opinions and commentary than offering "news," but the ethics of the communication process are remarkably similar for both bloggers and journalists, regardless of the content.

Even bloggers acknowledge the similarities. In May 2005, the Media Bloggers Association (yes, there is one) held an inaugural education session for bloggers. The subject: how to use computers to "cut through the PR cant and spin and get to the real underlying news on public policy issues"—a version of the computer-assisted reporting seminars that have long been successful training tools for journalists.[54] More than 300 bloggers attended the conference.

In fact, the Poynter Institute makes the parallels explicit, offering a pair of articles from online veteran Steve Outing describing what bloggers and journalists can learn from each other. Blogging, he quotes Wonkette.com's Ana Marie Cox as saying, is great fun—"all chocolate cake and no potatoes." But bloggers need to eat their vegetables too, Outing cautions, if they "expect to grow up and win the respect of larger audiences." Among the spinach he recommends: incorporating some sort of editorial oversight in an effort to catch problems before they are published, learning the value of journalistic legwork (talking to multiple sources, checking their credibility, avoiding anonymous sources), and sharpening their writing talons . . . uh, talents in order to get quickly to the point. Outing also reminds bloggers of the value of standard journalistic norms such as accuracy and fairness. Ultimately, he says, the key is using power wisely. "Journalists, as members of the 'Fourth Estate,' have long held power. Now bloggers are positioned to share some of that. Take care, please."[55]

In a companion piece, Outing turns to what bloggers can teach journalists. His ideas echo those with which we began our consideration of blogging ethics. They involve the approach to news as the product of a collective conversation, one in which the participants know rather a lot about each other and in which correcting erroneous information is part of the process rather than segregated from it. He concludes, however, that the two forms have a great deal in common and that "bloggers and mainstream journalists should be looking to one another for ideas on how to navigate our newly revised media world."[56]

So are bloggers journalists, and are their ethics interchangcable? No, they are different—but complementary rather than contradictory. Indeed, the relationship between bloggers and journalists perhaps can best be described as symbiotic. Interconnected blogs and their readers form a community that discusses, dissects, and extends the stories created by mainstream media, as well as producing its own commentary, fact-checking, and grassroots reporting. The mainstream media in turn feed upon this material, developing it as a pool of tips, sources, and story ideas[57]—not to mention bringing blogs and the issues raised by bloggers to the public's attention by covering them as newsworthy. "The revolution," declared *The New York Times* in assessing bloggers' influence on the 2004 election, "will be posted."[58]

One observer who himself is both a journalist and a blogger has coined the term "Estate 4.5" to describe the blogosphere, in "a nod both to the profession whose excesses galvanized many bloggers and to the medium they use." Bloggers, K. Daniel Glover says, are like inspectors general, "the independent watchdogs of government. Just as IGs are not part of the agencies they oversee, bloggers are neither part of government nor journalism, but they keep a wary and watchful eye on both. And in so doing they provide a valuable check against the arrogance, inadequacies, and abuses of all four estates."[59] Let us explore this idea of bloggers as watchdogs on the watchdogs a bit more.

Watchdogs on the Watchdogs

Bloggers and journalists, as we have seen, both value truth highly but take different paths toward it. In doing so, can they together attain something closer to truth than either can alone? We think they can.

For one thing, as we have already seen, bloggers are more dedicated in their adherence to a number of journalistic norms than are many journalists themselves. Bloggers' commitment to the idea of transparency seems deeper than the commitment of many journalists, or at least the media organizations they work for, to the related idea of accountability. Bloggers' incorporation of readers' feedback and viewpoints goes far beyond the limited opportunities offered through an op-ed page or letters to the editor section. And bloggers give "voice to the voiceless" more consistently than do journalists, who rely heavily on those in power for their information, despite their own code's reminder that "official and unofficial sources of information can be equally valid."[60] Fundamentally, the difference may be that the open, participatory, and interconnected nature of the Internet is integral to blogging in a way it is not to journalism. Although there are many examples of innovative journalistic uses of the medium, for most journalists the Internet remains a place to offer a souped-up version of a traditional product rather than the birthplace of wholly new media forms.

Of course, bloggers also rely on those in power for their information: They rely on the journalists. A great many of the items discussed on blogs of interest to a general audience are based on stories that originated in the mainstream media. And bloggers are quite fond of biting the hands that feed them. "For lazy columnists and defensive gatekeepers, it can seem as if the hounds from a mediocre hell have been unleashed," writes *Columbia Journalism Review* contributor Matt Welch. "But for curious professionals, it is a marvelous opportunity and entertaining spectacle; they discover what the audience finds important and encounter specialists who can rip apart the work of many a generalist. More than just A.J. Liebling-style press criticism, journalists finally have something approaching real peer review, in all its brutality."[61]

It can, indeed, be brutal. Just ask Dan Rather. After a rather stunning series of missteps at CBS News in fall 2004 surrounding the network's flawed reporting on President George W. Bush's disputed Air National Guard service as a young man, bloggers took the lead in challenging the leaked memos at the heart of the story. Although much of the "information" flying around the Internet was untrue,[62] the buzz it caused was real enough. The mainstream media quickly picked up the story, CBS launched an internal investigation, and, within weeks, the veteran journalist and long-time anchor announced his resignation. Bloggers triumphantly compared their "victory" to everything from Agincourt to the Boston Tea Party.[63] It was not the first, though. Barely a year earlier, they had flogged *New York Times* executive editor Howell Raines unmercifully for his role in the Jayson Blair scandal, creating a virtual chorus of indignation. Make that former executive editor.[64]

Political journalists across the country also know the feeling of having a blogger watching over their shoulder. Throughout much of the 2004 campaign, top-tier political reporters at the *Washington Post, The New York Times,* Reuters, and Associated Press were each "adopted" by a blogger who read every word and posted comments and critiques—and even, sometimes, praise. Many, but not all, of the bloggers' efforts had partisan overtones. *Columbia Journalism Review,* one of the oldest media watchdogs in the country, started its own nonpartisan group blog, called Campaign Desk, to oversee campaign coverage and, ideally, correct the record before the pack latched on to a mistake. "The narrative of [Al] Gore as arrogant but smart and Bush as honest but dumb really took hold and led to distorted coverage of the campaign" in 2000, said Campaign Desk's assistant managing editor, Bryan Keefer. "The idea was to start something to prevent that from happening again. The media serves as a filter for the way people see politics, and if that filter is distorted, people will get a distorted view."[65]

In general, "big journalism" is the target of a great deal of contempt and derision in the blogosphere. As Glenn Reynolds, a law professor who is behind the enormously popular InstaPundit political blog, explained, bloggers have very little power, but "what they have is influence. They have an ability to get ideas noticed that would otherwise be ignored and to shame people into doing their jobs better."[66] Many of those people are journalists. Indeed, at their best, blogs serve as a corrective mechanism for sloppy or erroneous reporting,[67] as well as a source of expert information that a journalist either did not or could not provide. Journalists can expect that virtually anything they write or say will be scrutinized by someone somewhere in the world who is able and more than willing to instantly publish the outcome of that scrutiny. Bloggers have famously fact-checked everything from war correspondents' stories about Iraq to opinion columnists' use of quotations.[68] Media executive and blogger Jeff Jarvis periodically points out on his BuzzMachine blog that it is foolish to do journalism today without realizing that bloggers are going to "fact check your ass." An editorial stance of arrogance or aloofness is becoming difficult if not impossible to sustain.[69]

Of course, bloggers also serve as watchdogs on others in power who might prefer to remain arrogant or aloof, as well. Bloggers' role in politics, for instance, extends well beyond the campaign period. Many Americans first became aware of bloggers thanks to their role in the political demise of former Senate Majority Leader Trent Lott. When Lott remarked, at a public event attended by plenty of reporters, that the country would have been better off if voters had elected segregationist presidential candidate Strom Thurmond in 1948, not a single media outlet picked up on the significance of that statement. Bloggers, though, who were watching coverage of the event on C-Span, not only were paying attention but kept the story alive in the blogosphere until, eventually, the mainstream media woke up. Within weeks, Lott had stepped down.[70] Other examples of bloggers' flogging a story until it makes the media agenda abound.

Blogs, then, seem to be carving out an important ethical role for themselves in our society. They serve as watchdogs on the watchdogs in a variety of ways, holding journalists accountable for what they report—and what they do not report but should. This role is another aspect of the complementary, even symbiotic, relationship between bloggers and journalists. We will finish this chapter with a brief look at the ethical implications when the relationship overlaps completely: when journalists run their own blogs.

Journalists Who Blog

Hundreds of American news organizations are turning their own journalists loose to blog. Are they cashing in on the cachet surrounding blogs, or do they recognize the value of less formal and more participatory ways to communicate with readers and viewers? Probably both.

Online journalist and media scholar Mark Deuze, from whom we will hear more in Chapter 8, suggests that blogging is a logical step for journalists. "When journalists blog, they do more of what they did when, for example, they were writing op-eds in newspapers, doing columns on the radio, or providing interpretation and analysis as a correspondent on television," he says. "All of these practices make the journalist more human."[71]

Many journalists who have pioneered the format in their newsrooms and in the industry as a whole agree. These "j-bloggers" cite, among other advantages, the ability to share valuable information that does not fit in the limited news hole of the traditional media format, to incorporate more voices in their reporting, to get potentially valuable feedback from the public, and even to counteract media corporatization. "Bloggers are the dam-busters of the media world," writes *Christian Science Monitor* j-blogger and former Online News Association executive director Tom Regan. "Long may they blow open holes in the gatekeepers' firewalls so that all the voices that are being ignored or silenced can find ways to be heard."[72] Blogs also enable journalists to cover big stories in novel ways, whether those stories are about politics (many journalists covering the 2004 campaigns and conventions did so as both news reporters and bloggers), wars (notably Iraq and the recent Israeli conflicts), tragedies (for example, the space shuttle *Columbia* explosion in 2003 and the 2004 tsunami in southern Asia), or sports events. *Newsweek* offered a blog about Martha Stewart's trial and tribulations; *The New York Times* took on climate shifts in the Arctic. On any topic that a major news organization is willing to devote resources to telling well online, the odds are rapidly increasing that the coverage will include a blog. By the time you read this, the trend may have spread to home-town media, as well; indeed, newspapers in relatively small communities such as Spokane, Washington, and Greensboro, North Carolina, have been among the biggest early innovators.

Editorial boards also have begun experimenting with blogs as a way of opening up their decision-making processes to public examination. The *Dallas Morning News,* for instance, required its board members to post daily and encouraged readers to respond. The blog was "a way for us to demystify what we do and how we do it," *Morning News* editorial page editor Keven Ann Willey says. It "shows the reader how we reach our decisions. We argue about things and we arm-wrestle and we dispute one another."[73] She says reader feedback was enormously positive. "Even in instances where people disagree with our point of view, they say, 'We like your openness, it helps us understand how you reach your point of view, it helps us understand that you're not a bunch of ivory tower people.'"[74] Similarly, the *Sacramento Bee,* which began blogging about the California recall election in 2003, retained its "Fly on the Wall" blog as a place for readers to read the "news, views, and musings posted by members of the *Bee*'s editorial board as they discuss issues of the day," as well as discuss ideas with board members.[75]

In 2005, the *Los Angeles Times* briefly experimented with even greater openness. It turned the paper's editorial into a wiki, a site that anyone can edit, and invited its online readers to jump in. Its first (and, as it turned out, only) "wikitorial" was on the subject of the war in Iraq. *Times* editors introduced the feature this way: "How do you like the linked editorial? A lot? Thanks! Not so much? Do you see fatuous reasoning, a selective reading of the facts, a lack of poetry? Well, what are you going to do about it? You could send us an e-mail (or even write us a letter, if you can find a stamp). But today you have a new option: Rewrite the editorial yourself."[76] Within three days, the wikitorial was gone—shut down after the site was flooded with obscene messages and photos in what one user described as less a national agora than a "virtual mosh pit."[75] All that remained a month later was this forlorn two-sentence notice, under a "Where is the wikitorial" headline in the middle of an otherwise blank page on the LATimes.com site: "Unfortunately, we have had to remove this feature, at least temporarily, because a few readers were flooding the site with inappropriate material. Thanks and apologies to the thousands of people who logged on in the right spirit."

As the *Times*'s experience suggests, the process of opening up the journalistic conversation to members of the public is not without its headaches, not least among them the difficulty of balancing a desire to maintain civic discourse with a desire to offer a place for unfettered views to be expressed. The tension results from a permutation of the norm we discussed early in this chapter: the process of verification as a necessary component of truth-telling. Indeed, perhaps the biggest issue for j-bloggers has been the role, or even the presence, of an editor. "Every time I mention blogs with newspaper editors, the first question is 'Who's editing it?'" says Andrew Nachison, director of the Media Center at the American Press Institute.[78]

The answer varies, as does the level of controversy. In Spokane, where the *Spokesman-Review* offers dozens of blogs on everything from basketball tournaments to the rumblings of the Mount St. Helens volcano, reporters have become accustomed to blogging from home and on the road. Online managing editor Ken Sands, himself a blogging pioneer, says editors regularly log on to keep an eye on things and catch mistakes, but reporters mostly publish unedited. "We haven't had to kill a single post," he said in a 2004 interview with *American Journalism Review.*[79]

If Spokane offers a best-case scenario for editors who are thinking about turning reporters loose to blog, the *New Republic* highlights the potential dark side. Senior editor Gregg Easterbrook used his unedited blog to criticize Hollywood executives after the release of Quentin Tarantino's violent film, *Kill Bill Vol. 1*. Easterbrook wrote that then-Disney head Michael Eisner and

Miramax chief Harvey Weinstein were "Jewish executives" who "worship money above all else." Having served as a delivery vehicle for the remark, though, the blog also served as the vehicle for Easterbrook's apology. "Maybe this is an object lesson in the new blog reality," he wrote. "I worked on this alone and posted the piece. . . . Twenty minutes after I pressed 'send,' the entire world had read it. When I reread my own words and beheld how I'd written things that could be misunderstood, I felt awful."[80]

In addition to the lack of a second set of eyes on their copy, journalists who blog may raise other ethical concerns. Perhaps the biggest problem is that blogging reporters may say something that compromises the premise that what emanates from those who work in a newsroom is objectively reported and presented. The list of reporters who have found themselves in trouble for expressing their opinions in blogs is fairly long. It includes, among others, a CNN correspondent whose bosses told him to stop blogging about his experiences covering the war in Iraq (and who later gained his own permanent blog space on Yahoo!); a *Hartford Courant* columnist who lost his column along with his blog after editors declared the latter a conflict of interest;[81] a *St. Louis Post-Dispatch* reporter who resigned after being criticized for writing a blog in which he lambasted the paper; and a *Houston Chronicle* bureau reporter fired after using his blog to assess politicians he covered for the paper.[82] The *Chronicle* reporter, who went by the online name of Banjo Jones, saw his blog as a harmless creative outlet; his editors, when they discovered his dual identity, saw it as an appalling conflict of interest.[83]

Jane Kirtley, former head of the Reporters Committee for Freedom of the Press and now a media ethics and law professor at the University of Minnesota, says blogs often are at odds with the reporter's traditional role. "We expect in the American tradition to maintain this role of detached observer and not cheerleader or insider," she notes. Blogs mostly rely on "the idea of inside information and commentary."[84] Others, however, find it troubling that an institution rooted in the First Amendment would muzzle its own members. They suggest that simply asking reporters to use discretion in personal expression would serve the purpose, as well as adhering to long-standing precedents, such as asking reporters to refrain from displaying a candidate's political campaign sign in their yard or participating in political demonstrations.[85] Then there is the argument that objectivity, particularly to the extent that it leads to superficial and formulaic "he said, she said" reporting of opposing views, is not all that great an idea anyway.[86] "Reporters are people, too (really)," New

York University journalism professor Adam Penenberg points out. "Just because they express opinions doesn't mean their reporting should be dismissed out of hand, as long as they arrive at their conclusions honestly, through rigorous reporting."[87]

Blogs by journalists raise a number of other issues for media organizations, as well. For instance, if a journalist runs a personal blog under his or her own name—a name that the public associates with a media outlet—does that constitute using a professional affiliation to personal advantage? When the journalist gets a good scoop, does it go first to the blog or first to the employer who pays the reporter's salary? If the journalist posts something libelous on the blog, who is responsible then, legally or ethically? Actually, that last question seems relatively easy to answer, at least from a legal standpoint. Newspapers offering reporter-written blogs are exposing themselves to legal liability. "It does create considerable additional libel risk for newspapers to have their reporters doing blogs," says Michael Rothberg, a media lawyer in Washington. "Newspapers are every bit as much responsible for these blogs legally as they are for their regular articles."[88]

With an eye to that concern, a number of media outlets that actively encourage various forms of "citizen journalism"—and that number is growing—have appointed someone to serve, officially or unofficially, as a "citizen media editor." Part chat moderator, part copy editor, and part ombudsman, these news staffers have the difficult job of finding a balance between giving people the freedom to tell their own stories (and the motivation to do so for little or no pay), protecting the media outlet's reputation for accuracy, and warding off anything that could lead to a lawsuit. The more editing is done, the more liability a publisher has. Different media outlets take different approaches. Some, such as the Northwest Voice in Bakersfield, California, have an editor look over every submission. "We have the same legal guidelines as any newspaper, and if we have a questionable submission, we won't run it until it has been checked," says the publisher of the site, which is affiliated with the Bakersfield *Californian*.[89] At MyMissourian, a citizen journalism effort associated with the Columbia *Missourian,* there are four major rules for content: no nudity, no profanity, no personal attacks, and no attacks on race, creed, or national origin. But when it comes to fact-checking, editors largely rely on the community to uncover inaccuracies.[90]

If you are getting the idea that there are few definitive answers to the questions we raised at the start of this chapter, you are right. Perhaps the best "solution" for journalists, at least, is to remember that their primary loyalty is to the public,[91] and the obligation to serve the public well is the same whether one is posting to a blog or writing an inverted pyramid news story. The best way to carry out the obligation may vary, but the underlying ethical precept does not. Media ethicist and veteran journalist Mike Kittross offers some final thoughts on this topic in Exhibit 5.3.

This chapter about bloggers has dealt with one particular aspect of online journalism fostered by the inherently interactive nature of the medium. Next we will look at some other issues raised by interactivity and the blurred boundaries between audiences and journalists.

Note: Portions of this chapter were included in a paper titled "Truth and Transparency: Bloggers' Challenge to Professional Autonomy in Defining and Enacting Two Journalistic Norms," presented to the Media Ethics Division of the Association for Education in Journalism and Mass Communication at its 2006 annual convention in San Francisco; and in an article titled "Contested Autonomy: Professional and Popular Claims on Journalistic Norms," published in *Journalism Studies* in 2007.

Exhibit 5.3
Who Is a Journalist?

John Michael Kittross is editor of Media Ethics *magazine and a former editor of the* Journal of Broadcasting. *He is the coauthor of several books, including* Stay Tuned: A History of American Broadcasting *and* Controversies in Media Ethics. *Kittross has taught at the University of Southern California, Temple University, and Emerson College, as well as in the U.S. Army Psychological Warfare School. His eclectic professional background includes work in both broadcast journalism and film; he is a widely published scholar who signs his e-mails "Curmudgeon, Iconoclast & Gadfly." Here, our curmudgeonly gadfly offers his thoughts about bloggers and journalists, law and ethics.*

Anatole France once said, "The law, in its majestic equality, forbids the rich as well as the poor to sleep under bridges, to beg in the streets, and to steal bread."[1] And I believe that today's laws apply to both old and new communications media and technologies.

(continued)

Exhibit 5.3 *(continued)*

Yet more than law applies to the use of the Web as a mass communications medium. There are ethical and moral standards, and there are practices subject to the same standards. These apply to Web communication just as surely as the "majestic equality" of the law does.

There are two sides to the coin of journalistic communication: rights and responsibilities. Both are important, and both can lead to the last-resort venue of the courtroom, where both victory and defeat are uncertain, and lawyers hold sway. Unfortunately, many journalists of every stripe often think much more about their real or imagined legal rights than about their responsibilities or about the concepts of a just society that lead to laws in the first place.

Take privacy, for example. Is there an ethical difference between a blogger who has never studied journalism (or, for that matter, one who has) and an experienced reporter for *The New York Times,* each rummaging through a subject's private life or private papers? Hardly. Both might try to justify this invasion by saying that "the public has the right to know," regardless of whether the public has a *"need* to know" or whether the information sought and published is of any importance to the reader. The *Times* may do a better job of editing, but that is of little comfort to the stripped-naked subject. The courts have long held that having a small staff is no excuse for harming someone else's reputation. And bloggers don't even really have the justification of a daily deadline forcing a premature publication since production is so simple, inexpensive, and immediate.

However, there are also some real differences in practice between the Weblog and the published newspaper. The *Times* is considered permanent. It will be found in libraries and archives for centuries to come, whereas the blogger can push the "delete" button on a story at any time—and it may be as if it never was. . . .

[For bloggers], there is a deadline every second. A conscientious blogger will continually update her or his offering, primarily because the typical blogger has only two things to sell: his or her insight, sources, reasoning, and writing skill on the one hand, and speed of presentation—measured by how early in the chain of borrowings of content one is—on the other. "Scooping" one's competition pays off in bragging points.

But is that an excuse for sloppy reporting, editing, and publishing? Nope. When a computer publishing program drops a paragraph while flowing from one page to another; when a link disappears; when a server

(continued)

Exhibit 5.3 *(continued)*

goes down; when a spell-check program is used to substitute for a copy editor; when experienced editorial personnel are replaced by hungry (and cheap) young newcomers who can pound a fast keyboard—quality is bound to suffer. It is the responsibility of those who own the paper, station, or Web site to develop methods to ensure greater availability, reliability, and validity of the news that they provide to the citizens who need it in order to make valid decisions in a democracy.

Military intelligence used to (and may still) mark each item with two rankings: one for the quality of the *source,* and the other for the quality of the *specific assertion.* A highly reliable source, one who has provided verifiable newsworthy information at other times, may have messed up *this* time. Both source and content rankings are needed. Journalists often use their professional judgment to select sources and stories, but editors backstop them. Shouldn't the reader be told what level of confidence the blogger has for these data and knowledge? For example, if a blogger is following the pack and relying to a great extent on the ideas and writing of other bloggers (which may create a moral as well as a copyright problem), then it might be thought of as taking in each other's washing. This doesn't give the objective reader much confidence.

I propose that all those—particularly bloggers—who do not have the resources to double check or document both the information they are publishing and the amount of verifiable and valid support their published opinions have should spell out the reasons for accepting *this* information and rejecting *that.* So, particularly because it doesn't go through a multistage editorial approval process, each online article should be assessed as to the trust that should be placed in both sources and the specific information that supports the thesis of the article. These assessments should be published at the top of every story, enabling the blogger to deal with rumors, solid facts, and everything in between, and pass along her or his confidence level to the reader. Reliance on an egocentric implied plea to "trust me" is insufficient.

If someone wants only to wallow in "friendly" political or other blogs, there shouldn't be a problem—unless the blogger fails to identify his or her biases, funding or memberships. If someone wants journalistic satire —the *Daily Show* on cable, or *Saturday Night Live,* for example—they should be able to get it. But the producers of such programs or features have, I believe, the same obligation to spell out any biases that the creative talent (writers, performers) might possess.

(continued)

Exhibit 5.3 *(continued)*

Let's look again at the question of whether, in a legal or ethical sense, online journalism is different from conventional or traditional journalism. I don't think it is. "Publication" can be on a huge rotary press or on a Web site. There is no bright line distinguishing a newspaper from an online edition of a newspaper, the online newspaper from an Internet publication like *Salon, Salon* from a blog—even though many, particularly those working in traditional media, think there is a large distinction between the beginning and end of this chain, between a newspaper and a blog.

So this legal Luddite holds that the law applies to content, not to form—and form is the only major difference between traditional media and those in cyberspace.

Source: John Michael Kittross sent this material to Jane Singer in an e-mail on February 22, 2005.

[1]Anatole France, "The Red Lily," 1899, www.classicreader.com/read.php/sid.1/bookid.2422/sec.8.

Case Study: Newspaper's Blog

(This case study involves an issue facing real journalists, but the specific circumstances, as well as the names used here, are fictional.)

Newsroom veteran Jim Harrison was the top political reporter at his metropolitan daily, the *Capital Courier.* He started covering city government in the 1980s, became the lead statehouse reporter in 1997, and is part of a three-person team that covered state and national campaigns in election years. He also wrote a weekly column about politics for the Sunday paper. Marketing surveys showed that a majority of subscribers know his name and regularly read his work.

In addition to being politically savvy, Harrison had a reputation within the newsroom for being tech savvy, too; as a political reporter, he was a newsroom leader in using online public records databases and computer-assisted reporting. So when *Courier* editors decided they needed to develop some promotion-worthy new features for the paper's affiliated Web site, they decided to make Harrison become a blogger.

If the editors expected an argument from Harrison, they were pleasantly surprised. A political junkie, he had little interest in either a different beat or a move to an editor's desk, but the routine of following the same basic story lines had begun to be a bore. He had followed the rise of the political blogs with interest, reading several regularly, picking up story ideas, and occasionally writing about the phenomenon in his column. Doing something similar at a local and state level excited him.

"Harrison's Harangue" was born.

The transition in writing style was a bit tricky, but he had used his weekly column as a platform for offering often-irreverent commentary on politics and politicians, and it was a short step from there to letting loose on the blog. He loved the quick-hit format, as well as the freedom to post any time he felt inspired about anything that struck his fancy. His editors—who quickly realized that if they insisted on editing his posts, they would be working any time of the day or night—pretty much left him alone. A few times, InstaPundit even linked to *him!*

Frankly, he was having more fun at his job than he had in years.

Readers liked the Harangue, too. Usage was high (though never in the same league as the stuff the sports guys wrote). Within a few weeks, the blog developed about a dozen regular contributors, plus an assortment of others who posted comments from time to time. Of course, posters never used their full real names, so Harrison was never certain who they were, though he was pretty sure he recognized a few longtime sources by the sorts of things they seemed to know a lot about.

There was just one problem. Although he had cut back on his daily reporting duties when he began blogging, he still wrote several stories a week for the news section. Or he tried to. The problem was that no one at the statehouse or in city hall seemed to want to talk to him on the record any more. They would talk about whatever was in the latest press release, and they remained happy to chat about sports and the weather. But Harrison was a skillful reporter whose success depended on his ability to get people in power and those around them to open up to him about what was really going on in city and state government. He thought he had earned their trust, and the chill hurt his feelings as well as the quality of his reporting.

Still, he was having such a good time that he happily continued the blog, figuring his sources would start talking again sooner or later. And they did—though not in a way he was prepared for.

One morning, he posted an innocuous item about the state senate majority leader's family vacation in South Florida. It was not the sort of item that usually generated any comments from readers, but this one did.

One of the Harangue's sporadic contributors, who went by the online name of Scoop, posted this:

> That was no family vacation. He was taking his little whore of a daughter to one of those boot camp places for rich people with kids they can't control. Little Angela is sixteen but hardly sweet. She's already had two abortions and lately she's been screwing the governor's kid brother, you know, the one who married into money and then found out his wife was a rich dyke? Anyway, Angela's safely locked away, and the senator hopes he took her far enough that no one will find her.

Other posters immediately piled on, claiming to have firsthand (or second- or third- or whatever) knowledge about Angela's activities—snorting coke, shoplifting, selling sex under the high school bleachers. The governor and his extended family also came in for some choice commentary—some of it about events that only insiders could possibly know.

Harrison, who had gone out for coffee after uploading his seemingly safe little post about the vacation, was stunned. Not only were the posts unsubstantiated and potentially libelous but they also violated many of the newspaper's ethics policies, such as refraining from naming minors accused of wrongdoing and avoiding highly offensive language. The posts, however, were now "out there"—published on, in effect, the newspaper's Web site. Under, in a way, Harrison's byline.

He fired off a post urging his readers to stop, asking them to think about how hurtful their comments were, and promising to look into the allegations. But the bloggers showed no self-restraint. After his second post, the blog exploded in all directions, from tirades against media hypocrisy to screams about censorship to lurid details about the less-than-saintly exploits of Angela's classmates at her private high school (including links and, in one case, photo attachments). Harrison recognized some screen names; many others he had never heard from before. It was a real blogswarm.

Then Harrison's phone began ringing, along with the phone at the news desk and in his editor's office. His call was from the senate majority leader's office; the senator's chief aide was suddenly quite eager to talk with Harrison, right away. He could only guess who was calling the newsroom phone and his editor . . . but out of the corner of his eye, he saw the elevator door open and the newspaper's attorney emerge, moving fast.

1. What should be the newspaper's first action, right now? Why? What should it tell its readers? How and by whom should that message be communicated? Try drafting the text of such a message.

2. What should Harrison do next in his role as a reporter? As a columnist? As a blogger? (Remember that his sources were reluctant to talk with him even before this incident. Now the only ones who will not be avoiding him will be those with axes to grind, such as political rivals of the various folks involved.) Do any of those roles conflict in this situation? If so, how should he resolve the conflict?

3. Afterward Harrison, his editors, and the newspaper's attorney agree it is time to establish a policy related to the paper's blogs. What points should they include in such a policy? How can they balance free speech, civic discourse, the newspaper's ethical standards, and individuals' right to privacy? How should they communicate this policy to the public? How should they enforce it?

Notes

1. Amanda Lenhart and Susannah Fox, "Bloggers: A Portrait of the Internet's New Storytellers," Pew Internet & American Life Project, July 19, 2006, www.pewinternet. org/PPF/r/186/report_display.asp.

2. Dave Sifry, "State of the Blogosphere, August 2006," Sifry's Alerts blog, August 7, 2006, www.sifry.com/alerts/archives/000436.html#summary.

3. Jeffrey Henning, "The Blogging Iceberg," Perseus Development Corp., 2003, www.perseus.com/blogsurvey/iceberg.html.

4. Wikipedia, "Statistics," "Wikipedia Statistics," 2006, http://en.wikipedia.org/wiki/Special:Statistics; http://en.wikipedia.org/wikistats/EN/Sitemap.htm; http://stats.wikimedia.org/EN/TablesArticlesNewPerDay.htm.

5. Wikinews, "Wikinews: Introduction," "Wikinews Statistics," 2006, http://en.wikinews.org/wiki/Wikinews:About; http://stats.wikimedia.org/wikinews/EN/Sitemap.htm; http://stats.wikimedia.org/wikinews/EN/TablesArticlesTotal.htm; http://stats.wikimedia.org/wikinews/EN/TablesWikipediansContributors.htm.

6. Lee Rainie and Mary Madden, "Podcasting Catches On," Pew Internet & American Life Project, April 3, 2005, www.pewinternet.org/PPF/r/154/report_display.asp.

7. Meredith Mandell, "Bloggers Come of Age in US Presidential Race," Agence France Press, July 6, 2004, www.inq7.net/inf/2004/jul/06/inf_4–1.htm.

8. Peter Johnson, "Bloggers to Join Mainstream at the Conventions," USA Today, July 13, 2004, www.usatoday.com/life/columnist/mediamix/ 2004–07–13-media-mix_x.htm.

9. Jay Rosen, "'There Is an Orthodoxy to Our Thinking': Thomas B. Edsall of the Washington Post on How Blogs Can Enliven Journalism," PressThink, July 29, 2004, http://journalism.nyu.edu/pubzone/weblogs/pressthink/2004/07/29/edsall_blogs.html.

10. Jeff Jarvis, "I Pledge Not to Pledge," BuzzMachine, July 23, 2005, www.buzzmachine.com/archives/2005_06_23.html#009915.

11. Bill Kovach and Tom Rosenstiel, *The Elements of Journalism: What Newspeople Should Know and the Public Should Expect* (New York: Crown, 2001).

12. Jay Black, Bob Steele, and Ralph Barney, *Doing Ethics in Journalism: A Handbook with Case Studies,* 3rd ed. (Boston: Allyn & Bacon, 1999).

13. Society of Professional Journalists (SPJ), "Code of Ethics," 1996, http://spj.org/ethics.

14. Kovach and Rosenstiel, *Elements of Journalism.*

15. Jane B. Singer, "The Marketplace of Ideas—with a Vengeance," *Media Ethics* 16 (Spring 2005): 1, 14–16.

16. Kovach and Rosenstiel, *Elements of Journalism.*

17. Singer, "Marketplace of Ideas."

18. Donald Matheson, "Weblogs and the Epistemology of the News: Some Trends in Online Journalism," *New Media & Society* 6 (August 2004): 443–468.

19. Singer, "Marketplace of Ideas."

20. Staci D. Kramer, "CBS Scandal Highlights Tension Between Bloggers and News Media," *Online Journalism Review,* October 4, 2004, www.ojr.org/ojr/workplace/1096589178.php.

21. Shayne Bowman and Chris Willis, *We Media: How Audiences Are Shaping the Future of News and Information* (Reston, VA: Media Center at American Press Institute), September 21, 2003, www.hypergene.net/wemedia/weblog.php?id=P41.

22. Jay Rosen, "Bloggers vs. Journalists Is Over," PressThink, January 15, 2005, http://journalism.nyu.edu/pubzone/weblogs/pressthink/2005/01/15/berk_essy.html.

23. Dan Gillmor, *We the Media: Grassroots Journalism by the People, for the People* (Sebastopol, CA: O'Reilly Media, 2004).

24. Black, Steele, and Barney, *Doing Ethics in Journalism.*

25. Society of Professional Journalists, "Code of Ethics."

26. Black, Steele, and Barney, *Doing Ethics in Journalism.*

27. Humphrey Taylor, "Trust in Priests and Clergy Falls 26 Points in Twelve Months," Harris Poll: Harris Interactive, November 27, 2002, www.harrisinteractive.com/harris_poll/index.asp?PID=342.

28. Project for Excellence in Journalism, "Overview: Public Attitudes," *The State of the News Media 2005,* www.stateofthemedia.org/2005/narrative_overview_publicattitudes.asp?cat=7&media=1.

29. J.D. Lasica, "The Cost of Ethics: Influence Peddling in the Blogosphere," *Online Journalism Review,* February 17, 2005, www.ojr.org/ojr/stories/050217lasica/index.cfm.

30. Bill Mitchell and Bob Steele, "Earn Your Own Trust, Roll Your Own Ethics: Transparency and Beyond" (paper presented to the Blogging, Journalism and Credibility conference at Harvard University, Cambridge, MA, January 17, 2005), http://cyber.law.harvard.edu/webcred/.

31. J.D. Lasica, "Transparency Begets Trust in the Ever-Expanding Blogosphere," *Online Journalism Review,* August 12, 2004, www.ojr.org/ojr/technology/1092267863.php.

32. Sheila Lennon, "Blogging Journalists Invite Outsiders' Reporting In," *Nieman Reports* 57 (Fall 2003): 76–79.

33. Steve Outing, "What Journalists Can Learn from Bloggers," PoynterOnline, December 20, 2004, www.poynter.org/content/content_view.asp?id=75383.

34. Gillmor, *We the Media.*

35. Matthew Klam, "Fear and Laptops on the Campaign Trail," *New York Times Magazine,* September 26, 2004, pp. 43–49, 115–116, 123.

36. Adam Cohen, "The Latest Rumbling in the Blogosphere: Questions About Ethics," *New York Times* Week in Review, May 8, 2005, p. 11.

37. J. Ryan, "Leading Internet Marketing Firm Pays Bloggers to Shill," Guerrilla News Network, May 13, 2005, http://bravo411.gnn.tv/articles/1366/Blogging_for_Dollars.

38. Forrester Research, "Forrester Research Releases US Online Advertising and Marketing Forecast—Market to Reach $26 Billion by 2010," Yahoo! News, May 3, 2005, www.forrester.com/er/press/release/0,1769,1003,00.htm.

39. Cohen, "Latest Rumbling."

40. Lasica, "Cost of Ethics."

41. Ibid.

42. Brian Morrissey, "Blogs Growing into the Ultimate Focus Group," *Adweek,* June 20, 2005, http://naa.missouri.edu/trade/05morrissey1.pdf.

43. Issue Dynamics, Inc., "Internet Services: Blogger Relations," 2005, www.idi.net/what-we-do/blogger-relations.html.

44. Black, Steele, and Barney, *Doing Ethics in Journalism.*

45. Singer, "Marketplace of Ideas."

46. Mark Glaser, "A Tale of Two Rumors: How Reagan, Kerry News Spread Online," *Online Journalism Review,* June 16, 2004, www.ojr.org/ojr/ethics/1087341701.php; Mark Glaser, "Exit Polls Bring Traffic Deluge, Scrutiny to Blogs, Slate," *Online Journalism Review,* November 5, 2004, www.ojr.org/ojr/glaser/1099616933.php.

47. Martin Kuhn, "Interactivity and Prioritizing the Human: A Code of Blogging Ethics" (paper presented to the Media Ethics Division of the Association for Education in Journalism and Mass Communication, San Antonio, TX, August 2005).

48. Dan Kennedy, "Cardiac Kids," *Boston Phoenix,* January 7–13, 2005, www.bostonphoenix.com/boston/news_features/dont_quote_me/multi-page/documents/04383304.asp.

49. Jonathan Dube, "A Blogger's Code of Ethics," CyberJournalist.net, April 15, 2003, www.cyberjournalist.net/news/000215.php.

50. Rebecca Blood, *The Weblog Handbook: Practical Advice on Creating and Maintaining Your Blog* (New York: Perseus Books Group, 2002), www.rebeccablood.net/handbook/excerpts/weblog_ethics.html.

51. Kuhn, "Interactivity and Prioritizing the Human."

52. Lasica, "Cost of Ethics."

53. *Online Journalism Review,* "What Are the Ethics of Online Journalism?" March 9, 2005, www.ojr.org/ojr/wiki/ethics.

54. Media Bloggers Association, "Media Bloggers Association Launches First-of-Its-Kind Journalism Education Program," March 21, 2005, www.mediabloggers.org/archives/2005/03/media_bloggers_5.php.

55. Steve Outing, "What Bloggers Can Learn from Journalists," PoynterOnline, December 22, 2004, http://poynter.org/content/content_view.asp?id=75665.

56. Outing, "What Journalists Can Learn from Bloggers."

57. J.D. Lasica, "Blogs and Journalism Need Each Other," *Nieman Reports* 57 (Fall 2003): 70–74.

58. *New York Times,* "The Revolution Will Be Posted," November 2, 2004, www.nytimes.com/2004/11/02/opinion/02blogger-final.html.

59. K. Daniel Glover, "Journalists vs. Bloggers," Beltway Blogroll, July 8, 2005, http://beltwayblogroll.nationaljournal.com/archives/2005/07/journalists_vs.html.

60. Society of Professional Journalists, "Code of Ethics."

61. Matt Welch, "The New Amateur Journalists Weigh In," *Columbia Journalism Review,* September/October 2003, www.cjr.org/issues/2003/5/blog-welch.asp.

62. Kramer, "CBS Scandal Highlights Tension."

63. Corey Pein, "Blog-gate," *Columbia Journalism Review,* January/February 2005, http://cjr.org/issues/2005/1/pein-blog.asp.

64. Hugh Hewitt, *Blog: Understanding the Information Revolution That's Changing Your World* (Nashville, TN: Thomas Nelson, 2005); Tom Regan, "Weblogs Threaten and Inform Traditional Journalism," *Nieman Reports* 57 (Fall 2003): 68–70.

65. Mark Glaser, "'Watchblogs' Put the Political Press Under the Microscope," *Online Journalism Review,* February 11, 2004, http://ojr.org/ojr/glaser/1076465317.php.

66. Rachel Smolkin, "The Expanding Blogosphere," *American Journalism Review,* June/July 2004, http://ajr.org/article.asp?id=3682.

67. Paul Andrews, "Is Blogging Journalism?" *Nieman Reports* 57 (Fall 2003): 63–64.

68. Welch, "New Amateur Journalists."

69. Mitchell and Steele, "Earn Your Own Trust."

70. Regan, "Weblogs Threaten and Inform."

71. Mark Deuze, posting to http://jethicsdialogues.blogspot.com (October 2004).

72. Regan, "Weblogs Threaten and Inform," p. 70.

73. Keven Ann Willey, "Editorial Board Goes Blogging," DallasNews.com, December 23, 2004, www.dallasnews.com//sharedcontent/dws/news/longterm/stories/blogexplain.60b329f.html.

74. Mark Glaser, "Papers' Online Units Allow Editorial Boards to Lift Veil with Video, Blogs," *Online Journalism Review,* March 9, 2004, www.ojr.org/ojr/glaser/1078877295.php.

75. "Fly on the Wall" blog of the *Sacramento Bee,* www.sacbee.com/static/weblogs/the_wall.

76. LATimes.com, "A Wiki for Your Thoughts," June 17, 2005, www.latimes.com/news/opinion/la-ed-wiki17jun17,0,4157492.story.

77. Elinor Mills, "*L.A. Times* Shuts Reader-Editorial Web Site," C/Net: News.com, June 2, 2005, http://news.com.com/L.A.+Times+shuts+reader-editorial+Web+site/2100–1023_3–5754202.html.

78. Kelly Heyboer, "Bloggin' in the Newsroom," *American Journalism Review,* December/January 2004, http://ajr.org/article.asp?id=3473.

79. Ibid.

80. Ibid.

81. Barb Palser, "Free to Blog?" *American Journalism Review,* June 2003, http://ajr.org/article.asp?id=3023.

82. David Kesmodel, "Should Newspapers Sponsor Blogs Written by Reporters?" *Wall Street Journal,* July 12, 2005, p. B1.

83. Steve Olafson, "A Reporter Is Fired for Writing a Weblog," *Nieman Reports* 57 (Fall 2003): 91–92.

84. Kesmodel, "Should Newspapers Sponsor Blogs?"

85. Palser, "Free to Blog?"

86. Brent Cunningham, "Re-thinking Objectivity," *Columbia Journalism Review,* July/August 2003, http://cjr.org/issues/2003/4/objective-cunningham.asp.

87. Adam L. Penenberg, "Heartaches of Journalist Bloggers," *Wired* News, January 13, 2005, www.wired.com/news/culture/0,1284,66251,00.html.

88. Kesmodel, "Should Newspapers Sponsor Blogs?"

89. Mark Glaser, "How to Succeed as a Citizen Media Editor," *Online Journalism Review,* March 22, 2005, www.ojr.org/ojr/stories/050322glaser/index.cfm.

90. Mark Glaser, "The New Voices: Hyperlocal Citizen Media Sites Want You (to Write)!" *Online Journalism Review,* November 27, 2004, www.ojr.org/ojr/glaser/1098833871.php.

91. Kovach and Rosenstiel, *Elements of Journalism.*

6

Beyond Blogs
Other Interactive News Forms

Cecilia Friend

People "formerly known as the audience" are engaging more fully with the news process in a variety of ways.[1] The last chapter considered the ethical implications of blogging—for reporters who blog, for readers who contribute to blogs, and for independent bloggers in their roles as media watchdogs. This chapter continues the discussion of interactive news forms, focusing more closely on citizen journalism, online polling, and e-mail, and investigating the ethical issues surrounding each.

In discussing citizen journalism, we will examine ways in which mainstream news organizations solicit and publish user contributions, including the use of open-source and distributed reporting, as well as how they set up and monitor user sites. We will also examine the roles and responsibilities associated with independent citizen news sites.

Polling has long been a way for audiences to interact with news organizations; today, however, the easy, immediate interactivity of the Web has made it a standard feature online. But poll questions answered only by users interested enough to vote skew results and can mislead others. And reporting even scientific poll results can raise ethical questions for journalists, especially during national elections.

Interactivity between journalists and citizens becomes personal in one-on-one communication. Reporters who are encouraged to embrace the freewheeling style of the Web may simultaneously be criticized for stepping outside standard journalistic personas on certain topics or with sensitive readers. Do we need some sort of prescriptive rhetoric for this kind of interactive dialogue?

User-Generated Content

Having readers contribute to the news report is not a new idea. Coverage has long been built on witness reports, person-on-the-street interviews, letters to the editor, and the like. In fact, the president of the Associated Press (AP) says his organization has accepted the importance of citizen journalism for more than a century, citing a collection of historic news photos taken over the decades by amateurs and distributed by the wire service. "The only difference now is that amateur and witness content is more ubiquitous," AP President Tom Curley told the Media Center's We Media conference in New York in 2005. Including citizen-created content "is something we have to do every day."[2]

Amateur news photography and reporting have become a significant part of recent breaking news coverage, from terrorist bombings to wars to natural disasters. Often called citizen journalism, the movement is also known as participatory journalism, grassroots or bottom-up media, or user-generated or citizen-created content, and it has been propelled and expanded by the interactive nature and technological convenience of the Web.

The July 2005 terrorist bombings in London, for example, brought thousands of e-mails, tips, photos, and videos from witnesses—content that led the BBC news package the day after the bombings, says Richard Sambrook, director of the BBC's global news division. The event was a "tipping point," according to Sambrook. "This isn't a toe in the water," he says. "It's a fundamental realignment" of BBC's citizen media strategy. Citizen reporting complementing professional reporting is here to stay, he notes. It is only a matter of figuring out how to do it better and deal with the issues of authenticity.[3]

Citizen journalism initiatives go beyond witness reports, of course. Citizen journalism is based in part on the idea that news should be a conversation rather than a monologue from professional journalists and mainstream news organizations. It strives to give the "former audience" a say in deciding what constitutes news at a time when many citizens are skeptical or distrustful of professional journalists. It welcomes customers and consumers as participants in the news process. The pioneers and champions of the movement assert the same fundamental ethical principle as traditional journalists: The purpose of news is to enable citizens to have the information needed to more fully participate in society and to be free and self-governing. "This news revolution, ultimately, is about citizenship," says Dan Gillmor, author of *We the Media* and a pioneer of the grassroots media movement.[4]

The more that citizens participate in the news, the more deeply engaged they tend to become in the democratic process. We saw in Chapter 5 how blogs have given citizens the ability to publish their own views on the issues of the day. Online users also participate in developing news stories for traditional news organizations as well as writing and editing their own citizen journalism sites. The symbiotic relationship between professional and citizen journalists that Sambrook describes leads to questions about the role and responsibility of mainstream news organizations that invite and host citizen contributors. And as users become producers of news and editors of independent news sites, ethical questions also arise about their roles and responsibilities to their audiences and the public:

- Should news organizations that sponsor citizen content moderate or edit contributions? Do they have a responsibility to make sure information is accurate and fair and does not libel or harm anyone before the information is published? Or is it OK to "publish, then filter"?
- Do independent news sites have any ethical responsibilities, either to their users or to the news report itself?

The ethical principles that underlie our examination of these issues are the same guiding principles of journalism that we have outlined in other chapters, including accuracy, verification, independence, and accountability to the public. These, along with the issue of authenticity of sources and information, are issues that must be faced by both traditional news organizations' citizen media initiatives and independent citizen media sites if they are to ethically fulfill their responsibilities to the public.

A broader ethical concern is voiced by Bill Kovach and Tom Rosenstiel, authors of the State of the Media 2006 report and *The Elements of Journalism*. They warn that while expanding technology has made the news forum more robust, it has also led to the paradox of more news outlets covering fewer stories.[5] The Project for Excellence in Journalism, which names this issue as one of the six major trends in its State of the Media report, says that as the number of places delivering news proliferates, the audience for each tends to shrink and the number of professional journalists in each organization is reduced. Since national news organizations still have to cover major stories, there are "more accounts of the same handful of stories each day." This concentration of personnel around a few stories also aids those who would like to control what the public knows:

> In the future, we may well rely more on citizens to be sentinels for one another. No doubt that will expand the public forum and enrich the range of voices. . . . Yet the changes will probably also make it easier for power to move in the dark. And the open technology that allows citizens to speak will also help special interests, posing as something else, to influence or even sometimes overwhelm what the rest of us know. The worry is not the wondrous addition of citizen media, but the decline of full-time, professional monitoring of powerful institutions.[6]

This chapter looks at the various kinds of citizen journalism and examines the promise and pitfalls of each.

News Organizations' Citizen Media Initiatives

Citizen journalism takes many forms. Steve Outing, online media columnist for *Editor & Publisher* and formerly PoynterOnline, describes what he calls "11 layers of citizen journalism." In it, he heralds experimentation by mainstream media to "harness the power of an audience permitted for the first time to truly participate in the news media."[7]

Nine of Outing's layers describe participatory journalism initiatives by mainstream news organizations, from letting readers attach comments to online articles to combining the work of professional journalists and citizen contributors. The other two go beyond the existing practices of American mainstream news organizations in 2005: integrating citizen and professional journalism equally under one roof and developing wiki journalism in which the readers serve as editors. (See Exhibit 6.1.)

Here are four ways news organizations incorporate citizen voices into their news processes and products:

• **Citizen blogs on mainstream news sites:** News organizations have taken various approaches to including citizen blogs on their Web sites. Some offer blog hosting services, allowing anyone in the community to start a blog. Others are more selective, inviting specific people to blog on specific topics. Unlike the independent bloggers that Chapter 5 focuses on, bloggers writing under a news site's brand are often monitored or edited. That oversight can be as heavy as having every submission read

Exhibit 6.1
The Eleven Layers of Citizen Journalism

Steve Outing is the interactive-media columnist for Editor & Publisher *where he writes on the intersection of news and the Internet. He is a former senior editor for the Poynter Institute and founder and publisher of Enthusiast Group. This is an abridged version of his June 15, 2005, PoynterOnline column.*

Citizen journalism isn't one simple concept that can be applied universally by all news organizations. It's much more complex, with many potential variations.

1. The first step: Opening up to public comment

For some publishers skittish about allowing anyone to publish under their brand name, enabling readers to attach comments to articles on the Web represents a start. At its simplest level, user comments offer the opportunity for readers to react to, criticize, praise or add to what's published by professional journalists.

2. Second step: The citizen add-on reporter

A small step up the ladder is to recruit citizen add-on contributions for stories written by professional journalists. . . . With selected stories, solicit information and experiences from members of the public, and add them to the main story to enhance it.

3. Now we're getting serious: Open-source reporting

The term generally is understood to mean a collaboration between a professional journalist and his/her readers on a story, where readers who are knowledgeable on the topic are asked to contribute their expertise, ask questions to provide guidance to the reporter, or even do actual reporting which will be included in the final journalistic product.

4. The citizen bloghouse

The real promise of blogs remains with nonjournalists, whom blogging has given a powerful and inexpensive publishing tool to reach out to

(continued)

Exhibit 6.1 *(continued)*

the world with their stories and thoughts. A great way to get citizens involved in a news Web site is to simply invite them to blog for it. A number of news sites do this now, and some citizen blogs are consistently interesting reads.

5. Newsroom citizen "transparency" blogs

A specific type of citizen blog deserves its own category here. It plays on the notion of news organization "transparency," or sharing the inner workings of the newsroom with readers or viewers. This involves inviting a reader or readers to blog with public complaints, criticism, or praise for the news organization's ongoing work. A reader panel can be empowered via a publicly accessible blog to serve as citizen ombudsmen, of a sort, offering public commentary on how the news organization is performing.

6. The stand-alone citizen-journalism site: Edited version

This next step involves establishing a stand-alone citizen-journalism Web site that is separate from the core news brand. It means establishing a news-oriented Web site that is comprised entirely or nearly entirely of contributions from the community.

  Most such sites focus on local news—very local news. Citizen contributors can submit whatever they want, from an account of a kids' soccer game, to observations from an audience member at last night's city council meeting, to an opinion piece by a state legislator, to a high-school student telling of her prom-night experience. The site's editors monitor and perform a modest degree of editing to submissions, in order to maintain some degree of "editorial integrity" of content placed under the publisher's brand name.

7. The stand-alone citizen-journalism site: Unedited version

This model is identical to No. 6 above, except that citizen submissions are not edited. What people write goes on the site: blemishes, misspellings and all.

(continued)

Exhibit 6.1 *(continued)*

With this model of stand-alone citizen-journalism site, it is important to have safeguards against inappropriate content being posted. Having a site editor review all submissions as soon as possible after they've been automatically published is ideal—but impractical. . . .

A more practical model is to include "Report Misconduct" buttons on every citizen-submitted story and photograph.

8. Add a print edition

For this model, take either No. 6 or No. 7 above and add a print edition. A number of newspapers have tried this, using a print edition distributed freely once a week as an insert into a traditional daily or weekly paper, or as a stand-alone print product delivered to people's doorsteps and/or delivered to local retailers and placed in news boxes for consumers to pick up.

9. The hybrid: Pro + citizen journalism

The next step up the ladder creates a news organization that combines citizen journalism with the work of professionals. South Korean site OhmyNews is the best example of this approach. It has recruited, to date, some 38,000 "citizen reporters," who contribute articles for review by OhmyNews's editorial staff. A small team of professional reporters also create content for the site. Citizen reports account for about 70 percent of the site's content, and pro reporters create the rest, so the emphasis clearly is on the citizen.

Not everything submitted by the citizen reporters is accepted for publication on OhmyNews. And some of the contributors who submit quality content are paid modest fees for their writing and/or photography. This is a different approach than is taken by most U.S. citizen-journalism sites, which rarely pay for submissions. OhmyNews treats its citizen reporters as though they are journalists (albeit low-paid ones).

10. Integrating citizen and pro journalism under one roof

Now we enter the world of theory, because I've yet to find anyone taking this bold step yet. Imagine, then, a news Web site comprised of reports

(continued)

Exhibit 6.1 *(continued)*

by professional journalists directly alongside submissions from everyday citizens. This is slightly different than No. 9, above, because on any one page there will be a mix of professionally written (paid) and citizen-submitted (free) content—labeled appropriately so that the reader knows what he/she is getting—rather than the more typical walling-off of citizen content as a way of differentiating it from the work of professionals.

(OhmyNews and Bluffton Today come close to this, and Greensboro's *News & Record* perhaps is heading in this direction.)

11. Wiki journalism: Where the readers are editors

Finally, in the "way out there" category, comes wiki news. The most well known example is the WikiNews site, a spinoff of the famed Wikipedia public encyclopedia, which allows anyone to write and post a news story, and anyone to edit any story that's been posted. It's an experimental concept operating on the theory that the knowledge and intelligence of the group can produce credible, well-balanced news accounts.

The jury is still out on whether or not WikiNews will work, but the wiki model does seem to succeed with Wikipedia. The online encyclopedia is now one of the top information sources on the Web, and its entries are, for the most part, accurate and useful. WikiNews, at this writing, is a less compelling service.

Traditional news organizations are unlikely to copy WikiNews, but the wiki concept might be useful to them in certain situations. For example, an obituary might work as a wiki. A family member might write the initial article, then friends and family add remembrances, photos, etc. . . . News Web sites might better experiment with information rather than news. A city guide that's part of a news Web site, for instance, could benefit from the public being allowed to build on it and improve it over time.

Source: Steve Outing, "The 11 Layers of Citizen Journalism," PoynterOnline, June 15, 2005, www.poynter.org/11layers.

and vetted by professional journalists before publication, or it can be as light as an editor only periodically perusing submissions or responding to complaints about specific posts.

Traditional journalism ethics dictate that news organizations have a responsibility to make sure the information they offer to the public is accurate. They also usually have standards of good taste and a policy of minimizing harm, including trying to ensure that no one is libeled, for both ethical and legal reasons. Enforcing these standards on citizen submissions conflicts with the blogger-inspired ideal that the Web should be a free forum where users are allowed to write whatever they want, free from the censorship of editors.

• **Citizen reporting:** Setting up reader and viewer tip lines is not new to many news organizations. But the interactive nature of the Web and the effort to tap into the reservoir of citizen expertise have prompted an effort to engage citizens more deeply in the news-gathering process. Some news organizations are even setting up open-source and distributed-reporting projects—online collaborations between reporters and their readers.

In open-source reporting, a reporter might announce a topic under investigation and invite readers to contribute leads, sources, or ideas. The idea is that the site's users may know as much or more about a topic or have more sources or resources than the professional journalist. Opening up the reporting process to engage the online user community may allow reporting with greater depth and speed than could be produced by a single journalist. [8]

Distributed-reporting projects can take different forms, but they rely heavily on users to contribute concrete information for stories in addition to ideas and opinions. Distributed reporting could mean putting a draft story online and soliciting public feedback before publishing a final version online or in print. Or it might mean asking readers to do original reporting, which could then become part of the finished story package, or aggregating user information into a database that could then be published. [9]

Potential problems with these kinds of projects are both practical and ethical. Part of a journalist's instinct and training is to be the first to get a story out. Announcing a story project publicly would alert other writers and competitors to the story idea.

The ethical questions revolve around the traditional norms of accuracy, independence, minimizing harm, and avoiding libel. How can journalists or a news organization be sure the furnished information is accurate? How can they know whether a contributor has a hidden agenda? How can they make sure that a distributed reporting effort will not "degenerate into an anonymous bulletin board, with false reports and defamation," as one journalism review article puts it? [10]

Responsible design may be the answer, according to *Online Journalism Review*. "If a journalist designs his or her distributed reporting effort responsibly, sourcing all information and requiring readers to verify their identity to post (such as verifying an e-mail address), distributed reporting can produce a massive quantity of well-organized information in a fraction of the time it would take a traditional newsroom to do the same work."[11]

That is what Minnesota Public Radio (MPR) is doing with its Public Insight Journalism initiative. Since 2002, it has kept track of more than 15,000 public sources who have shared their experiences and expertise to contribute to more than a hundred stories. "We don't want opinion, we want knowledge," says Michael Skoler, managing director of news.[12] For example, the newsroom invited those with knowledge about health care to review plans for the seven-part Prescription for Change series that aired in January 2006.[13]

In fall 2005, MPR tapped those sources and others for a story on a mechanics' strike and bankruptcy of Minnesota-based Northwest Airlines. MPR analysts handed out contact cards at the airport, posted links on online bulletin boards and chat rooms popular with airline staff, and sent e-mails to those in the public source network. In response, more than 200 people called a toll-free number or filled out an online survey to share their experiences as passengers, employees, or replacement workers. Then MPR staffers verified new sources, confirmed information, and passed vetted leads to reporters, editors, and talk show producers. One source told of an FBI investigation into possible crew tampering—a story MPR confirmed and broke. A Federal Aviation Administration inspector offered access to an online database for tracking aircraft maintenance problems. Sources helped track and report on passenger service problems. Tapping into audience expertise "vastly speeds up the process of collecting information and sources," says reporter Dan Olson. "And it gives more credibility to the reporting because it draws on many more voices."[14]

• **Citizen sites set up by traditional news organizations:** Some news organizations are creating citizen journalism sites that are distinct from the main news pages but are still run by the news organization. Usually these sites are hyperlocal, focusing on neighborhoods, and the information can be all citizen-generated or a combination of professional and citizen content.

YourHub.com is a Web site affiliated with the local newspapers of the E.W. Scripps news organization. Operating in six states and more than one hundred communities, YourHub.com is one of a number of sites that has its own brand and may seem to the casual eye to be an independent, user-generated site. It is not obvious that YourHub is part of a larger news organization, although much of its news is written by professional journalists, who make up most of the paid staff. YourHub does not screen, edit, or vet citizen contributions, thus protecting itself from legal responsibility for the content, as we saw in Chapter 4. The terms of use in YourHub and sites that operate similarly also absolve the news organizations of any ethical responsibility for the content, including its accuracy, although they usually ask contributors to be factual and civil and to minimize harm to others, often including a way for users to comment on or flag content they deem offensive. The news organizations also relinquish adherence to other traditional journalistic values, such as independence, by allowing contributors to keep hidden possible conflicts of interest and sometimes even their identity.

News organizations stake their reputation and credibility on the ethical principles of accuracy, verification, independence, and minimizing harm, but often suspend those values when using citizen-created content. One motive for this suspension is the desire to incorporate unfettered citizen voices into the news process. The trend also may signal news organizations' growing willingness to embrace the bloggers' definition of truth as emerging from shared, collective knowledge, as described in Chapter 5. Many journalists applaud these attempts by mainstream news organizations to include audiences in the news conversation. But others are wary, seeing the open forum as a first step in the abdication of journalistic responsibility. "In this new age, it is more important, not less, that this public discussion be built on the same principles as the rest of journalism—starting with truthfulness, facts and verification," Bill Kovach and Tom Rosenstiel say in *The Elements of Journalism*. "For a forum without regard for facts fails to inform. A debate steeped in prejudice and supposition only inflames."[15]

• **Independent citizen media sites:** These kinds of sites are not sponsored by or associated with traditional news organizations, but like those sites, most independent sites are hyperlocal, focusing on news of a geographic community, and solicit citizen-created content.

Many do not screen or edit contributions, vouch for the accuracy or completeness of the site's information, or make claims for the authenticity or impartiality of their contributors. Backfence.com, a group of sites headquartered near Washington, DC, tells its users to "take what you find on

Backfence.com with a grain of salt." Backfence, which calls itself a leader in citizen journalism, includes this typical disclaimer in its community agreement: "While we urge our members to post only accurate information, we cannot guarantee that member postings are accurate, impartial or objective, and we make no assurances or representations as to the veracity of our members or the quality of the information posted to our site."[16]

While most sites require registration with a verifiable e-mail address, many, including Backfence, allow users to post anonymously, using only their self-selected user names. Hiding identities in this manner violates not only traditional journalism values, but also the principle of transparency, enshrined by bloggers and increasingly embraced by mainstream news organizations. Transparency, which includes revealing news processes and identifying sources, is not consistent with anonymous posting.

"Transparency is a form of currency in a medium particularly susceptible to fraud," says Jim Durbin in his blog Brandstorming.

> The ability to form relationships with fellow bloggers online is hampered when one or more participants is providing false statements, hiding their identity, or providing information that is designed to falsely show evidence of expertise when none exists. As most of the early bloggers were motivated by politics and media, the desire to "root out" the dishonest led to a desire to provide access to all comprehensive and factual information that could affect an issue under discussion. This is not a special quality of bloggers, but a necessary community strategy for any digital formation.[17]

Tom Grubisich, who surveyed citizen journalism sites and reported his findings in *Online Journalism Review*, criticized the practice, but also suggested that the very appeal of anonymity might undermine its usefulness, ultimately reducing such sites to the status of chat rooms. "By allowing users to create fake screen names during the registration process, the site virtually invites contributors to be anonymous in their postings. But why would anyone want to get in a serious online discussion about a local issue with someone who is known only as 'woodslope' or 'nomdebytes'?"[18]

WestportNow, in Westport, Connecticut, operates under a somewhat different model. It vets contributors' submissions and now requires users to post under their real names. "I could no longer allow WestportNow to be used for anonymous sniping and personal attacks—no matter what the courts have ruled," said editor and publisher Gordon Joseloff. "WestportNow's success (125,000 visits a month in a town of 26,000) and credibility have been due in large measure to bringing professional standards to local Web journalism."[19]

Kovach and Rosenstiel share those sentiments:

> As rich or empty as the new forums may be, they cannot supplant the search for fact and context that the traditional journalism of verification supplies. If those who gather and then deliver the news no longer spend the time and money to report and verify and synthesize—if they fear that applying judgment is an act of elitism, or that the technology now frees them of these old burdens—then who will exist to find out which of the assertions in any chat room are actually true? Who will explore the backgrounds and motives of the various factions? . . .
>
> Unless the forum is based on a foundation of fact and context, the questions citizens ask will become simply rhetorical. The debate will cease to educate; it will only reinforce the prejudgments people arrive with. The public will be less able to participate in solutions. Public discourse will not be something we can learn from. It will dissolve into noise, which the majority of the public will tune out. So first, the journalistic forum should adhere to all the other journalistic principles.[20]

Dan Gillmor, an early proponent of citizen journalism and author of *We the Media*, says citizen sites should complement, not replace mainstream media. He expresses his concern about the economic threat to institutional journalism posed by competitors such as craigslist and eBay, which may undermine mainstream media's ability to perform public service work that amateur media cannot:

> Who will do big investigative projects, backed by deep pockets and the ability to pay expensive lawyers when powerful interests try to punish those who exposed them, if the business model collapses? Who would have exposed the Watergate crimes in the absence of powerful publishers, especially the *Washington Post*'s Katharine Graham, who had the financial and moral fortitude to stand up to Richard Nixon and his henchmen? At a more prosaic level, who will serve, for better or worse, as a principal voice of a community or region?
>
> Flawed as we may be in the business of journalism, anarchy in news is not my idea of a solution. . . . Credibility matters. People need, and want, trusted sources—and those sources have been, for the most part, serious journalists. Instead of journalism organizations with the critical mass to fight the good fights, we may be left with the equivalent of countless pamphleteers and people shouting from soapboxes.[21]

Polling and the Web

Engaging audiences through the interactivity made possible by the Web has made unscientific audience polling more ubiquitous than it is in print media. It also has made the reporting of election polls online more problematic and controversial.

Even before the advent of the Web, many news organizations ran opinion polls in print in an attempt to involve readers. Instead of using a random sample necessary for an accurate measure of opinion, news organizations print question coupons or call-in numbers that only newspaper customers have access to. And of those customers, only those who are moved enough by an issue to call or fill out and mail a coupon are counted. Respondents also can skew results by repeated voting or campaigning to have like-minded readers vote. That kind of self-selection and opportunity to answer more than once divests the poll of any scientific grounding and makes the responses impossible to generalize to a group, which is what scientific polls try to do.

Such flawed readings of public opinion are made even more common by online polls in which users are invited to vote on the hot issues of the day with the click of a mouse. Many such polls have no safeguards against repeat responses, which are even easier online than by telephone or mailed coupon. Even when constraints are in place, such polls are based on a self-selecting pool of respondents—those who use the site and are sufficiently motivated by strong or critical feelings about the issue to vote. That is not the kind of representative sample of the community that is required for scientific polling.

Even though news organizations usually, though not always, mention in a boilerplate disclaimer that a poll is unscientific, many nonetheless use the "data" to write news stories that generalize about the opinion of their audiences—or at least sanction the newsworthiness of the information collected. While everyone is interested in what other people think, writing a story from unscientific poll responses can easily give a false impression of group attitudes, as well as a false sense of validity and substance usually generated by statistical evidence. Not only can a news organization lose credibility by publishing distorted information, but doing so violates the fundamental journalism ethic to seek truth and report it.

"There are at least two excellent reasons not to release horse-race exit poll data," says Doug Feaver, executive editor at WashingtonPost.com.

"There is a distinct possibility it will be wrong, which doesn't help the credibility of the news business. Additionally, early release of the information might unfairly influence an election in a state where polls are still open. Just because you can do something doesn't mean you should."[22]

The Rutland, Vermont, *Herald* had to pull its online election poll in 2004 after a radio talk-show host urged listeners to vote and skew results. The host, Tim Philbin, told listeners that the poll was biased, and he wanted to show how easy it was to affect its results. "The point is, please don't tell me that represents reality," Philbin said. "That's called manufactured news." He suspected the newspaper's reason for posting the poll was to shape public opinion about political candidates, not reflect it. City editor John Dolan denied the charge and defended the *Herald*'s online polling. "It's valuable because it lets people participate willingly instead of waiting to be called and asked," he said. "And while the results are not scientifically accurate, they give some indication of what the community is thinking."[23]

Al Tompkins, broadcast and online group leader at PoynterOnline, commenting on the *Herald* and similar polls, says, "The big issue with online polling is that no matter how many responses you get, it's not 100 percent accurate. What you end up with is a very lopsided demographic. . . . Most of the time, I've found the online polls to be a complete waste of time because they're so wildly unscientific. They're called polls, but they're not really polls at all. One is borderline voodoo, the other is scientific polling."[24] The proliferation of "online pseudo-polls" by traditional media also irks Richard Morin, director of polling at the *Washington Post*. "The consistent failure of online surveys to accurately measure public attitudes is well documented; the reasons they're so unreliable are well understood. Still, the media continue to report these ghastly little horrors as if they were real barometers of public attitudes," he says.[25]

Steve Yelvington on PoynterOnline is more lenient about online polls: "They're fun, and they're a good tool for luring users into an interactive relationship with a Web site," he says, even though "we all know better than to take online polls seriously."[26]

As with edit-proof forums and anonymous or pseudonymous postings, the immediate attractions of online polling often contradict and overrule long-term news judgment. The immediacy of the Web experience itself becomes a hook for users, and the financial incentive to hook as many users as possible, as often as possible, can gradually erode the newsroom's core commitment to accuracy and balance.

Critics also argue that even news stories about reliable polls can unfairly influence public opinion at times. People tend to be influenced by the opinions of others in their community, so reading about prevailing views can affect election results, critics say.

Election polls might provide a snapshot of where candidates stand at a particular moment. But the momentary value of that news may be outweighed by the effect it can have on voters. Voters who support a promising but little-known candidate may be discouraged by polls that show the candidate getting scant support and, as a result, may switch their allegiance to a better-known candidate. This bandwagon effect can be repeated millions of times. Do polls eliminate good but lesser-known candidates early in a campaign by inadvertently boosting front-runners and prominent figures? Do they discourage voting on Election Day by suggesting that a candidate with a big lead is a sure thing? Critics say yes. Supporters say no, arguing that voters with firm opinions resist the bandwagon effect and that less certain voters are at least being influenced by accurate information rather than campaign rhetoric.[27]

While journalists may struggle with the ethical dimensions of the technology, politicians are more likely to use election polls to manipulate voters. "Politicians apparently take them seriously—not as good research, but for their potential to sway public opinion," says Steve Yelvington at PoynterOnline. "As all good marketers know, consumers love to jump on bandwagons." As an example, he cited a 2004 CBS News report that Democrats had encouraged the party faithful to vote in online polls "in order to get an edge in the 'post-debate spin.'"[28]

For those reasons, most news organizations refrain from running last-minute polls before an election. But on election night, TV networks and online sites do make predictions about who won before all the votes are cast, basing their predictions on exit polls. Exit poll data is collected from voters leaving polling places who are asked how they voted and why. Exit polls have been used for years to predict winners before all the actual votes are in and sometimes before voting locations have closed in some states and voting districts.

Historically, exit polls are the most accurate polls because they ask people not how they might vote, but how they already voted. The pollsters identify key voting precincts and demographics, then extrapolate how voters in the rest of the state will behave. The pollsters have a history of dramatic success in making accurate predictions, so the news media have relied on exit polls to be able to announce as quickly as possible who won an election.

But critics worry that, thanks to the three-hour difference in time zones, when East Coast networks announce that a certain candidate has "won" a national election after all East Coast polling places have closed but while West Coast citizens are still voting, West Coast voters might not even bother to cast ballots. Or some indecisive voters might change whom they intended to vote for in order to be on the "winning" side. If that is true, then journalists are no longer just reporting the news; they have become players in the political process and are no longer independent from it. And the information they are dispensing may be misleading.

Two presidential Election Day fiascos highlight these concerns: in 2000, when exit poll predictions by the major networks changed several times during the night, and in 2004, when bloggers publicized preliminary and misleading exit polling data. In both cases, not only were voters potentially influenced by polling information before voting stations closed, but the information they got was flawed.

In 2000, the main TV networks and the Associated Press all relied on one exit poll company, Voter News Service (VNS), which had a good record of predicting winners. However, VNS first called Florida for Al Gore, then said the result was still undecided, then said George Bush won, then again said the race was too close to call.

"This was a terrible election night for journalists," Tom Rosenstiel says. "There is no proof that the outcome was altered by premature predictions of victories in Florida or elsewhere. But the press has special freedoms in the United States to facilitate democracy. I worry that some might want to restrict those freedoms if they thought the press was inhibiting, rather than facilitating, the democratic process." Rosenstiel says the lesson for journalists should be to wait for more voting stations to close and more actual votes to be counted before making predictions.[29]

By 2004, networks had created the National Election Pool (NEP) to replace VNS and established more prudent rules about making early projections based on partial data. But while journalists reined in their predictions as an ethical response to the 2000 fiasco, bloggers felt no such compunction. Some bloggers published the first rounds of leaked exit poll numbers that showed John Kerry leading. From early afternoon to past midnight, leading blogs such as Andrew Sullivan, Daily Kos, Wonkette, Drudge, and Slate gave users the impression that Kerry would win. Until the actual votes showed that George Bush had won, Kerry fans celebrated and the stock market plunged nearly one hundred points in the last two hours of trading based on this "news."[30]

Slate, one of the sites that posted the early leaked poll numbers, was "demystifying a process controlled by the media elite," says Jack Shafer, who ran the exit poll page. "Think of the exit poll as a secret tracking poll conducted for the elite," Shafer says. "All Slate is doing is giving civilians a look at the process that they've been locked out of previously. The exit poll numbers are being swapped from NEP to its clients to politicians and journalists to boardroom big shots today like crazy, so why shouldn't civilians have access to the information? I trust readers and voters to see the exit polls for what they are."[31]

Blogger and political consultant Markos Moulitsas, who runs the popular left-wing blog Daily Kos, says that, unlike the mainstream media, he is not hemmed in by corporate rules or journalistic ethics. "If someone says I'm being irresponsible, I can just say, 'Screw you,'" he told Mark Glaser on *Online Journalism Review*.[32]

The motive for publishing exit polls might be at least partially self-serving: Like traditional media, bloggers have a vested interest in increasing interaction with their audience. Glaser reports that according to Nielsen/NetRatings, Slate had the fourth biggest jump in traffic of all sites on Election Day, growing 169 percent to 412,000 unique visitors. The Drudge Report reportedly had 36 million visits on Election Day, its best showing ever. According to Moulitsas, who says he turned off his traffic meters and stripped down his site to handle the traffic, his Daily Kos site was getting three to five time its normal traffic of about 800,000 visits per day.[33]

Eric Engberg, writing for CBSnews.com, charges that the bloggers were

> spreading a story that the network and wire service bosses knew to be incorrect because their own experts—and their journalistic experience—had warned them of the weaknesses in such data.
>
> Kerry was "in striking distance" in Florida and Ohio, said the Drudge Report. The popular and smutty Wonkette site [run by Ana Marie Cox] claimed it had "information" from "little birdies" showing Kerry up 52–47 in Ohio and 50–49 in Florida. . . . After repeating some of Wonkette's numbers, [Andrew] Sullivan, a *Time* magazine columnist and author of the popular blog The Daily Dish, mused, "A Kerry landslide? Could be. Could be." He cautioned the numbers could be misleading, even as he was publicizing them.
>
> . . . It was clear to me, from following their efforts that night, that, unlike journalists, some blog operators who are quick to trash the MSM not

only don't care about the veracity of the stories they are spreading, they do not understand when there is a live hand grenade on their keyboard. They appear not to care. Their concern is for controversy and "hits."[34]

The popularity of polling stories and their ability to pull in audiences make them likely to continue as a staple of news coverage in all media. Internet technology and the increasing use of unscientific polling online have made those stories especially vulnerable to ethical difficulties and especially problematic for online journalists.

Interactive Dialogue Through E-mail

News organizations traditionally welcomed readers' views and story reactions in letters to the editor. Reader expectations for feedback have risen along with the tide of digital interactivity, however, engendering a culture where readers expect not only to be able to talk back, but also to be heard and acknowledged. Many news organizations have responded by offering reporters' e-mail addresses along with their bylines. The *New York Times,* long resistant to what it regarded as digital gimmickry, even added a clickable e-mail form with reporters' bylines in early 2006. *Times* reporters now have become an interactive feature of their stories and, like many other journalists, must factor reader responses into their reporting duties.

Used smartly, interaction with informed readers can expand reporters' options by giving them an opportunity to develop new and more diverse sources. But e-mail also subjects reporters to a barrage of junk mail as well as messages from those pushing their own agendas, such as political spinmeisters who now routinely deluge reporters' e-boxes with their messages. Such one-on-one communication between journalists and readers is a lot more personalized than a letter to the editor. And reporters who respond to e-mails are no longer so easily insulated behind the "objective" voice of the conventional news story. While reporters often are asked to embrace the more freewheeling style of the Web in dealing with readers, they also may face criticism—or even punishment—when they step outside standard journalistic personas.

E-mail as Resource and Headache

Reviewing and culling reader e-mails requires time, but it can also be an opportunity and a resource if used in an organized way, says Jan Schaffer of J-Lab: the Institute for Interactive Journalism at the University of Maryland. She cites beat reporters in Spokane, Washington, who organize e-mail comments from readers by topic, geography, gender, and expertise to create databases of sources that they can call on when they need insight or comments. Journalists who no longer can cover every community meeting are cultivating e-mail correspondents to tip them on stories that need following, Schaffer says.[35]

Dick Meyer, editorial director of CBSNews.com, says that he enjoys the feedback he gets for his online column "Against the Grain." And reader feedback can counter the elitism that traditional media are often charged with, he told Mark Glaser in *Online Journalism Review*. But not every journalist is in a position to answer a lot of e-mail, and Meyer believes e-mail addresses should be posted only if reporters can respond. "I don't think it makes sense to do it unless you can give a meaningful response to people who are writing in," Meyer says. "I think if you can't give a meaningful response, then what you're engaging in is a marketing gimmick, which cheapens both your organization and the process of interactivity."[36]

Chicago Tribune travel writer Alan Solomon sings the praises of e-mailing readers as well. "I simply don't understand the logic in not communicating with the people we're actually working for," he says. "The readers are why we do what we do. Without them, we're nothing, zero, bupkiss."[37]

The difficulty is that those sentiments do not always reflect newsroom realities, especially at small newspapers and stations, where reporters must produce a great volume of stories with limited clerical help. A writer who is conscientious about responding to e-mail daily may be overwhelmed by the in-basket while working on an ongoing, controversial topic. At exactly the point where more readers or viewers want and deserve a thoughtful dialogue, the reporter is least able to provide it. In addition, all beats are not created equal when it comes to the volume and intensity of audience response. A travel beat such as Solomon's may inspire only a fraction of the responses sparked by a sportswriter or political columnist.

E-mail may be one way to welcome readers into the news conversation, but e-mail overload, flaming, and spamming are the unwanted side effects. Campaign strategists often overload reporters with e-mail spin. Advocacy groups sometimes send out mass e-mails to support their causes. The avalanche of mail may be overwhelming, and not always easy to sort out. Journalists need to be aware of who is e-mailing what, Schaffer says.

Glaser is hopeful that the benefits will outweigh the difficulties. "As e-mail becomes an indispensable tool, it will likely become more ingrained in a reporter's day-to-day life," he says. "And the result will mean more tips and feedback for reporters, and a better understanding of the newsroom process for readers."[38] That insight into the news process is a key to transparency, a value that many Web advocates say has been lacking in mainstream media.

Responding to E-mail

Once a policy has been established that reporters should respond to all—or at least all rational—e-mail, another ethical door is opened. How should those responses be written? What are the standards and guidelines for such exchanges?

This is not merely a question of style or etiquette. A journalist's professional identity and authority is profoundly linked to his or her voice, which is partly individual and partly institutional. The dispassionate, analytical tone and organizational balance of the conventional inverted pyramid story are critical facets of that voice in the mainstream media, and while the inverted pyramid and its pretense of objectivity have been widely challenged, few newsrooms are ready to abandon them altogether.

Stepping outside the conventions of standard journalistic discourse cost editor Rosemary Armao her job in 2002. Armao, who was managing editor for the *Sarasota Herald-Tribune* in Florida, had been e-mailed by a reader who took exception to a piece about a Republican congressional candidate, Katherine Harris. Armao's candid response included a statement that she assumed that Harris would win but that Armao would not vote for her. Armao also blamed Democrats "for not finding a better candidate . . . and our culture for craving, as its public figures, women like Katherine who are very pretty, hard-working and without original ideas that I can find." Armao's candor "compromised our impartiality and cast questions on our ability to cover that race," executive editor Janet Weaver said. "As journalists, I don't believe we reveal our personal views." [39] Armao resigned rather than be fired.

According to *Washington Post* editor Leonard Downie Jr., the *Post* takes a similar view. "Our policy says [reporters] are not supposed to express any opinions in public about things they cover," including private e-mails, he says.[40]

A policy such as Weaver's and Downie's boasts the virtues of consistency and continuity: Reporters and editors simply bring their print voices and principles whole to the realm of digital discourse. But there are larger implications. Cautious, considered, opinion-free e-mail strikes most Web denizens as a contradiction in terms. To the extent that it is possible at all, it may mark the reporter who writes it as afraid of debate, cold and aloof, or otherwise disengaged—precisely the opposite of the effect intended by interacting with readers in the first place.

One promising model as journalists attempt to develop a prescriptive rhetoric for e-mail is a familiar one—the newsroom phone call. Reporters and editors have long practice in fielding news tips, allowing callers to vent, explaining coverage, and handling corrections. These conversations are typically carried out with civility, and ideally callers come away with insight into the news process as well as a sense that their contributions are needed and valued. At the same time, journalists know never to promise specific coverage or story placement, never to permit sources to vet stories, and never to be coaxed into agreeing with slurs or slander.

But while telephone protocols offer some guidance, they are far from foolproof. As a technology, e-mail is an example of what Walter J. Ong has called a "secondary orality," a form of electronic discourse that borrows from both the oral traditions of past millennia and the more recent conventions of print. Such hybrids can breed ethical confusion. Specifically, e-mail encourages the spontaneity of conversation, but it also gives one's words the document status of writing. It can be saved, reproduced, taken out of context, and distributed in ways never intended by the writer.

When Are Reporters' Personal E-mails Public?

Another dilemma regarding the appropriateness of reporters' e-mail correspondence emerges when reporters send personal messages about their work that become public. These are especially sensitive when they concern war or other potentially divisive news.

One high-profile example is the case of Farnaz Fassihi, a *Wall Street Journal* reporter stationed in Baghdad, who wrote to friends about life in Iraq in an e-mail that was widely circulated on the Web. Her moving account included descriptions of her daily life—a car bomb blowing out the windows of her house, her feeling of being under virtual house arrest—as well as her assessment of the war in Iraq. Her statement on the war's progress was candid and bleak: "Despite President Bush's rosy assessments, Iraq remains a disaster. If under Saddam it was a 'potential' threat, under the Americans it has been transformed to 'imminent and active threat,' a foreign policy failure bound to haunt the United States for decades to come. . . . One could argue that Iraq is already lost beyond salvation. For those of us on the ground it's hard to imagine what if anything could salvage it from its violent downward spiral."[41]

"This was a private correspondence that has been thrust into the public domain without my consent," Fassihi told *Editor & Publisher*.[42] And in an e-mail to *Washington Post* reporter Howard Kurtz, she wrote, "As a human being, you make observations and form opinions. But what distinguishes good journalists is their ability to separate opinion from fact. I've done that throughout my career and plan to continue doing it, and would never cover any story where my mind isn't open to new facts and new ideas."[43]

Wall Street Journal managing editor Paul Steiger defended the objectivity of Fassihi's *Journal* stories. "Ms. Fassihi's private opinions have in no way distorted her coverage, which has been a model of intelligent and courageous reporting, and scrupulous accuracy and fairness."[44]

On the other hand, Jay Rosen, in his blog PressThink, argued that her news reports were too objective: While the e-mail is a personal account, "it's not intimate speech. It's really journalism, an eyewitness report, giving impressions and conclusions about the struggle to prevail in Iraq." Part of what gives the e-mail account its power is that it is told by an "authorized knower," speaking directly, not through sources and quotes. Rosen said the e-mail conveyed a sense of the situation that had not come through in other accounts. "Fassihi's mistake, if you could call it that, was not doing a better job of getting those observations . . . onto the pages of *The Wall Street Journal*."[45]

As with so many ethical dilemmas in the digital realm, the question of e-mail protocol is ultimately a question about objectivity and its continued value in what Mark Deuze calls the "media ecosystem." Deuze points out that there is not a firm, clear line between "interactive engagement" and "professional detachment," as much as most working journalists and some scholars would like to believe that such a line exists. Instead, one's concept of objectivity shifts with the medium and its technological possibilities:

> The discourse of professional distance clearly stands in stark contrast to the rhetoric of inclusivity so often found in the debates and studies

about online journalism and convergence. Online and multimedia's careful embrace of interactivity as well as a merging of different cultures (print, broadcast, online; "hard" and "soft" news, marketing and editorial) within the news organization—a perceived necessary byproduct of convergence—confronts the individual professional with multiple interpretations of objectivity. It is therefore not surprising that journalists' main response to such changes and challenges is nostalgia (and stress). Yet at the same time reporters involved in the frontlines claim to have gained a new appreciation of different ways to do things. . . . If journalists start blogging, start interacting with colleagues and publics, their professional identity becomes at once more autonomous as well as less self-centered.[46]

Is this process of adjustment and exploration only a personal one, or might it also be an institutional one? As newspapers, newsmagazines, and broadcasters devote greater resources to their Web operations while opening their doors to bloggers and other citizen journalists, the "rhetoric of inclusivity" will almost certainly redefine the conventions of "professional distance" that have dominated mainstream journalistic discourse for a century. But it is not likely to be a one-way process. The values of distance, perspective, and balance are too deeply embedded in newsroom culture to be simply cast aside.

Exhibit 6.2
A New Kind of Reporter
Jeff Jarvis in BuzzMachine

Jeff Jarvis blogs about media and news at Buzzmachine.com. He is the director of the interactive journalism program at the City University of New York's Graduate School of Journalism and the former president and creative director of Advance.net. This is an abridged version of a May 23, 2005, posting on Buzzmachine.

Editor as News Gatherer

I think we're getting ready to define a new job description of the journalist.

(continued)

Exhibit 6.2 *(continued)*

One of my favorite soundbites . . . is that we in the press need to think of ourselves not just as news creators but also as news gatherers, collecting news from inside and outside our newsrooms and sharing it wherever, whenever, and however people want.

Or to say it in another obnoxious soundbite: We need to stop being controllers and start being enablers.

I read Stephen Baker's post on the Businessweek Blogspotting blog recounting lunch at a Korean restaurant . . . with a media exec who argued that we will soon see the rise of a new kind of newsperson. They see it as a new kind of reporter.

I think it's a new kind of editor who gathers and sifts and vets and shares and guides and goads—and does all that not just with beat reporters but with beat citizens: readers turned writers.

From their lunch: He said that the day of the classic "beat reporter," is coming to an end. Replacing the legions of beat reporters banging out their stories in newsrooms, he predicts, will be a far smaller group of so-called multimedia journalists. These people will be higher paid. They will know how to harvest the knowledge of experts and citizen reporters alike, and will fashion new journalistic products out of various media. They will have entrepreneurial skills and many will create their own brands. . . .

So imagine the job description of a *real* city editor of the near future. Duties include:

1. *Aggregate, organize, and highlight the best of newsroom and citizen media:* good reporting, good story ideas, new viewpoints, public pulse points.
2. *Make assignments inside and outside the newsroom:* You need someone to cover a school-board meeting where there's a controversy brewing, you might allocate one of your staff reporters. For another meeting, you might go out to bid with citizen information entrepreneurs, picking someone who has your trust because she has training and a track record. For another meeting, you know that the event will be covered by citizens anyway—some with a stated viewpoint—and you'll aggregate those. But you'll make sure that what needs to be covered gets covered. The insiders will be on salary.

(continued)

Exhibit 6.2 *(continued)*

The outsiders may get a payment or may be part of your company's ad network or may just get promotion that benefits them when they sell the ads.

3. *Identify, train, and support reporting talent:* What you have done in the newsroom, you will need to do outside. You will find promising and motivated citizen reporters and put the best into a company training program—or take the best from journalism schools that now serve the industry and the public with citizen training. On an ongoing basis, you will work with this distributed reporting base to improve their work. You won't be able to edit every line of every report to which you link, but you will try to educate them—and earn their respect as they earn yours.

4. *Share news anywhere, anytime, in any medium:* You will package and enable news gatherers to share news as it happens in and through any appropriate medium—text, photo, audio, video, conversation, shared resources.

5. *Converse:* It's important to stay in conversation with the community: Get out, meet people, read their blogs, read their comments, respond to them, be a member of the community.

Source: Jeff Jarvis, "Editor as News Gatherer," Buzzmachine.com, May 23, 2005, www.buzzmachine.com/archives/2005_05_23.html#009724.

Case Study: A Citizen's Initiative

Imagine you are the editor of the *News Observer,* a midsize circulation paper in New York State, and its online site, NO.com. You want to increase citizen participation in your news organization and decide that inviting readers' comments would be a good way to start.

Many issues must be decided before launching your citizen initiative. You make a list of questions to circulate to other editors and reporters for comment. But first you want to think about how you would answer them yourself. Write out your decisions and the thought processes that led you to them, along with any other considerations that you think relevant.

1. Should you set up a comment response form for every story or only for major or local ones? Or should there be a separate,

general comment area on the newspapers' Web site instead of, or in addition to, specific story response forms?

2. Should you also, or instead, set up a system that allows readers to privately contact reporters, such as making local bylines clickable with an e-mail form to write reporters directly?

3. Should you require commenters to register with real, verifiable names and addresses before being allowed to publicly post, as is now required for printed letters to the editor? Should commenters (registered or not) be allowed to post comments anonymously or using only their usernames?

4. Should comments on individual stories be publicly posted along with the story itself? Or should comments be sent directly to the relevant reporter or editor? Or should all comments go to a separate comment area on the site?

5. Should you "thread" comments so that all comments relating to a specific topic are seen together? Should you set up an e-mail alert system so that commenters know when others have responded or posted comments on the same topic?

6. If comments are to be publicly posted, should those comments be read or edited before posting? Should allegations be fact-checked before posting?

7. How would you deal with posted comments that are derogatory, in poor taste, or possibly libelous? What about those that are very critical of an article, the reporter, or the news organization? Should a reporter or editor be allowed or required to publicly post responses to such postings?

8. Should there be a way for commenters to flag other comments they deem objectionable? How should the news organization deal with those? Should every comment someone deems objectionable be removed? Only after a certain number of complaints? Only if the editors also decide a comment is objectionable?

9. Should reporters be required to respond to e-mails sent to them directly or about their stories? If so, should there be standards regarding those personal e-mails, such as requiring all reporter responses to maintain objectivity regarding issues or people in the news? Or should the more informal, personal style of bloggers be allowed?

10. Should comments be actively solicited from print readers by listing the URL with stories? Should all or some of the online comments be printed in the paper's editorial section?

Notes

1. Jay Rosen, "Top Ten Ideas of '04: News Turns from a Lecture to a Conversation," PressThink, December 29, 2004, http://journalism.nyu.edu/pubzone/weblogs/press-think/2004/12/29/tp04_lctr.html.

2. Steve Outing, "We Media: Something Old, Something New," E-Media Tidbits, PoynterOnline, October 5, 2005, www.poynter.org/column.asp?id=31&aid=90098&.

3. Outing, "We Media."

4. Dan Gillmor, "Web 2.0, Journalism and Nicholas Carr," October 23, 2005, http://bayosphere.com/blog/dan_gillmor/20051023/rough_type_nicholas_carrs_blog_the_amorality_of_web_2_0?highlight=about%2Ccitizen%2Cjournalism.

5. Project for Excellence in Journalism, State of the News Media 2006, www.stateofthenewsmedia.org/2006/narrative_overview_intro.asp?media=1; Bill Kovach and Tom Rosenstiel, The Elements of Journalism: What Newspeople Should Know and the Public Should Expect (New York: Crown, 2001), p. 135.

6. Project for Excellence in Journalism, 2006.

7. Steve Outing, "The 11 Layers of Citizen Journalism," PoynterOnline, June 15, 2005, www.poynter.org/11layers.

8. "How to Report a News Story Online," Online Journalism Review, www.ojr.org/ojr/wiki/Reporting.

9. "How to Report"; Outing, "11 Layers."

10. "How to Report."

11. Ibid.

12. Michael Skoler, "Fear, Loathing and the Promise of Public Insight Journalism," Citizen Journalism, Nieman Reports, Winter 2005, www.nieman.harvard.edu/reports/contents.html.

13. Stephanie Xenos, "Opening Up the Newsroom," Minnesota Public Radio, June 2006, http://minnesota.publicradio.org/about/features/2006/06/pij/. (This article also appeared in Minnesota Monthly, June 2006.)

14. Skoler, "Fear, Loathing."

15. Kovach and Rosenstiel, Elements of Journalism, p. 136.

16. Backfence.com Community Agreement, www.backfence.com/about/index.cfm?page=/members/commAgree&mycomm=BE.

17. Jim Durbin, Brandstorming blog, Durbin Media Group, May 22, 2006, http://durbinmedia.com/brandstorming/2006/05/myth-4-blogs-should-never-be-censored.asp.

18. Tom Grubisich, "Grassroots Journalism: Actual Content vs. Shining Ideal," Online Journalism Review, October 6, 2005, www.ojr.org/ojr/stories/051006.

19. Grubisich, "Grassroots Journalism."

20. Kovach and Rosenstiel, Elements of Journalism, p. 145.

21. Gillmor, "Web 2.0, Journalism and Nicholas Carr."

22. Mark Glaser, "Exit Polls Bring Traffic Deluge, Scrutiny to Blogs, Slate," Online Journalism Review, November 5, 2004, http://ojr.org/ojr/glaser/1099616933.php.

23. Brent Curtis, "Herald Pulls Manipulated Poll," September 30, 2004, www.timesargus.com/apps/pbcs.dll/article?AID=/20040930/NEWS/409300323/1003/NEWS02.

24. Ibid.

25. Richard Morin, "Online Polling: No Substitute for the Real Thing," WashingtonPost.com, September 7, 1999, www.washingtonpost.com/wp-srv/politics/polls/wat/archive/wat090799.htm.

26. Steve Yelvington, "Taking Online Polls Seriously," PoynterOnline, October 11, 2004, www.poynter.org/content/content_view.asp?id=72662.

27. Cecilia Friend, Donald Challenger, and Katherine C. Adams, *Contemporary Editing*, 2nd. ed. (New York: McGraw-Hill, 2005), p. 266.

28. Yelvington, "Taking Online Polls Seriously," his CBS information linked from www.cbsnews.com/stories/2004/10/01/politics/main646915.shtml.

29. Tom Rosenstiel, "Media's Role in Calling Elections," CNN.com, Allpolitics Chat, November 9, 2000, www.cnn.com/chat/transcript/2000/11/9/rosenstiel/.

30. Richard Morin, "Surveying the Damage: Exit Polls Can't Always Predict Winners, So Don't Expect Them To," WashingtonPost.com, November 21, 2004, www.washingtonpost.com/ac2/wp-dyn/articles/A64906-2004Nov20.htm. Morin is the director of polling at the *Washington Post*.

31. Glaser, "Exit Polls."

32. Ibid.

33. Ibid.

34. Eric Engberg, "Blogging as Typing, Not Journalism: For Real News, Stick with the Dinosaurs," CBS News.com, November 8, 2004, www.cbsnews.com/stories/2004/11/08/opinion/main654285.shtml.

35. Jan Schaffer, Dialogues on Online Journalism Ethics, http://jethicsdialogues.blogspot.com.

36. Mark Glaser, "Is a Reporter's E-mail Address Really Anyone's Business?" *Online Journalism Review*, March 3, 2004, www.ojr.org/ojr/glaser/1079478749.php.

37. Ibid.

38. Ibid.

39. Howard Kurtz, "E-Mail Deriding Katherine Harris Costs Editor's Job," WashingtonPost.com, June 28, 2002, www.washintonpost.com/ac2/wp-dyn/A58769–2002Jun27?.

40. Joe Strupp, "Is It OK for Journalists to Put Opinions in Personal E-mails?" Romenesko, PoynterOnline, October 15, 2004, www.poynter.org/content/content_view.asp?id=72851.

41. Romenesko, "WSJ Reporter Fassihi's E-mail to Friends," PoynterOnline, September 29, 2004, www.poynter.org/column.asp?id=45&aid=72659&.

42. Jay Rosen, "Authorized Knower: Farnaz Fassihi's Accidental Baghdad Dispatch," PressThink, October 8, 2004, http://journalism.nyu.edu/pubzone/weblogs/pressthink/2004/10/08/e_fassihi.html. Rosen cites an *Editor & Publisher* story at www.editorandpublisher.com/eandp/news/article_display.jsp?vnu_content_id=1000653324, accessible only with subscription.

43. Howard Kurtz, "When Private Passions Meet Public Journalism," WashingtonPost.com, October 11, 2004, www.washingtonpost.com/wp-dyn/articles/A23086–20040ct10.html.

44. Jim Romenesko, "What Did WSJ's Fassihi Do Wrong?" PoynterOnline, October 5, 2004, http://poynter.org/forum/view_post.asp?id=8105.

45. Rosen, "Authorized Knower."

46. Mark Deuze, Dialogues: Online Journalism Ethics, October 2004, http://jethicsdialogues.blogspot.com.

7

Commercial Issues and Content Linking

Cecilia Friend

In a Web environment, journalists must sometimes struggle to adapt traditional ethical standards to a new realm of proprietary information, sponsored content, and advertisers. The design and nature of the medium itself make it difficult to separate on occasion—or even distinguish between—editorial and commercial content in the same way they are separated in print and broadcast. For that reason, the ethical principles that have governed print and broadcast sometimes seem inadequate or even irrelevant to the task. This chapter looks at such traditional church-state issues and how news organizations handle them in an interactive medium.

The chapter also examines the ethical issues involving linking to sites that may be controversial, highly partisan, graphic in nature, or otherwise likely to inflame sensitivities. Sending users to such sites may imply endorsement. Some news organizations also are reluctant to link to outside sites, even if the sites are unobjectionable and the links valuable to users, because linking takes those users away from the original site. Again, traditional ethical norms may be difficult to apply, especially since linking itself is an interactive format, and following a link is a user option with no equivalents in print or broadcast. This chapter discusses these issues and the evolving principles that online media are applying to linking, one of the hallmarks of the Web.

Specifically, this chapter will consider:

- Church-state issues, or the separation of editorial and commercial content:

Clearly separating advertising from news and editorial content has been a standard journalistic principle in print for almost a hundred years. Should the principle be different for online news sites that are struggling for economic viability? Should advertising be considered simply another form of "information" that consumers might like to have without news organizations worrying about how to isolate or label it adequately on a Web page?

Some sites use an ad-within-editorial-text technique that turns words in articles into clickable ads when users mouse over them. Some place commercial links alongside informational links without clearly labeling them as paid advertising. Do those practices cross the line between editorial and advertising?

- Linking to other sites:

Content linking poses its own ethical questions. Should a news organization link to a site that may be repugnant, either philosophically or graphically, or vehemently one-sided on a complex issue? Should users be given the opportunity to see for themselves if material is objectionable or one-sided? Is there an ethical distinction between physically providing a link and merely citing the URL for the site? Is linking tantamount to an endorsement? Does it matter where in the story the link appears, such as within text or at the bottom or side of an article? Do disclaimers take care of possible ethical issues?

Church-State Separation of Advertising and News

The church-state divide originally referred to the literal constitutional issue of keeping religion free from governmental endorsement or control. In journalism, it has come to mean the separation of news copy from commercial content. Perhaps the reason journalism has borrowed this phrasing is because of the complexity and sacrosanct nature of both issues: In both cases, the church-state divide is an absolute ideal that can become extremely fuzzy when applied to real-life situations. That complexity has only deepened with news organizations' creation of Web sites, where traditional print and broadcast conventions of separating content do not easily translate.

The practice of labeling ads was not universal in print news until 1912, when Congress made it a federal requirement related to newspapers' mailing privileges. Until that time, publishers often disguised ads to resemble news stories and editorials. Congress passed the Newspaper Publicity Act in part to regulate that practice, requiring newspapers to clearly identify ads that bore a typographical resemblance to news stories or editorials. The law passed constitutional muster in 1913. The press eventually embraced the practice, and it has been a hallmark of journalistic ethics for most of the last century.[1]

With greater graphic and typographic capabilities, contemporary newspapers usually distinguish news from advertising by using different typefaces for news and commercial content. But since Web users can control how type is presented on screen and since the range of readable typefaces and fonts is quite limited, that practice does not always work online. The interactive nature of the Web also permits new forms of advertising that in turn require new approaches and design parameters for clearly distinguishing them from news matter.

Some sites do carry over the visual page division of print newspapers and magazines to the Web, using a side rail of a Web page for advertising and sponsored links that are so labeled. Display ads in the middle of articles also are becoming more common, but those are usually boxed and easily identified as advertising.

More insidious, because it may not as easily be perceived as ad delivery, is the technique of having words in a story turn into clickable ads or commercial links when users merely mouse over them. Users are used to seeing clickable words in stories—word links placed by a writer or editor that lead users to related information elsewhere on that or another site. Using the same technique to rope readers into refocusing on an advertising pitch is, to many, unethical because it is a form of misrepresentation. In individual instances the technique may simply be an irritant, but its habitual use ultimately obliterates the distinction between information gathered according to established news methods and standards and information that is not.

One practice offers companies the right to purchase keywords in stories. If a story mentions "IBM," for example, that term becomes a pop-up ad each time the user's mouse slides over it. Actually clicking on it takes you to the company's Web site. While at first glance that may not seem such a stretch from what writers often do—offering users an easy way to get more information on a company mentioned in a story—the difference is that the link is paid for and the writer may not even know that the link was created.

That technique is taken a step further by the IntelliTXT ad system developed by Vibrant Media, which describes itself as contextual keyword advertising. It scans article content for words that are merely related in some way to the services or products of paid advertisers, and then it creates links that look like common editorial-driven links.[2] Clicking on the word takes users to the advertiser's Web site. Clicking on the word "homecoming" in a story about a solder's return to his family, for example, might take the users to a commercial people-finder site where they are encouraged to hunt for former high school classmates for a fee.

Forbes.com experimented with the IntelliTXT ad-within-editorial-text system in 2004 but dropped it within the year. Staffers complained that it encroached on their work because they had no control over what words were linked to ads or what products or services were being advertised.[3] Jim Spanfeller, president and chief executive at Forbes.com, likened the ad-in-text technology to the "Buy This Book" ad links common in Web-based reviews and features.[4] But even that practice was controversial when it was first introduced in the late 1990s and when consumers were unaware that the links were paid spots. The *New York Times* online received criticism for putting "Buy This Book" boxes at the end of its book reviews because readers were not told that the *Times* received a commission from the bookseller Barnes & Noble, whose site was linked to the boxes. The *Times* no longer uses that type of advertising in its book reviews.

In February 2005, the *New York Post* experimented with an ad-in-text technique in business stories on nypost.com. In a story on rising oil prices, for example, there was a reference to the conference board that issues the consumer confidence index. The word "conference" appeared in green and was underlined. Clicking it took users not to a site linked to the conference board, but to GoToMeeting, an online conference service from Citrix Online. Executives at the *Post* later said the experiment was not intended to be live and they were unsure how the ads wound up on the paper's public Web site.[5]

Many sites use the IntelliTXT system and another similar technique developed by Kontera, which claimed 1,100 clients in 2006, but Forbes and the *Post* are two of the very few pure news sites to have tried the technology as of this writing. The promise of this technique to generate Web-specific advertising revenue, at a time when many news sites are not economically viable in themselves, may still tempt other news organizations to give it a try, especially in soft, consumer-oriented coverage, such as travel, home, and health pages.

While the advertising strategy may increase ad revenue, its use on news sites has attracted controversy. Aly Colón, who taught ethics at the Poynter Institute and is now its reporting, writing, and editing group leader, said that the biggest risk may be turning off readers. "If we want to be taken seriously for the work that we do as journalists, we should try to devise a way of presenting our material so the users, the readers, know that we are first and foremost about the news," he says. Articles scattered with paid advertiser links could create the impression that advertising shaped the reporting, which, in turn, could undermine the value of advertising in those articles in the first place: "Advertising wants to be associated with a news product that has integrity."[6]

The idea that ads-in-text advertising could shape—or appear to shape—news content was a concern of Forbes's journalists and was a worry also expressed by Larry Kramer, then chief executive at CBS Marketwatch and now president of CBS Digital Media. He says the system has the potential to seriously erode the barrier between advertising and news content. "Are we going to start writing stories that use words that we think will bring us more revenue?" he asks. "While I don't think anybody is doing anything untoward now, I do think there is potential for that."[7]

Steven Klein in PoynterOnline says the "firestorm" over Forbes.com's use of the in-text ads was much ado about nothing new. The technique "is hardly trailblazing," he says. "We've already been there, done that, and, more importantly, fixed that," he notes, referring to the 1912 Newspaper Publicity Act that first mandated clearly separating ads from news: "Editorial integrity is demanded of newspapers. It should be no different online."[8]

But while the historical parallel is important, so is the historical distinction. The 1912 Newspaper Publicity Act took effect with a maturing journalistic philosophy of independence, professionalism, and objectivity in the ascendant, and it codified the relationship—or nonrelationship—between news and advertising within that philosophy. In the twenty-first century, objectivity remains the dominant ideal among mainstream news organizations, but it faces accusations from various camps that it is outdated, misconstrued, manipulated, and, particularly, largely a product of print culture. A twenty-first-century online version of the Newspaper Publicity Act would still have legal authority, but it is less certain that it would carry the same ethical weight of its predecessor.

Robert Berkman, coauthor of *Digital Dilemmas: Ethical Issues for*

Online Media Professionals, thinks that the big issue is clarity and distinction—making sure there's no confusion or mixing together of different types of information. "Mixing up of ads and editorial, including the mouse-over of words in text to become ads, is a bad idea," he says, especially because trust of the media has become such a big and contentious issue. Berkman says readers and viewers are already cynical and skeptical about their information sources. "The successful and ethical news organization (in print or online) will figure out how to get the trust of their readers and build audience and revenue that way. And there may be lots of ways to do this . . . I could potentially see a very well marked online sidebar, stating something like 'directory of commercial providers,' apart from the story, like the buyers guides that trade magazines offer . . . with a list of links. But I don't like the idea of a hotlink, or story reference link, where commercial information is embedded, thereby mixed up, and therefore potentially confusing of the two purposes for the reader."[9]

In a statement issued in 2003, the Society of Professional Journalists (SPJ) called on the news media to maintain the clear separation of news and advertising. The release specifically targeted broadcast organizations that allow sponsored segments where businesses pay for a chance to be interviewed on the air, calling them "clear violations of the basic tenets of ethical journalism that threaten the independence of the press guaranteed by the Constitution." But the release also reiterated the importance of the church-state separation of news and advertising in every medium, reminding news organizations of the SPJ Code of Ethics on the issue: "Distinguish news from advertising and shun hybrids that blur the lines between the two."[10]

The principles of the Online News Association, a group of professional online journalists, also speak to editorial integrity: "Responsible journalism on the Internet means that the distinction between news and other information must always be clear, so that individuals can readily distinguish independent editorial information from paid promotional information and other non-news."[11]

In one case posted on PoynterOnline, clarity and distinction were so lacking that a reader of an online *Guardian Observer* story read most of it before she realized that it was not written by a *Guardian* staffer but by a member of an interest group, Amnesty International. (See Exhibit 7.1.)

Still, observing the wall between church and state has been a bigger problem for bloggers, as discussed in Chapter 5. Many bloggers are both editors and publishers of their sites, responsible for both content and advertising, and may lack a grounding in or allegiance to traditional journalistic ethics. Advertisers have sponsored blogs; for example, Sony paid the Gawker Media group $25,000 a month in exchange for sponsorship of Gawker's Lifehacker blog about personal gadgetry software. Such direct payments from advertisers have been criticized by some in the blogging community, as noted in Chapter 5, but the practice has not abated.

Linking and Implied Endorsement of Linked-to Content

Linking to online ads is an ethical dilemma, but at least we can look to its ethical underpinnings in the traditional journalistic mandate of separating news from ads. Content linking, however, poses unique ethical questions because linking readers to off-site content from news stories is a practice that has no direct parallel in print or broadcast, making traditional ethical norms hard to apply.

Linking is central to the architecture, appeal, and power of the Web. Making instant connections between sites and related information is what Tim Berners-Lee sought in creating the World Wide Web. It is the cornerstone of the world of distributed hypertext. "On the Web, to make reference without making a link is possible but ineffective—like speaking but with a paper bag over your head," Berners-Lee says in "Links and Law: Myths about Links"[12] (see Exhibit 7.2). Bloggers have taken this philosophy to heart. Most blogs not only have in-text links to most references they make, but also use side rails for lists of links to outside sites.

Most mainstream news organization sites, however, do not link to outside sites. This is one of the sharpest and most fundamental differences between the two forms. While many news organizations offer links, almost all are links to content elsewhere on the same site. Even obvious links, such as linking from health stories that reference studies in the *New England Journal of Medicine* or the journal *Nature* to the original study articles themselves, are extremely rare among mainstream media. News organizations have two reasons for their reluctance to link to outside sites. The first has to do with the implied endorsement of a site that may not conform to the same journalistic standards. The second justification is more economic: News organizations want to keep users on-site rather than steering them to other sites out of the purview of income-generating site advertisements.

Exhibit 7.1
Minor Identity Crisis at the *Observer* Blog

Amy Gahran, a conversational media consultant and content strategist based in Boulder, Colorado, posted this column on June 16, 2006, on PoynterOnline's Weblog E-Media Tidbits, which she edits. Gahran is also the editor of her own Weblog, Contentious, where she offers news and musings on communication in the online age.

Context is crucial in online media, especially in weblogs. Readers should never have to wonder, even for an instant, who authored a posting. Momentary confusion or hesitation can easily translate into lost online readers.

Given that, perhaps the weblog associated with the *Guardian*'s Sunday *Observer* paper might want to tweak the format for its postings and feeds.

Here's what I mean—check out this June 12 *Observer* blog posting: Google "soul searches" over censorship (http://blogs.guardian.co.uk/observer/archives/2006/06/12/we_are_irrepres_1.html).

The dateline for that posting reads: "By Observer/International 12:01 am." That led me to believe that this was a staff-written post. So I got very interested when I read the lead: "Our irrepressible.info campaign, to combat Internet repression has continued to gather pace and support this last fortnight."

"Cool!" I thought, impressed that a news organization would launch such a campaign.

In the next paragraph, however, I started getting confused: "Since the campaign launched in *The Observer* two weeks ago, over 21,000 people have now gone online and signed our pledge for Internet freedom, writes Kate Allen, director of Amnesty International."

Reading further, my confusion deepened as I encountered lines such as, "At Amnesty we believe there is much that Internet companies can do in China and elsewhere to protect human rights." (That was not presented as a quote in the posting, but as a direct editorial statement.)

"Hmmmm . . ." I wondered. "So whose campaign is this, the *Observer*'s or Amnesty's?"

The link to irrepressible.info leads to a site that says it's "an Amnesty International Campaign" and that the campaign is supported by the *Observer*. The "launched" link leads to this special reports page on the

(continued)

Exhibit 7.1 *(continued)*

Observer site, where it says: "Some 45 years after an *Observer* article launched Amnesty, *The Observer* and Amnesty International have teamed up again to campaign against a new threat to our freedom—Internet repression."

Interesting! I had no idea of the close historical connection between the *Observer* and Amnesty. Scrolling down that page, I found this announcement of the campaign, which supplied more current context. (The campaign, called irrepressible.com, calls for governments to stop censoring websites, blocking e-mails, and shutting down blogs—and big corporations to stop helping them.)

OK, finally it became clear to me: irrepressible.info is a partnership campaign between the *Observer* and Amnesty International—and a very intriguing effort worth checking out, in my opinion. It struck me as odd for a news organization to partner so closely with an advocacy group, but in this case the two organizations' deeply intertwined historical roots made this partnership understandable.

Still, I expected to see, maybe at the bottom of the "soul searching" blog posting, a note clarifying who actually wrote the article—or at least indicating that it was written by staff at Amnesty, not the *Observer*. But no, to all appearances this is presented as an *Observer*-authored item.

Lesson: You never know where your online audience is coming from, and what background or context they have. If you're presenting any content that might possibly cause a newcomer to stop and wonder, or perhaps question your intentions or credibility, it helps to clarify such issues *with every posting*. If I'd been less intrigued or more rushed, I wouldn't have bothered clicking around to figure out this puzzle.

In this case the *Observer* blog could have included a box at the top of the right-hand sidebar briefly clarifying the partnership nature of the campaign. They also could have modified the byline to say something like "By Amnesty International for the *Observer*." The site's feed also should clearly indicate authorship of the posting, and the posting itself could be reworded to clarify the relationship.

Such minor tweaks can prevent confusion and thus allow readers to engage more effectively with your content. As more news organizations experiment creatively with collaborative content and projects, clarity about who's who will only grow more crucial.

Source: Amy Gahran, "Minor Identity Crisis at the *Observer* Blog," PoynterOnline, June 16, 2006, www.poynter.org/tidbit_observer.

Exhibit 7.2
Links and Law: Myths About Links

This list of link myths by Tim Berners-Lee, who invented the World Wide Web in 1989 while working at the European Organization for Nuclear Research (CERN), is part of a statement of principles by the World Wide Web Consortium (W3C), an industry group dedicated to building consensus around Web technologies. They were written in April 1997 and updated in 2004. Berners-Lee with others created the W3C, and Berners-Lee has served as its director since it was founded in 1994. This list, part of a larger document on Web architectural and philosophical principles, are Berners-Lee's personal notes expressing "fundamental understandings upon which the practical uses and power of the Web rest."

Myth One

Myth: A normal link is an incitement to copy the linked document in a way which infringes copyright.

This is a serious misunderstanding. The ability to refer to a document (or a person or anything else) is in general a fundamental right of free speech to the same extent that speech is free. Making the reference with a hypertext link is more efficient but changes nothing else.

When the "speech" itself is illegal, whether or not it contains hypertext links, then its illegality should not be affected by the fact that it is in electronic form.

Users and information providers and lawyers have to share this convention. If they do not, people will be frightened to make links for fear of legal implications. I received a mail message asking for "permission" to link to our site. I refused as I insisted that permission was not needed.

There is no reason to have to ask before making a link to another site.

But by the same token, you are responsible for what you say about other people, and their sites, etc., on the Web as anywhere.

Myth Two

Myth: Making a link to a document makes your document more valuable and therefore is a right you should pay for.

(continued)

Exhibit 7.2 *(continued)*

This is another dangerous one. It is of course true that your document is made more valuable by links to high quality relevant other documents. A review in a consumer magazine has added value because of the quality of the products to which it refers the reader. I may be more valuable to you as a person if I refer you to other people by name, phone number or URL. This doesn't mean I owe those people something.

We cannot regard anyone as having the "right not to be referred to" without completely pulling the rug out from under free speech.

Myth Three

Myth: Making a link to someone's publicly readable document is an infringement of privacy.

The "security by obscurity" method of hiding things behind secret URLs has the property that anyone knowing the URL (like a password) can pass it on. This is only a breach of confidentiality if there is some confidentiality agreement which has been made.

Hall of Flame

Famous cases in which people tried to prevent others linking to their Web pages include, if I recall correctly, Ticketmaster trying to stop the Seattle Sidewalk site linking into its pages, so that those looking through the site about the town could follow a link and buy tickets to the events. This was widely perceived not only as philosophically wrong by falling for the myths above, but also crazy, as it was a protest against Seattle Sidewalk bringing traffic and hence business to the Ticketmaster site.

In 2002, a Danish court made an injunction preventing a Danish news filtering service (effectively a sort of search engine) from linking to pages of a Danish newspaper. . . . I assume that the appeals process will clear up this after this time of writing (2002/07). If such decisions are accepted, the whole working of the Web would break down.

In 2004, a comment to the W3C TAG [World Wide Web Consortium Technical Architecture Group] noted that the Athens Olympic site, no less, tried to prevent deep linking to pages such as their sports page. Thus, a vast set of rather unique resources were supposed to be not really part

(continued)

Exhibit 7.2 *(continued)*

of the Web. They even tried to constrain how one will link to the entry page. The Athens site violates the principles above and sets a very bad example. A pity, when the Olympics celebrate what is best in humanity, that the Web presence should exclude itself from the global discourse.

Conclusions About Links

There are some fundamental principles about links on which the Web is based. These are principles that allow the world of distributed hypertext to work. Lawyers, users, and technology and content providers must all agree to respect these principles which have been outlined.

It is difficult to emphasize how important these issues are for society. The first amendment to the Constitution of the United States, for example, addresses the right to speak. The right to make reference to something is inherent in that right. On the Web, to make reference without making a link is possible but ineffective—like speaking but with a paper bag over your head.

A reminder that this is personal opinion, not related to W3C or MIT [Massachusetts Institute of Technology] policy. I reserve the right to re-phrase this if misunderstandings occur, as it's always difficult to express this sort of thing to a mixed and varied audience.

Source: Tim Berners-Lee, "Links and Law: Myths About Links," April 1997, www.w3.0rg/DesignIssues/LinkMyths.html. This statement is part of W3C's De-sign Issues: Architectural and Philosophical Points, www.w3.org/DesignIssues/ Overview.html. Copyright © 1997 World Wide Web Consortium (Massachusetts Institute of Technology, European Research Consortium for Informatics and Mathematics, Keio University). All rights reserved. www.w3.org/Consortium/ Legal/2002/copyright-documents-20021231.

The Risk of Implied Endorsement

One clear ethical predisposition emerging online is that linking carries an underlying implication of a relationship with or tacit endorsement of the site or information linked to. Many journalists therefore regard linking as a compromise of their and their newsrooms' independence. Journalists are especially reluctant to link to possibly objectionable sites unless the link is necessary and truly benefits readers.

"We should think of links like we think of a disturbing photograph. If it's gratuitous, you don't use it. If it's vital to the understanding of a story, you do," says Will Tracy, former managing editor of the *New York Times* Web site. "Some practitioners, utilizing the television model, provide warnings that alert users when a link will take them to potentially objectionable sites. Some routinely provide disclaimers that information on external Web sites is not endorsed by the online news site."[13]

Digital Dilemmas author Berkman also reads the issue in the context of traditional media. "I'd say that each case is different," says Berkman. "The decision to include a link to a site that contains offensive, graphic, or other problematic content will depend on the newsroom's own policies and standards on what they would and would not permit in their own paper." Editors and reporters need to discuss honestly and thoroughly which links are compatible with the role and mission of the news organization. "In general, I would lean to not linking to a site that includes anything (including, say, naming of rape victims) that the paper would not put in its own paper that would violate its own standards," Berkman says. "A news organization is still a filter, and just because something is 'out there' and accessible, I don't buy the well, then 'anything goes' type argument."[14]

The decision becomes especially troublesome when a story sparks substantial worldwide interest but also is gruesomely graphic, such as the beheading of an American hostage in Iraq. Most U.S. news organizations report on these events but do not link to sites where beheading videos are available or even provide the URLs of those sites. Some, such as Foxnews .com in the case of Nicholas Berg in 2004, allow viewers to link to edited video on their own site. But one South African broadcasting corporation did link to the beheading video of American hostage Eugene Armstrong in October 2004. Matthew Buckland, editor of South Africa's *Mail & Guardian Online,* defends the practice. Buckland says if a site has warnings for sensitive viewers, such a video can be acceptable because "it is newsworthy and brings home the horror and chaos on the ground in Iraq, contrary to what many politicians are saying." Buckland's argument is that on the Web, users can make a conscious choice of what to view "by actively clicking on the link we provide to the video stream."[15]

The publisher of an alternative Boston newspaper, the *Boston Phoenix,* also defends linking to execution videos. In 2002, the newspaper's Web site linked to the video of the beheading of *Wall Street Journal* reporter Daniel Pearl. "The general public goes to films that are far more gory, and for no purpose other than to affect emotions," publisher Stephen Mindich says. "This is the real world, an enormously important event; the picture speaks a thousand words."[16]

Poynter's Colón said that given the amount of reporting and information available on the Pearl case, he is "challenged by the idea that linkage to that event was really needed. There are new and emerging technologies that raise new environments and issues and opportunities that didn't exist before," he said. "That doesn't mean ethics don't apply. It means you have to enlarge the way you think of those things. The ethics aren't different. The circumstances are."[17]

The difference between what a news organization prints or airs and what it links to from its Web site is that readers and viewers have little choice over whether they see newspaper pictures or videos. Providing links to graphic material, however, requires online users to make an active choice and to physically enact that choice by clicking—an important difference. News organizations should still consider whether graphic material is gratuitous or newsworthy and should provide a warning. But if the material advances the readers' understanding of the story, leaving the choice to the user seems to embody what the Web is all about.

Economic Justifications

Yet most major news organizations link very little if at all to outside sites. That seems to be the case even when other sites offer valuable information some users may want to see directly and even when those sites are not direct competitors. Common examples are health stories based on medical studies in research journals, government policy stories that cite think tanks, and pop culture stories that cite fanzines, independent music sites, and grassroots video sites, such as YouTube.com. The reluctance is tied to the conventional wisdom that keeping users on the news organization's own site is the way to economic viability.

Bill Grueskin, managing editor of WSJ.com, the *Wall Street Journal*'s Web site, says the perception has been "that if people leave our site then they'll never come back." But he notes that WSJ.com, which is a paid subscription site, has a loyal readership: "So if they go to ESPN.com, it's not like they're not going to come back." He also says that WSJ's links are not an endorsement of the accuracy of a story: "We leave it to the readers to make up their own mind whether it's valid or not."[18]

Adrian Holovaty, an Internet developer and now editor of editorial innovations at Washingtonpost.Newsweek Interactive, says that restricting links to outside sites sells a news site short.

> I think it's more than a question of news judgment; it's also a question of business rules. Some site managers see outside links as a threat, and they make the business decision not to include them, or at least to limit their use. . . . It's a classic example of *not* embracing the Web.
>
> The way I see it, editors who are afraid of linking to other sites clearly don't trust the value of their content. If an editor is really proud of his or her site, why on earth would he or she worry about users clicking away to other sites? Wouldn't it make sense that a well-done site would be visited regularly by people who are interested in its contents? Where's the trust? Where's the professional pride?[19]

Ironically, a news site that eschews links to external content may be "plastered with distracting advertisements that are clickable and do take users away to other sites," says Mindy McAdams, holder of the Knight Chair in Journalism at the University of Florida and author of *Flash Journalism*.[20] But that may be changing. In August 2006, the *Washington Post* announced that it had contracted with the news aggregator Inform.com, which scans news and blog sites and then delivers article-related links to clients. The links then appear either in the text of a story or in a sidebar box. Clicking on a link opens a new window in the user's browser, but leaves the original site page up as well. The agreement was prompted not by cooperation across the industry but as a counterattack against Google and Yahoo, whose search engines and aggregation services have enticed readers and advertisers away from newspapers in recent years, according to a story in the *New York Times,* which said it will not join the move to Inform. "These deals with Inform are but one indication that newspapers may be reconsidering long-held beliefs about how to compete, and cooperate, with other publishers," the *Times* article said. [21]

Yet the *Washington Post* planned at first to link only to related stories from other Washingtonpost.Newsweek Interactive sites, such as Slate.com, Newsweek.com, and BudgetTravelOnline.com. It planned eventually to include links to stories from sites not affiliated with the *Post,* Caroline H. Little, chief executive and publisher of the online division of the *Washington Post,* told the *Times.* "Five years ago, everybody said you have to keep readers on your site, with no links out to other sites," Little said. "But ultimately, people will go where they want to go."[22]

"We think it's the right thing to do," said Jim Brady, the executive editor of WashingtonPost.com. "It seems limiting to tell people about something another news organization has reported and not point them to it. It goes against the Web's DNA."[23]

The need for broader definitions of journalistic principles to apply to such online practices has been recognized by the American Society of Newspaper Editors, which created a revised set of core values. Linking is included under the topic of balance, broadened to the category: "Balance/ fairness/wholeness: Hypertext links to more information can guarantee thorough reporting." The posting asked editors to consider:

- When should we link to ads, to editorials or columns, to sites of partisan organizations, hate groups, charities seeking contributions, other news media?
- What should we do about readers leaving a report (via links) before they read all sides?
- Since we can, when should we use all the photos and words from the scene? [24]

Case Study: Linking to YouTube.com

(Some of the elements of this hypothetical case are based on similar real events.)

You are an online reporter at a major TV news organization and have been told that a group of white border patrol policemen beat several Mexicans without provocation as they approached the U.S.-Mexican border. The news tip came from a friend who had seen the beatings on YouTube.com. You watch the video and then call the border patrol. An officer tells you that there was an "incident" at the border town named in the video and that the border patrol is still investigating.

Convinced the video is not a hoax, you do some further investigating and write a story. But because the details of the beatings are available only on the video, you and your editors have to decide how to handle that part of the story. Users' understanding of the story would no doubt be advanced by their seeing the video for themselves. General company policy is to avoid linking to outside sites, but since this is an unusual case, you have some leeway in considering your options.

- Should you provide a link from your story to the YouTube site so users can see the extent and nature of the beatings themselves?
- Instead of directly linking, should you provide the URL to the YouTube video page?
- Should you just report that a video is available on the YouTube site and let users search the site for themselves?
- Should you copy the video, put it on your own site, and provide an internal link?
- Would your decision be any different if you now learned that the independent reporter/videographer who shot the footage is going to sue YouTube for copyright infringement because someone copied the video and posted it without his knowledge? When you talk to YouTube, you learn that the site is going to remove the video by the end of the day. What is your decision now?

Notes

1. Linda Lawson, *Truth in Publishing: Federal Regulation of the Press's Business Practices, 1880–1920* (Carbondale: Southern Illinois University Press, 1993), reviewed in *Newspaper Research Journal,* Fall 1994, by Stephen Vaughn and cited by Steven Klein, "Forbes.com Isn't Trying Anything New," PoynterOnline, August 10, 2004, www.poynter.org/content/content_view.asp?id=69632.

2. John Giuffo, "Ad-monishment at Forbes.com: A Newsroom Says No to a Dodgy New Ad Scheme," *Columbia Journalism Review,* January/February 2005, www.cjr.org/issues/2005/2/onthejob-giuffo.asp.

3. Ibid.

4. Ibid.

5. Nat Ives, "Ads Embedded in Online News Raise Questions," *New York Times,* February 24, 2005, www.nytimes.com/2005/02/24/business/media/24post.html?ex=1267160400&en=4418aad7a972216d&ei=5088&partner=rssnyt.

6. Ibid.

7. Nat Ives, "Marketing Entwined with Journalism on Forbes.com," August 3, 2004, www.nytimes.com/2004/08/03/business/media/03adco.html.

8. Klein, "Forbes.com Isn't Trying Anything New."

9. Robert L. Berkman, Dialogues: Online Journalism Ethics, October 2004, http://jethicsdialogues.blogspot.com.

10. "SPJ Calls on News Media to Maintain Clear Separation of News and Advertising," SPJ.org, November 10, 2003, www.spj.org/news.asp?ref=351.

11. Online News Association, "About ONA," June 20, 2004, http://journalist.org/about/archives/000012.php.

12. Tim Berners-Lee, "Links and Law: Myths About Links," April 1997, www.w3.org/DesignIssues/LinkMyths.html.

13. Bonnie Bressers, "Ethical Considerations of the Web Link," April 30, 2003, www.asne.org/index.cfm?ID=4645.

14. Berkman, Dialogues.

15. Steve Outing, "Is Linking to Beheading Video OK on Web, Not TV?" October 14, 2004, www.poynter.org/content/content_view.asp?id=72830.

16. Ron DePasqulae, "Boston Phoenix Runs Pearl Execution Photos; Weekly Defends Decision to Run Video Online," *Editor & Publisher,* June 12, 2006.

17. Bressers, "Ethical Considerations."

18. Mark Glaser, "Open Season: News Sites Add Outside Links, Free Content," *Online Journalism Review,* October 19, 2004, www.ojr.org/ojr/glaser/1098225187.php.

19. Adrian Holovaty, OJR Interview Transcript: Linking Policies, holovaty.com, September 16, 2003, www.holovaty.com/blog/archive/2003/09/16/2101/?highlight=linking%2520AND%2520interview%2520transcript.

20. Mindy McAdams, Dialogues: Online Journalism Ethics, October 2004, http://jethicsdialogues.blogspot.com.

21. Bob Tedeschi, "Newspapers to Use Links to Rivals on Web Sites," *New York Times,* July 31, 2006, www.nytimes.com/2006/07/31/technology/31ecom.html?ex=1311998400&en=5af81a57cf62ddf3&ci=5088&partner=rssnyt&emc=rss.

22. Ibid.

23. Ibid.

24. Joann Byrd, "Online Journalism Ethics: A New Frontier," American Society of Newspaper Editors, March 22, 1996, updated March 23, 1997, www.asne.org/kiosk/editor/november/byrd.htm.

8

Cross-Platform Journalism, Partnering, and Cross-Ownership

Jane B. Singer

By 2006, news organizations in about seventy-five U.S. markets were engaged in what the American Press Institute describes as some form of "convergence activity."[1] Such activities range from newspaper and television journalists in partnered organizations cross-promoting each other's stories to reporters producing content for print, on-air, and online distribution. In general, such cross-platform journalism or "convergence" refers to a combination of news staffs, technologies, products, or geography from previously distinct print, television, and online media.[2]

The overarching ethical issue related to cross-platform journalism is whether it enhances or detracts from the journalist's commitment to public service. If the purpose of journalism is to provide citizens with the information they need to be free and self-governing,[3] then an ethical approach to convergence must consider whether combining resources helps journalists fulfill that responsibility. Is the public better served by converged or partnered news organizations, which can provide more comprehensive and multifaceted coverage of important stories, or do such arrangements mainly curtail the number of voices a community hears? This chapter starts by exploring both arguments.

For individual journalists in converged organizations, overcoming ingrained newsroom cultures can be difficult. Though all journalists share broad ethical principles, they can and do vary in the way they put those principles into practice. Typically, journalists identify with both their profession and the specific media outlet for which they work; for instance, research indicates that a newspaper serves as the vehicle for an individual's expression of professional beliefs, particularly during times of restructuring or management change.[4] Restructured newsrooms seeking cross-platform content ask journalists to loosen allegiance to their organization in favor of a stronger allegiance to the more broadly defined profession of journalism. Ethical issues can quickly become apparent, including the following:

- Translation of ethical standards across media platforms. Print journalists tend to cover different sorts of stories in different ways than their television counterparts. What happens when news judgment and professional approaches to a story conflict?
- Stress created by "us" and "them" culture clashes. When the "blow-dried airheads" have to cooperate with the "arrogant slobs," things can get ugly.

In addition to challenging beliefs, values, and approaches to news, management-driven partnerships also push journalists toward new roles oriented toward product branding and marketing. For example:

- In many converged operations, newspaper journalists are asked to provide "talkbacks" for the television news program, meaning they appear on air to discuss a story they are covering—turning print reporters into news sources for the viewing audience.
- Cross-platform promotions, most commonly the use of time within a newscast to encourage viewers to read the next day's newspaper for details about a particular story, take up valuable air time—turning TV reporters or anchors into salespeople for the partnered newspaper.

Finally, convergence poses issues related to an organization's ethical obligations to the journalists who work for it. In most converged news organizations, journalists' salaries have not substantially increased—if they have increased at all—to accommodate increased job expectations. Nor, in most cases, have their responsibilities to their primary employer lessened. Throughout most of this book, we have talked about ethics in relation to the journalist's professional roles and his or her responsibilities to the public. But what ethical responsibilities do employers owe to journalists, and how might managers carry out those responsibilities? What are the consequences of asking journalists to simply make it "part of the job" to provide content for multiple media outlets?

Much of the information, including many of the quotes, in this chapter comes from research in converged newsrooms by one of the authors of this book in 2003. Because she promised the journalists in her study confidentiality, no names are used with those quotes.

Public Service

A few years ago, Robert Haiman, president emeritus of the prestigious Poynter Institute, published a stinging critique of convergence on the institute's Web site, warning that while convergence might be good for media companies, it would necessarily undermine the public service mission of the journalists who work for those companies. "Even if it goes as well as it possibly can," he said, "I believe that it is going to distract journalists, journalism teachers, and journalism students away from that single most important imperative of the craft—to create an informed society capable of intelligently governing itself. And if it does not go well, I fear it is going to subject journalists to time, resource, craft, and ethical pressures, all of which will be bad for journalists, bad for journalism, and bad for the country."[5] The evolution of convergence has largely been a debate over whether Haiman was right.

A common rationale offered by media managers for converging their news operations has been the ability to explore new ways to tell stories and to facilitate communication with and among audiences.[6] Newsroom supporters say the combination of print, on-air, and online formats allows them to provide a "360 perspective on a story" that any one medium alone can never match, providing the public with news in multiple, complementary ways tailored to each media format. For example, an exploration of safety hazards faced by American workers won a Pulitzer Prize for Public Service in 2004. Although the prize officially went to *The New York Times,* the newspaper's stories were complemented by Canadian Broadcasting Corporation and PBS *Frontline* pieces timed to air in conjunction with the print stories, as well as by extensive companion Web sites from all three news organizations.[7]

Critics, however, say the impetus for partnerships and cross-platform journalism has been economic—the tantalizing prospect that converging news operations ultimately will allow organizations to do more with fewer people—and that the inevitable result is a decline in the number of voices providing information to a community, both within and across media outlets.

The concern that convergence is yet another step toward media mo-

---

Exhibit 8.1
The Power of Convergence

Carole Tarrant talks about how the Forum, *the 51,000-circulation daily in Fargo, North Dakota, used multimedia to tell an important community story. Tarrant, who is now managing editor at the* Roanoke Times *in Virginia, was the managing editor at the* Forum, *whose parent, Forum Communications Co., owns a TV and radio station in the market. Its affiliated Web site, www.in-forum.com, has received national awards from the Associated Press Managing Editors and Newspaper Association of America. Tarrant's comments come from a 2004 Web site discussion associated with the book.*

The multimedia approach, when used for the common good, can be incredibly powerful. Instead of just the newspaper calling attention to a public ill, TV can join in, radio can add another layer, then online can bring them together with the interactive element allowing readers to comment on the issue. Our 2002 series on population loss in North Dakota—a very public service issue—greatly benefitted from this approach. Our megaphone was that much louder. The important wording here, however, is "public service role." The power of convergence is such that it should be used carefully. In the wrong hands. . . .

---

nopoly and thus toward an economically motivated homogenization of information comes largely from outside observers. Much of it has focused on corporate and technological convergence, which together work to eliminate traditional distinctions between media (including news) and communications sectors.[8] Giant conglomerates control both the content and the means of distributing it—think of the enormous family of products and services owned by Time Warner, for instance, or the News Corporation—and such concentration of power over information is widely seen as inherently dangerous and antidemocratic.

But convergence within the newsroom also has drawn its share of critics on public service grounds. One key concern is the potential for fewer journalists to be hired and thus fewer reporters to perform watchdog and other democratic roles.[9] Another has been that when managers ask journalists to do multiple tasks, including some for which they have little or no expertise, the result will be a mediocre product[10] that fails to meet its public service obligations. In particular, detailed investigative reporting and sustained critical coverage of public affairs potentially could suffer in a converged environment that values speed, quantity, and content adaptability; major spectacles and planned events yield the kinds of formulaic stories most easily incorporated in a variety of media formats.[11]

Among the more than one hundred journalists interviewed by Jane Singer in 2003, however, most discounted the idea that competition had been reduced in the current media environment, by convergence or any other factor. "That was the great mantra of all this: 'Oh, consumers will be short-changed.' I think that's something for ivory-tower critics to say, but it hasn't panned out," said a veteran television reporter in one converged newsroom. Moreover, both news executives and newsroom staffers point out, their audience already has "converged." People now get information from multiple sources throughout the day rather than relying on the morning newspaper or the evening newscast for a single daily dose of news.

Nor does the evidence seem to suggest that producing content across media platforms has reduced newsroom staff size. News organizations went through rounds of layoffs and hiring freezes earlier in the 2000s, and while convergence does offer one potentially appealing way to do more with less, it has not brought further staff cuts. On the contrary, an increase in news personnel, particularly among the online staff, has marked many partnership efforts. "I can't find one of these that is a bottom-line success—whether it's in ratings, circulation, or revenue—that hasn't added staff," says the Poynter Institute's Al Tompkins. "Those that do it on the cheap, those that do it with a thin staff, ultimately will find that they're not successful."[12]

But journalists do have other concerns related to public service in a market served by news partnerships. One is that there is one less competitor for local news and a corresponding decrease in the impetus to hustle to get a story no one else has. Particularly in smaller markets, a single reporter may now do the courthouse or police blotter checks that used to be done separately by both television and print journalists, each hoping to scoop the other. The loss of the competitive edge diminishes the possibility of finding a story that may lie below the smooth surface provided by official sources.

A related concern is that cross-platform journalism decreases the time available for good reporting—for investigating a story thoroughly, learning the background about an issue or process, or simply nosing around a beat in search of interesting tidbits of information that no sources are volunteering. Generating content for more than one medium simply takes time, which is always a limited resource. "The more TV stuff I do, the less time I have for the kinds of things that don't go into the story but get you there, like walking around City Hall," said one reporter, who cited a memo on a cubicle wall about an unofficial hiring chill as an important story he got by just cruising around. Although he may still get the same number of stories, he added, their quality is affected by the need to allow time for generating content for online and on-air partners. "If I have to just go to meetings," he said, "I'm trapped."

Although cross-platform journalism is a relatively new newsroom phenomenon, early evidence suggests clear value in using the power of distinct media forms—print, television, and online—to bring important stories to the public's attention. Not only does conveying a story through multiple platforms increase its exposure to different audiences, but it also provides an opportunity to convey different aspects of the story in ways ideally suited to each format, with words, still and moving images, sound, background, documentation, and supporting links. However, few if any media organizations are likely to commit the resources needed to plan and produce that "360 perspective" on every story; they are far more apt to throw everything they have at the big investigative pieces that already were examples of what journalism does best.

Public service problems related to convergence stem from the more routine stories that constitute most media coverage. These are harder to see. Some are invisible because they are too big: for example, the global machinations of vast corporate entities whose real effects can be difficult to recognize as they play out in your hometown. Others are invisible because they are too small; they affect decisions made by individual journalists and often involve things that do not happen rather than those that do. A journalist with less time and less incentive to dig for information simply does less digging; she interviews the readily available source or chooses to do the quick and easy story rather than the difficult and time-consuming one. The public may never know what voices went unheard and what stories went untold.

Culture Clashes

Under the umbrella norm of public service are a variety of concrete ethical issues related to the ways that journalists make news. Convergence

Exhibit 8.2
Conversing About Convergence

Mark Deuze is a former Dutch newspaper and online journalist. A Fulbright Scholar with a PhD from the University of Amsterdam and a widely published expert on online journalism, Deuze currently is an assistant professor at Indiana University and associate editor of the journal Convergence: The International Journal of Research into New Media Technologies. *Here are his thoughts on the ethics of convergence, in response to questions posed by the authors in an e-mail in February 2005.*

Q: Where are the ethical pressure points when journalists are asked to do multiple tasks, and which are most significant?

A: Convergence should be broadly understood as the integration of telecommunications, computing, and (news) media. This also means the various ways in which people use these technologies—such as the mobile phone, the desktop computer, and the television—converge. For journalists, this means that performing multiple tasks includes understanding and dealing with different expectations of people using multimedia. This in turn creates ethical dilemmas. The newspaper is hardly interactive and requires a story be told in as coherent and linear a way as possible to an interested audience. Put this story on television, and the audience tends to be more passive, expecting the images to do most of the interpretation of the news. Online people don't want to be audiences anymore—they want to talk back. The ethical pressure points will have to do with establishing a delicate balance between finding your own voice as a journalist and engaging with active users in their dialogue.

Q: Some observers have criticized convergence on the grounds that it reduces the number of voices providing information in a community; others dismiss this concern, pointing to the media explosion in recent years, including cable and Internet outlets. Many journalists say that the ability to tell an important story to more people, particularly when it can be told in different but complementary ways, actually enhances their public service role. What are your views about the impact of convergence on the news that reaches the public?

A: If convergence means distributing the same story across different media, journalists never have to rethink who they are and why they do

(continued)

Exhibit 8.2 *(continued)*

what they do. Only if you understand the different characteristics of the different media and try to analyze what happens if these converge will you be able to harness the additional possibilities this brings for new kinds of storytelling. Most importantly, journalistic storytelling in a multimedia environment may not be about gathering and distributing news at all—it may just be about managing and editing communication and information flows of others, such as publics, other journalists, news sources, agencies, and so on. The shift in journalism from writing to editing will prove to be the biggest ethical challenge.

Q: Television, print, and online newsrooms each have their own "culture," tied to the nature of the content that each produces. What ethical issues are raised when journalists work across cultures different from the one they are most comfortable in? How can these issues be resolved?

A: No culture is always the same, nor is it immutable. Culture means learned behavior. This also means certain ways of doing things can be unlearned. Convergence, when pushed from above (board of directors, management), will not have its intended effects. Convergence supported from below (the newsroom and the audience) has more chance of succeeding, while maintaining ethical safeguards and standards that are necessary for editorial autonomy.

Experiences and research of news organizations engaged in convergence consistently suggest the culture of different journalisms (print vs. broadcast, online vs. offline, hard vs. soft news) or even the "nature" of journalists (as rather egocentric individuals) as the No. 1 issue determining success or failure. On the other hand, research on codes of journalism ethics points out the similarities in such codes around the world . . . the same notions of objectivity and public service. Perhaps we should develop a code of ethics in convergence journalism as a tool to guide newsrooms as they move towards collaboration and integration?

Q: Journalists in many converged newsrooms are being asked to serve as sources for other media partners; newspaper journalists, for instance, are being interviewed on television about issues on their beats, or are fielding questions from online users in Web-based chats. What are the ethical issues when a journalist becomes an "expert"? Is this any differ-

(continued)

Exhibit 8.2 *(continued)*

ent in a converged environment than it is in a decades-old cable news environment in which journalists frequently appear as commentators on talk or news shows?

A: Journalists talking with journalists about the news—and thus "making" the news—is indeed an old phenomenon, although in recent years journalists increasingly have become sources of their own news. There is a fine line between using a reporter because of her expertise and using a journalist from your own organization in order to cut corners and save time. Ultimately, the top expert about any news story can never be the journalist, as she is supposed to observe, select, edit and present the expertise of those directly involved in the news.

Q: In many converged operations, one visible change has been an increase in cross-promotion of stories among outlets; for instance, newscasters will urge viewers to pick up tomorrow's paper for more information, or print reporters will advise readers to check the Web site for additional details. Is such cross-promotion appropriate? Does it present any ethical issues?

A: Cross-promotion is an intelligent marketing strategy for converged news operations, and as such is appropriate. Its practice does create ethical issues regarding the increasing so-called "intertextuality" of the news media. This means that news organizations increasingly rely on each other to determine what is news as they feed off each other's scoops and leads. What is on the evening news will be a lead story in the next day's paper even if these media are not part of the same company, as editors everywhere are afraid to miss out on "the big story." It makes good sense if this practice results in giving the public added value every time they access the story—regardless of medium. But if audiences basically get the same story over and over again, this practice will contribute to the public disconnecting from news altogether.

Q: In most converged news organizations, journalists' salaries have not been substantially increased—if they have been increased at all—to accommodate increased job expectations. Nor, in many cases, have their responsibilities to their primary employer been lessened. What ethical

(continued)

Exhibit 8.2 *(continued)*

responsibilities do employers owe to journalists? What consequences are there of asking journalists to simply make it "part of the job" to provide content to multiple media outlets?

A: Ultimately, convergence in media organizations is carried by individual media professionals. If they are overworked, frustrated, underpaid, stressed out and still expected to do more without additional rewards or benefits, the quality of the news suffers. If the quality goes down, the public will look somewhere else for its news. Exploitation of media professionals goes on everywhere, but is ultimately self-defeating. This is an important argument to be used by reporters and editors when faced with increasing top-down pressure to do more with fewer people or resources. Journalism organizations, unions, and other media interest groups should include such concerns in their charters and policies.

asks journalists from different media organizations to cooperate in that news-production process, and challenges relate to work routines, information gathering, storytelling methods, and other aspects of the journalist's job. The culture of a newsroom socializes journalists who work there to conform to accepted work practices and provides them with defenses to withstand pressure for change.[13] Numerous accounts of partnership efforts document the strength of those defenses, making culture clashes the "toughest hurdle" in the minds of many managers trying to get staffers to accept convergence.[14]

Those tensions create ethical conflicts, as well. Reports from converged newsrooms suggest that although most journalists subscribe to similar norms—and one effect of cross-platform journalism has been a realization that ethical standards are shared across media—journalists do tend to see convergence partners as comparatively less diligent than themselves about upholding those norms. Particularly in small markets, where online staffs are likely to be tiny and television staffs inexperienced, veteran journalists express concern about mistakes creeping into news coverage, reflecting negatively on all the partners. In general, convergence confirms for many journalists the existence of considerable variation in both news judgment and professional approaches to a story.

One example involves the relative importance given to different types of stories. Crime, accident, and fire stories with strong visual elements typically get better play on television than in print, for example; in large markets, the newspaper might not run them at all. The partnered Web site also may display such stories prominently because their "breaking news" qualities play to the medium's strength in up-to-the-minute timeliness. Indeed, the demand for high traffic numbers can put considerable pressure on journalists creating content for the Web, whose users gravitate toward crime and "anything to do with sex," in the words of an online editor.

In addition, the Web's constant demand for fresh information can create ethical pressures that are less urgent for television journalists with three daily newscasts to worry about and less urgent still for print journalists with one deadline a day. Increasingly, both print and television journalists are expected to feed whatever they know to online staffers as soon as it is available, directly from the scene if possible. The emerging online philosophy of "get it up and fix it later" makes many journalists in the traditional media uneasy, although the basic idea has served high-quality wire services such as the Associated Press well for a long time. Also troubling and ethically dubious is the practice, reported in a number of converged newsrooms, of online staffers using morning news budgets or story rundowns—lists of anticipated stories that commonly are shared electronically among media partners—as the basis for brief online items. As anyone who has worked in a newsroom knows, those in-house budgets are more often wish lists than reliable accounts of verified information, and publishing anything they contain is a recipe for egg on the faces of all involved.

Journalists in converged environments also see a real or potential clash between news values, which journalists define as providing what they believe the public needs, and entertainment values that cater to what they see as baser interests. Although all commercial media must attract and keep an audience, that concern is part of the reality of daily news work to varying degrees. Newspaper journalists are not under constant pressure from circulation numbers in the way that television journalists are from ratings and online journalists from usage reports. Some journalists are concerned that entertainment values will become more dominant throughout a converged operation than they might be otherwise, leading to a trend toward "sensationalized" content for all the partnered outlets.

In addition to concerns about the kinds of stories that might be covered, print journalists are worried that they as individuals will become a bigger part of their own stories than in the past, drawn into the "cult of personality" that they see as dominating television journalism. They express concern that how they look, the way they speak, and what they wear (and the number of wrinkles in both their clothes and their faces) will become considerations in reporting the news. They worry about having to do the sorts of promotional ads for the newspaper that television journalists have to do for their newscast. "When we see that and it's part of their world, that's why we don't get it," one newspaper reporter said. "We're here because we don't want to be that. Then the corporate masters come down and say 'Think about that'." Ultimately, many print journalists continue to denigrate their on-air counterparts as little more than pretty faces. In the words of another newspaper reporter, television is simple: "Thirty seconds, look good, have pearly whites."

Television and Web journalists have their own concerns about their print colleagues' way of doing news. In particular, they are impatient with how long it takes to grind out a newspaper story. From their perspective, print journalists have no proper sense of urgency; information gathered in the morning can be digested slowly with lunch, followed by a leisurely afternoon of gearing up to sit down and, eventually, write. By then, they say, the story is no longer even news, and the journalist's commitment to keeping audiences informed has been undermined. Online journalists (and users), in particular, have little tolerance for the same day-old information as the morning paper contains. What is the point of having more reporters gathering news, a key benefit of convergence for short-staffed online and television news operations, if reporters do not share what they know when they know it?

Many newspaper journalists, needless to say, believe the time they spend makes their stories better. The time, at least in theory, allows them to make the extra phone call, run the story by one more source, and reflect on what the story is about. "One reason that newspapers are thought of as being more complete, balanced, and thoughtful is that we have time to think about a story," said a veteran editor. Still, some say that the "infectious urgency" of their colleagues has been energizing. Others describe their affiliated Web site, in particular, as a "beautiful thing" because of the timely news service that it provides. Traffic logs and audience research provide evidence that people are turning to their local media—in whatever permutation best suits their immediate needs—for credible information. That may be the Web site for traffic conditions after an afternoon accident, the TV newscast for reactions from the scene, and the newspaper for a consideration of what the city is doing about its hazardous intersections. As we will see in the next section, many journalists as well as their editors and managers see such cross-media "branding" opportunities as a key benefit of convergence.

However, disagreements over issues such as how fast information should be provided and the importance of personal appearance for journalists highlight one of the biggest obstacles to effective partnerships: the persistence of an "us" and "them" attitude within each newsroom. In fact, many journalists seem to be resisting the change as long as they can; they continue to see cross-media colleagues as sufficiently unlike themselves to constitute a different "species" of journalist with whom they are not likely to produce viable offspring—good stories. In addition to the misgivings already discussed, many journalists continue to feel possessive about "their" stories and unwilling to share with people whom they have long regarded as competitors. Especially rankling to online and television journalists are requests for embargoes so the once-a-day newspaper can break a story first. Instead of concentrating on which medium can tell a story best, annoyed managers say, the issue becomes which outlet the story "belongs" to. In fact, they argue, the story belongs to the public, not the journalist, and the journalist's obligation should be to convey that story to the public as soon as it is ready to tell.

In reality, observers have noted that most converged operations remain exercises in just this sort of "coopetition," in which journalists share information, with varying degrees of reluctance, on some stories but also continue to compete for news.[15] True convergence, in which content is planned and shared throughout the news cycle, has remained elusive. "Many of the convergence situations have gotten stuck at coopetition," said researcher Larry Dailey of Ball State University. Journalists "don't know how much to compete and how much to cooperate. From there, you start sharing content but not really integrating the other into your organization. 'True convergence' is where you share from the planning process. 'What's Web gonna do that's gonna be best on the Web, what's print gonna do, what's TV gonna do, and how are we gonna market it all together to make something new out of it?' We call this true convergence, or hugging and singing 'Kumbaya.'"[16]

But if nirvana remains out of reach, there is evidence that cross-platform journalism has had at least one perhaps unexpectedly beneficial consequence with ethical implications beyond the concrete professional norms considered so far: Many journalists have gained respect for each other and have discovered that they actually enjoy working with people with different professional strengths. "I've learned quite a bit and have had my opinions changed and have had some of the print-side arrogance knocked out of me," one newspaper editor confessed.[17] An anecdote from Sarasota, Florida, sums up both the fears and their ongoing resolution. In 1995, when the *Herald Journal* began its pioneering convergence experiments with the local cable news channel, a popular columnist wrote a piece titled "Klingons Coming." In it, he compared himself to *Star Trek*'s Captain Kirk, suddenly ordered to make peace with aliens who will be, among other things, "elbowing us out of the way to do their makeup at our restroom mirrors." Even worse, "We are supposed to become them! Well, it will never happen to me," he concluded. But in retrospect, he said nearly a decade later, things turned out pretty much the way they did on *Star Trek:* The Klingons became friends and allies, radically different styles and all.[18]

Branding and Cross-Promotion

As we have seen, convergence compels journalists to reconsider the way they do their existing jobs, raising ethical issues in the process. In addition, it introduces new demands that can push journalists toward more marketing-oriented roles. Unlike new professional expectations that stretch journalists' news-gathering or production skills—for instance, a newspaper writer having to learn the basics of videography—these new roles are intended largely to bolster the partnered organizations' brand and audience and, ultimately, its bottom line. They include the increasing use of reporters as news sources or even commentators and the increasing use of news time or space for cross-promotion.

Partnered organizations have struggled with the fact that newspaper journalists lack either the skills or the time to produce broadcast-quality television news. One solution has been to steer print people toward contributing to television newscasts through "talkbacks" and to Web sites through chats. Talkbacks typically are short, live, on-air segments in which television anchors interview print journalists about a story they are working on. Chats invite the online audience to talk about stories with newspaper reporters and columnists, touting the writers' knowledge of selected topics;[19] WashingtonPost.com, for instance, offers an assortment in its Live Online section each day.

Talkbacks and chats position the journalist as an expert on a particular topic and thus a primary source of information about that topic. In other words, the reporter in one medium becomes the source in another. Of course, many journalists are indeed experts on their beats, and national news talk shows—from PBS's sedate *Washington Week in Review* to vitriolic cable news shoutfests—long ago made this blurring of roles commonplace. The resulting "argument culture" has drawn criticism on a variety of grounds, from its emphasis on entertainment to its penchant for polarization. Such talk shows are driven largely by the economic reality that it is much cheaper to produce a show in which people talk about news than to produce one that involves gathering and disseminating it.[20]

Before convergence, the journalist as expert source was mainly a national phenomenon. Now that role has been extended to the local news level, albeit in a relatively low-key form. The economic rationale is less about saving money (for instance, by reducing staff, a widespread but mainly unfounded fear among journalists in converged newsrooms) than about making more of it: Executives see convergence as a prime opportunity to create or extend their organization's brand as the leading information source in the community. The print partner benefits in competitive newspaper markets such as Tampa, where the *Tribune* and the *St. Petersburg Times* have been embroiled in an intense rivalry for decades. But regardless of the print environment, the television partner benefits from the not-so-subtle reminder to viewers that it has a leg up on the other local affiliates—dozens or even hundreds of legs, actually, belonging to the newspaper reporters who are now positioned as part of its news-gathering team.

Using reporters as means to a marketing end is not new; commercial media have touted their news-gathering resources, in one way or another, for a hundred years and more. And a reporter appearing on the television news show to talk about a story does provide potentially valuable information to those members of the public who will never see the newspaper. But talkbacks can put a reporter in ethically dubious situations. For instance, questions from an anchor may encourage a reporter to shift from conveying information to engaging in what one journalist calls "opinionizing." One government reporter was asked to make an on-air prediction of who he thought would win a local election. "I wasn't too happy about that!" he said. "So I declined to answer and made sure it didn't happen again." With journalistic objectivity already under fire, on-air speculation by local news reporters can add to the public perception that it is a myth.

The use of newspaper reporters to deliver updates on the newscast may not be a terribly subtle form of brand-name marketing, but the overt cross-promotion of a partner's news product is even more blatant. Using one news vehicle to pitch another is designed to drive traffic to the Web site, to encourage television viewers to buy the morning newspaper, or to get readers to tune in to the television news for live coverage. The jury is largely out on whether the efforts are working. As of the mid-2000s, only about a quarter of newspapers were actively working to boost efforts to promote their stories on-air,[21] but there was some evidence that cross-platform promotion can enhance the brands of participating news organizations. For example, research in Tampa suggests a correlation between cross-promotion and an improved public perception of the newspaper, the broadcast news outlet, and the Web site.[22]

But unlike putting a newspaper reporter on television to discuss a story, pure cross-promotion has little or no news value—and, for many television journalists in particular, a big annoyance factor at being used as an adjunct to the circulation department. "I feel like every other thing we say is 'get the newspaper,'" one cable television reporter complained. "I joke that I wait for the day when I have to take my backpack around town and sell papers." Another television reporter in the same market said such cross-promotions were insulting to the public. "I think, 'Gee whiz, if you've got the facts, give them to me now, don't tell me to go pick up a paper tomorrow. Have you withheld information, telling me to go out and spend money?'" In addition, promotions obviously take up time and space that could be used for conveying news. "My responsibility should be to my story and not to furthering corporate goals" to promote a product, one newspaper reporter in a larger market said.

Moreover, cross-promotion can backfire as a public relations tool if it serves to remind the public that the media products they think of as separate entities actually are interconnected. Executives in converged markets say they are sensitive to this issue—or at least to public perception of it. Former *Tampa Tribune* president and publisher Gil Thelen says market research indicated

> there was not a concern among citizens that there was any diminution of citizens' voices, of sources, diversity of news, and viewpoints. We were very concerned about this going in, and I think it's important that everybody pays attention. In a time of almost corrosive skepticism about the intentions and performance of the news media, we have to safeguard the multiple strings of information and diversity. Our critics, I think, were

right early on to say that this could degenerate into simply a huge cross-advertising campaign for the separate platforms. And I think it's very important to be sure that when we are referring customers to one another, it's for specific content and not simply for brand building.[23]

Journalists working in partnered newsrooms are not so sure. Some, particularly among the newspaper staffers, like having their stories plugged and see clear benefits to creating a brand image as the top news provider in a market. In particular, many approvingly regard the affiliated Web site primarily as a key branding tool for the traditional media partners, rather than as a viable news medium in its own right. Others, however, are disturbed by the implications of a new way to blur lines between commercial and editorial missions. "I really don't care about the business principles. I don't think journalists ought to care" about them, a television anchor said. "If there's a collision between standards of journalism and [convergence], I think they should err on the side of journalism. Journalism comes first."

Finally, convergence raises ethical concerns along more traditional "church and state" lines related to what one editor called the "smushed-together" relationship of advertising and editorial content, particularly on sponsored Web sites and television programs. However, direct advertising influence on editorial content seems to be a potential problem rather than a real one in many partnered operations. For example, a newspaper reporter whose once-a-week television piece is sponsored said that while the arrangement gave him an uncomfortable "journalistic hair-on-the-back-of-the-neck feeling," the sponsor had never actually sought to influence his story. Uneasiness about affiliated Web sites, however, is substantiated by working arrangements in some markets where, in the words of one print journalist, "their charge is, above all else, make money." In another market, editorial and advertising staffers work side by side; in a third, online news staffers work on classified ads, and advertising staffers have a say in overall site design. Even in markets where the line between news and advertising is seen as inviolable, Web staffers are explicitly reminded that "there is no paycheck fairy," an online manager said—money to support the enterprise has to come from somewhere.[24]

Employer Ethics

Finally, convergence brings to the fore the issue of what ethical obligations an employer has to an employee. Journalists in some converged newsrooms now are expected to contribute to more than one medium, including those in which they have little or no training or experience. And although there are a great many permutations, reports from the field suggest that, in general, journalists' salaries have not increased along with the increase in their duties. More commonly, news managers have reconfigured job descriptions to include convergence activities; employees who contribute significantly to the company's convergence efforts may or may not receive bigger raises, depending on how important their bosses think those efforts are in relation to other aspects of the job. In other words, most employers have successfully positioned new convergence-related tasks as simply part of the job.

Nor have journalists, by and large, seen a decrease in responsibilities to their "parent" medium with the addition of responsibilities to its partners. Newspaper and television reporters still are expected to regularly produce the same quality and quantity of stories for print or broadcast as before. Contributing to the partnered outlets comes in addition to, not instead of, contributing to the outlet that hired them. That means more work to do and more bosses to please. Combined with a widely perceived lack of adequate training to perform new tasks, the result can be long hours and a fair share of frustration. "Leaves us feeling a bit used now and then," one reporter said. "I wish it paid something beyond skill building and experience and job security. Money would be nice."[25]

Such issues related to what employers can ask of their employees may be one reason so many convergence efforts to date have been in the South—nine of them in Florida alone as of this writing.[26] Unionized newsrooms, which are rare in the South, face challenges to convergence that others do not. "It puts an incredible amount of stress on the reporters themselves, because they're expected to serve many masters," says Newspaper Guild president Linda Foley. "It's very difficult to produce news and do stories for various media." Foley says the Guild has no problem with the concept of convergence—except when it means that individuals have to do more work for the same pay, which impinges on their rights as employees.[27]

Anthony Moor, the editor at OrlandoSentinel.com, has explicitly cited the lack of unions in Florida newsrooms for the popularity of convergence there. Moor says labor concerns slowed convergence in two markets where he previously worked, San Francisco and Rochester, New York (though both now are convergence sites). "In Orlando, we don't have unions, but we still have to be careful about what we ask our staff to do because if they don't buy in to change, it won't happen, and that's not union-specific," he says. "It's just that we don't need to do a formal union-dance at the negotiating table for every change we undertake."[28]

Ultimately, successful newsrooms are ones with healthy working relationships—those in which employers and employees trust and respect each other. Successful convergence efforts also are built on mutual trust. In Singer's studies, the most successfully converged operation was one in which the three media outlets were all locally owned, the longtime family business of a man whom employees seemed universally to like and respect. They were willing to give his goals, including cross-platform journalism, a chance to work.

In the large markets, whose media outlets are owned by large corporations, newsroom staffers are much more likely to see convergence as economically motivated—to the detriment of a commitment to strong news product serving the public interest. And having ascribed revenue enhancement as the company's primary if not sole motive, they are more likely to resist convergence as a means for achieving that goal and to distrust any management assertions that the intention is to create a stronger news product. "The company wants to make more money at no extra labor cost," said a veteran television reporter. "Bottom line: fewer reporters, less real news gathering." A newspaper reporter in another Top 20 market said that no matter how many times management denied that convergence was intended as a money-saving move, "no one believes them." Another questioned whether the public was being served at all despite management's claims about its desire to provide more and better news to more people. "I hate to use the term cost-effective, but that's pretty much what convergence is all about—robbing Peter to pay Paul," this reporter said. He described essentially a zero-sum game: the more he did for the television station, the less he did for the newspaper.

Convergence itself is neither ethical nor unethical. Everything depends on how journalists, managers, and corporate owners choose to enact it, and this chapter has outlined a range of both real and potential concerns with that process. The core of any ethical consideration is the way people treat each other—with respect for the human dignity of each individual or as the means to an end, with an eye to the common good or an eye to more self-serving goals. As the philosophers whose ideas were outlined in the introduction remind us, an ethical approach also entails responsibility, which gives such an approach value equal to or even greater than the more legalistic concept of rights. Barring explicit contract specifications, employers are within their rights to demand more of employees. But they also have ethical responsibilities to those employees, just as journalists in our democratic society have a responsibility to the public they serve that is central to whatever enterprise they undertake. If the practices fall short of the principles, both employers and employees should work to bring the two more closely in line.

Conclusion

There is a reason why we have ended this book with a chapter that considers not just online journalism but the more traditional forms of print and television, as well. It is because we agree with the many journalists who told Singer they were convinced that multiplatform storytelling is the future—for journalists, for media companies, and for the profession as a whole. We also believe the centerpiece of this ongoing change will be the Internet. The online medium is rapidly becoming home to all previously distinct forms of journalism. Print and television may continue to thrive separately, and journalists will continue to develop their expertise with particular modes of communication. But that will not preclude either journalists or their products from coming together online. As the Project for Excellence in Journalism's 2005 State of the News Media report put it, "The Web—and a converged multimedia news environment—seem more clearly than ever to be journalism's future."[29] Although the forms will coexist, the Web will provide a place where the public can and will get, in whatever format it chooses, the information it needs to be free and self-governing.

This book has offered a look at key ethical issues facing journalists in a media world increasingly dominated by an unconstrained, networked, global form of communication unlike any that has preceded it. The Internet is so fundamentally different that it raises doubts about whether journalism, increasingly beleaguered by criticism from both inside and outside the profession, even has a future. In particular, the explosion of blogs and other citizen-generated forms of all sorts of news and information, discussed primarily in Chapter 5, raises the question whether our society needs journalists at all. We believe that the answer is yes, more than ever—and that, more than ever, an understanding of ethical challenges and a commitment to meeting them are vital.

Journalists are needed precisely because information has become so ubiquitous. The world in which there is no distinction between news audiences and news producers, a world in which anyone can publish anything and instantly disseminate it globally, is indeed incredibly empowering. But an exponentially expanded number of people generating information creates an exponentially greater need for help in sorting through it all. Journalists can no longer be information gatekeepers in a world in which gates on information no longer exist. Yet the need for sense-makers has never been more urgent.[30] Gatekeeping in this world is not about keeping an item out of circulation; it is about vetting items for their veracity and placing them within the broader context that is easily lost under the daily tidal wave of "new" information. As Michael Schudson pointed out more than a decade ago, in a world in which each of us is our own journalist, calls for the abolition of journalism as a seemingly superfluous profession, as some bloggers claim it has become, would be quickly followed by calls for its reinvention.[31]

But what, exactly, will make this journalism distinguishable from the rest of what is "out there" in this limitless information space? Old definitions of journalism, mostly based on a particular process of regularly producing a product labeled "news," no longer fit when everyone can be, at the very least, a publisher. Instead, we suggest that what will distinguish journalists and secure their future is the centrality of an ethical approach to information grounded in both independence from faction and commitment to public service, an approach that values both the individual and the common good.

Media forms will continue to evolve, bringing new challenges along with the changes; this book has explored some of those challenges specific to today's online medium. Whatever the future holds, journalists will be needed as long as people feel they can trust the information that journalists provide.

Case Study: The TV Critic in a Partnered Newsroom

(This case study involves an issue facing real journalists, but the specific circumstances, as well as the names used here, are fictional.)

To Tina Warren's way of thinking, she has the most fun job in the world: She gets paid to be a couch potato.

Warner has been an entertainment writer for fifteen years. She started as a movie critic for her college paper and worked her way through a series of successively larger newsrooms to her current position as an award-winning TV reporter and critic for the *Standard*. The *Standard* is a major metropolitan newspaper with a daily circulation of more than 500,000 readers and an affiliated Web site that draws an average of 800,000 unique visitors a day.

Earlier this month, Info Inc., which owns more than 50 media outlets around the country, including the *Standard,* announced it was purchasing the local ABC affiliate, WGIN-TV. Within a week, the paper's news executives called a staff meeting, telling the assembled reporters and editors that the *Standard* and WGIN-TV were to be convergence partners, effective immediately. The announcement came as no surprise to many of the journalists, who had worked out the whole scenario over beers at their favorite bar just hours after news of Info Inc.'s purchase hit the wires.

A handful of Warren's colleagues were excited about the opportunity to be on television. Most, however, were less than enthusiastic about the increased workload in the service of what they saw as yet another corporate money-making scheme—one that would have them buddying up to competitors with pretty faces and good hair.

But Warren had a different concern. As she saw it, her job had just become impossible.

Like all TV writers, Warren wrote a lot about national entertainment programming and waded through her share of Hollywood press releases every day to do it. And she did, in fact, spend many hours each week on her couch in front of the tube. But she prided herself on her reporting abilities, and that meant writing about the local media.

It was by far her favorite part of the job, and she was good at it. She already had won several awards, including an SPJ Sigma Delta Chi award, for a series of stories about how diversity in the four local television newsrooms affected their news coverage. She also had landed on the *Standard*'s front page—and on the Web site's Weekly Top Ten hit lists—with hard-hitting pieces about crime coverage, a sexual harassment lawsuit at the top-rated station, and local tactics in the evening news ratings war.

But now the *Standard* and WGIN-TV were to be partners—a big conflict-of-interest problem no matter what she did. If she wrote critically about the station's competitors, her stories would be discredited because readers would assume that her motivation was to help WGIN. If she wrote critically about WGIN, her editors would be put in an awkward position with their own bosses—and her new colleagues would be furious. If WGIN did something good, she really could not cover that either if she wanted to maintain any credibility with her readers.

In short, she saw the best part of her job—the part she enjoyed the most and the part she thought provided the most value to her readers, who after all could get information about their favorite prime-time drama from many other sources—disappearing.

What should Warren do?

1. Make a list of her options. What would be the likely consequences of each one? Which is best?
2. Now consider this development: One of her longtime sources gives Warren an off-the-record tip: WGIN-TV is under investigation by the Federal Communications Commission for having made fraudulent claims on its license renewal application last year. What should Warren do with this information?
3. And this one: An executive producer at WGIN-TV approaches Warren with what he thinks is a brilliant idea. He wants her to do a weekly segment at the end of the 6 P.M. newscast on Sundays (always a slow news day, leaving time to fill), giving viewers her picks for prime-time programming in the coming week. She can talk about any shows she likes most of the time, but he hopes she might highlight an ABC show at least once a month . . . more would be great, of course, if she sees fit. He says he already has suggested the idea to her editor at the paper, who thinks it would provide excellent visibility for both Warren and the *Standard*'s TV section. How should Warren respond to this idea?

Acknowledgment

Some of the material in this chapter has previously appeared in these academic journals:

Jane B. Singer, "Partnerships and Public Service: Normative Issues for Journalists in Converged Newsrooms," *Journal of Mass Media Ethics* 21 (Winter 2006): 30–53.

Jane B. Singer, "More Than Ink-Stained Wretches: The Resocialization of Print Journalists in Converged Newsrooms," *Journalism & Mass Communication Quarterly* 81 (Winter 2004): 838–856.

Jane B. Singer, "Strange Bedfellows? Diffusion of Convergence in Four News Organizations," *Journalism Studies* 5 (February 2004): 3–18.

Notes

1. Media Center at the American Press Institute, "Convergence Tracker Search Page," 2006, www.mediacenter.org/convergencetracker/search/.

2. Jane B. Singer, "More Than Ink-Stained Wretches: The Resocialization of Print Journalists in Converged Newsrooms," *Journalism & Mass Communication Quarterly* 81 (Winter 2004): 838–856.

3. Bill Kovach and Tom Rosenstiel, *The Elements of Journalism: What Newspeople Should Know and the Public Should Expect* (New York: Crown, 2001).

4. Tracy Callaway Russo, "Organizational and Professional Identification: A Case of Newspaper Journalists," *Management Communication Quarterly* 12 (August 1998): 72–111.

5. Robert J. Haiman, "Can Convergence Float?" PoynterOnline, December 18, 2002, www.poynter.org/content/content_view.asp?id=14540.

6. Rich Gordon, "Convergence Defined," *Online Journalism Review,* November 13, 2003, www.ojr.org/ojr/business/1068686368.php.

7. Jonathan Dube, "Convergence Landmark: Pulitzer Prize," CyberJournalist.net, April 5, 2004, www.cyberjournalist.net/news/001144.php.

8. Robert W. McChesney, *Rich Media, Poor Democracy: Communication Politics in Dubious Times* (Urbana: University of Illinois Press, 1999).

9. James C. Foust, *Online Journalism: Principles and Practices of News for the Web* (Scottsdale, AZ: Holcomb Hathaway, 2005).

10. Martha Stone, "The Backpack Journalist Is a 'Mush of Mediocrity'," *Online Journalism Review*, April 2, 2002, www.ojr.org/ojr/workplace/1017771634.php.

11. Robert I. Berkman and Christopher A. Shumway, *Digital Dilemmas: Ethical Issues for Online Media Professionals* (Ames: Iowa State Press, 2003).

12. Mark Glaser, "Business Side of Convergence Has Myths, Some Real Benefits," *Online Journalism Review,* May 19, 2004, www.ojr.org/ojr/business/1084948706.php.

13. Frank E. Fee Jr., "New(s) Players and New(s) Values? A Test of Convergence in the Newsroom" (paper presented at the annual meeting of the Association for Education in Journalism and Mass Communication, Miami Beach, August 2002).

14. Mark Glaser, "Lack of Unions Makes Florida the Convergence State," *Online Journalism Review,* April 7, 2004, www.ojr.org/ojr/glaser/1081317274.php.

15. Lori Demo, Mary Spillman, and Larry L. Dailey, "Newsroom Partnership Survey Executive Summary," Ball State University Center for Media Design (n.d.), http://web.bsu.edu/mediasurvey.

16. Glaser, "Lack of Unions."

17. Singer, "More Than Ink-Stained Wretches."

18. Jane B. Singer, "Strange Bedfellows? The Diffusion of Convergence in Four News Organizations," *Journalism Studies* 5 (February 2004): 3–18.

19. Jeffrey R. Young, "The Journalist in the Chat Room: An Analysis of WashingtonPost.com's Live Online," *Journal of Electronic Publishing*, June 2000, www.press.umich.edu/jep/05-04/young.html.

20. Kovach and Rosenstiel, *Elements of Journalism.*

21. Demo, Spillman, and Dailey, "Newsroom Partnership."

22. Glaser, "Business Side of Convergence."

23. Pew Center for Civic Journalism, "Convergence and the Community: All Bells and Whistles?" Batten Symposium Panel, 2001, www.pewcenter.org/batten/convergence.html.

24. Jane B. Singer, "Partnerships and Public Service: Normative Issues for Journalists in Converged Newsrooms," *Journal of Mass Media Ethics* 21, no. 1 (2006): 30–53.

25. Singer, "Strange Bedfellows?"

26. Media Center, "Convergence Tracker."

27. Glaser, "Lack of Unions."

28. Ibid.

29. Project for Excellence in Journalism, *The State of the News Media 2005*: Online Intro," http://stateofthemedia.org/2005/narrative_online_intro.asp?cat=1&media=3.

30. Tom Rosenstiel, "The Future of News: Sense-Making and Other Strategies for Survival," PoynterOnline, June 21, 2006, www.poynter.org/column.asp?id=34&aid=102671.

31. Michael Schudson, *The Power of News* (Cambridge, MA: Harvard University Press, 1995).

Appendix A

Code of Ethics of the Society of Professional Journalists

Preamble

Members of the Society of Professional Journalists believe that public enlightenment is the forerunner of justice and the foundation of democracy. The duty of the journalist is to further those ends by seeking truth and providing a fair and comprehensive account of events and issues. Conscientious journalists from all media and specialties strive to serve the public with thoroughness and honesty. Professional integrity is the cornerstone of a journalist's credibility. Members of the Society share a dedication to ethical behavior and adopt this code to declare the Society's principles and standards of practice.

Seek Truth and Report It

Journalists should be honest, fair and courageous in gathering, reporting and interpreting information.

Journalists should:

* Test the accuracy of information from all sources and exercise care to avoid inadvertent error. Deliberate distortion is never permissible.
* Diligently seek out subjects of news stories to give them the opportunity to respond to allegations of wrongdoing.
* Identify sources whenever feasible. The public is entitled to as much information as possible on sources' reliability.

* Always question sources' motives before promising anonymity. Clarify conditions attached to any promise made in exchange for information. Keep promises.
* Make certain that headlines, news teases and promotional material, photos, video, audio, graphics, sound bites and quotations do not misrepresent. They should not oversimplify or highlight incidents out of context.
* Never distort the content of news photos or video. Image enhancement for technical clarity is always permissible. Label montages and photo illustrations.
* Avoid misleading re-enactments or staged news events. If re-enactment is necessary to tell a story, label it.
* Avoid undercover or other surreptitious methods of gathering information except when traditional open methods will not yield information vital to the public. Use of such methods should be explained as part of the story.
* Never plagiarize.
* Tell the story of the diversity and magnitude of the human experience boldly, even when it is unpopular to do so.
* Examine their own cultural values and avoid imposing those values on others.
* Avoid stereotyping by race, gender, age, religion, ethnicity, geography, sexual orientation, disability, physical appearance or social status.
* Support the open exchange of views, even views they find repugnant.
* Give voice to the voiceless; official and unofficial sources of information can be equally valid.
* Distinguish between advocacy and news reporting. Analysis and commentary should be labeled and not misrepresent fact or context.
* Distinguish news from advertising and shun hybrids that blur the lines between the two.
* Recognize a special obligation to ensure that the public's business is conducted in the open and that government records are open to inspection.

Minimize Harm

Ethical journalists treat sources, subjects and colleagues as human beings deserving of respect.

Journalists should:

* Show compassion for those who may be affected adversely by news coverage. Use special sensitivity when dealing with children and inexperienced sources or subjects.
* Be sensitive when seeking or using interviews or photographs of those affected by tragedy or grief.
* Recognize that gathering and reporting information may cause harm or discomfort. Pursuit of the news is not a license for arrogance.
* Recognize that private people have a greater right to control information about themselves than do public officials and others who seek power, influence or attention. Only an overriding public need can justify intrusion into anyone's privacy.
* Show good taste. Avoid pandering to lurid curiosity.
* Be cautious about identifying juvenile suspects or victims of sex crimes.
* Be judicious about naming criminal suspects before the formal filing of charges.
* Balance a criminal suspect's fair trial rights with the public's right to be informed.

Act Independently

Journalists should be free of obligation to any interest other than the public's right to know.

Journalists should:

* Avoid conflicts of interest, real or perceived.
* Remain free of associations and activities that may compromise integrity or damage credibility.
* Refuse gifts, favors, fees, free travel and special treatment, and shun secondary employment, political involvement, public office and service in community organizations if they compromise journalistic integrity.
* Disclose unavoidable conflicts.
* Be vigilant and courageous about holding those with power accountable.
* Deny favored treatment to advertisers and special interests and resist their pressure to influence news coverage.

* Be wary of sources offering information for favors or money; avoid bidding for news.

Be Accountable

Journalists are accountable to their readers, listeners, viewers and each other.

Journalists should:

* Clarify and explain news coverage and invite dialogue with the public over journalistic conduct.
* Encourage the public to voice grievances against the news media.
* Admit mistakes and correct them promptly.
* Expose unethical practices of journalists and the news media.
* Abide by the same high standards to which they hold others.

The SPJ Code of Ethics is voluntarily embraced by thousands of writers, editors and other news professionals. The present version of the code was adopted by the 1996 SPJ National Convention, after months of study and debate among the Society's members.

Sigma Delta Chi's first Code of Ethics was borrowed from the American Society of Newspaper Editors in 1926. In 1973, Sigma Delta Chi wrote its own code and changed its name to Society of Professional Journalists, Sigma Delta Chi. It dropped Sigma Delta Chi from its name entirely in 1988. The code was revised again in 1984, 1987, and 1996.

Appendix B

Founding Principles of the Online News Association

OUR FOUNDING PRINCIPLES: We believe that the Internet is the most powerful communications medium to arise since the dawn of television. As the Net becomes a primary source of news for a growing segment of the world's population, it presents complex challenges and opportunities for journalists as well as the news audience.

EDITORIAL INTEGRITY: The unique permeability of Web publications allows for the linking and joining of information resources of all kinds as intimately as if they were published by a single organization. Responsible journalism on the Internet means that the distinction between news and other information must always be clear, so that individuals can readily distinguish independent editorial information from paid promotional information and other non-news.

EDITORIAL INDEPENDENCE: Online journalists should maintain the highest principles of fairness, accuracy, objectivity and responsible independent reporting.

JOURNALISTIC EXCELLENCE: Online journalists should uphold traditional high principles in reporting original news for the Internet and in reviewing and corroborating information from other sources.

FREEDOM OF EXPRESSION: The ubiquity and global reach of information published on the Internet offers new information and educational resources to a worldwide audience, access to which must be unrestricted.

FREEDOM OF ACCESS: News organizations reporting on the Internet must be afforded access to information and events equal to that enjoyed by other news organizations in order to further freedom of information.

Note: More information about the Online News Association is available at www.journalist.org. Copyright © 1999 by Online News Association. Reprinted by permission.

Appendix C

Key Concepts from
The Elements of Journalism

There are "clear principles that journalists agree on—and that citizens have a right to expect. They are principles that have ebbed and flowed over time, but they have always in some manner been evident. They are the elements of journalism.

"The first among them is that the purpose of journalism is to provide people with the information they need to be free and self-governing.

"To fulfill this task:

1. Journalism's first obligation is to the truth.
2. Its first loyalty is to citizens.
3. Its essence is a discipline of verification.
4. Its practitioners must maintain an independence from those they cover.
5. It must serve as an independent monitor of power.
6. It must provide a forum for public criticism and compromise.
7. It must strive to make the significant interesting and relevant.
8. It must keep the news comprehensive and proportional.
9. Its practitioners must be allowed to exercise their personal conscience."

Index

About the Authors

Cecilia Friend is a professor of journalism at Utica College in upstate New York. She spent ten years as a full-time reporter and editor and has since worked as a newsroom writing coach and special projects editor. She is the lead author of *Contemporary Editing*, which is in its second edition.

Jane B. Singer worked for fifteen years in print and online newsrooms and was the first news manager of the Prodigy service, one of the earliest to enable people to receive news by computer. She holds a PhD in journalism from the University of Missouri, as well as degrees from New York University and the University of Georgia. Her research has appeared in a variety of publications. She is on the editorial board of *Journal of Mass Media Ethics* and is a contributing editor of *Media Ethics* magazine.